LIVING IN THE EIGHTIES

VIEWPOINTS ON AMERICAN CULTURE

Catherine Clinton, Series Editor

Viewpoints on American Culture offers timely reflections for twenty-first century readers. A sensible guide to knowledge in a scholarly field, something one can pick up—literally and figuratively—seems to be facing extinction. Volumes in our series will provide intellectual relief and practical solutions.

The series targets topics in which debates have flourished and brings together the voices of established and emerging writers to share their own points of view in a compact and compelling format. Our books offer sophisticated, yet accessible, introductions into an array of issues under our broad and expanding banner.

Sifters: Native American Women's Lives
Edited by Theda Perdue

Long Time Gone: Sixties America Then and Now
Edited by Alexander Bloom

Votes for Women: The Struggle for Suffrage Revisited
Edited by Jean H. Baker

Race on Trial: Law and Justice in American History
Edited by Annette Gordon-Reed

Latina Legacies: Identity, Biography, and Community
Edited by Vicki L. Ruiz and Virginia Sánchez Korrol

Living in the Eighties
Edited by Gil Troy and Vincent J. Cannato

LIVING IN THE
eighties

**Edited by Gil Troy and
Vincent J. Cannato**

OXFORD
UNIVERSITY PRESS

2009

OXFORD
UNIVERSITY PRESS

Oxford University Press, Inc., publishes works that further
Oxford University's objective of excellence
in research, scholarship, and education.

Oxford   New York
Auckland   Cape Town   Dar es Salaam   Hong Kong   Karachi
Kuala Lumpur   Madrid   Melbourne   Mexico City   Nairobi
New Delhi   Shanghai   Taipei   Toronto

With offices in
Argentina   Austria   Brazil   Chile   Czech Republic   France   Greece
Guatemala   Hungary   Italy   Japan   Poland   Portugal   Singapore
South Korea   Switzerland   Thailand   Turkey   Ukraine   Vietnam

Copyright © 2009 by Oxford University Press, Inc.

Published by Oxford University Press, Inc.
198 Madison Avenue, New York, New York 10016

www.oup.com

Oxford is a registered trademark of Oxford University Press

Library of Congress Cataloging-in-Publication Data
Living in the eighties / edited by Gil Troy and Vincent J. Cannato.
     p. cm.—(Viewpoints on American culture)
Includes bibliographical references and index.
ISBN 978-0-19-518786-1; 978-0-19-518787-8 (pbk.)
1. United States—Social conditions—1980–   2. Popular culture—United States—History—20th
century.   3. United States—Politics and government—1981–1989.   4. United States—
Civilization—20th century.   I. Troy, Gil.   II. Cannato, Vincent J., 1967–
E169.12.L5557 2009
973.927—dc22   2009010770

9 8 7 6 5 4 3 2 1
Printed in the United States of America
on acid-free paper

CONTENTS

CONTRIBUTORS

MARK BRILLIANT is an assistant professor in the Department of History and Program in American Studies at the University of California, Berkeley. His book on civil rights in California from World War II to *Bakke* is forthcoming from Oxford University Press.

VINCENT J. CANNATO is an associate professor of history at the University of Massachusetts, Boston. He received his Ph.D. from Columbia University and is the author of *The Ungovernable City: John Lindsay and His Struggle to Save New York* (Basic Books, 2001) and *American Passage: The History of Ellis Island.*

JOSEPH CRESPINO is an associate professor of history at Emory University in Atlanta. He is the author of *In Search of Another Country: Mississippi and the Conservative Counterrevolution.*

SARA M. EVANS, a Regents Professor Emerita at the University of Minnesota, is an historian of feminism in the United States. Her books include *Personal Politics: The Roots of Women's Liberation in the Civil Rights Movement & the New Left; Tidal Wave: How Women Changed America at Century's End;* and *Born for Liberty: A History of Women in America.*

DAVID GREENBERG is an associate professor of history and journalism and media studies at Rutgers University and holds a Ph.D. in history from Columbia University. He is the author of *Nixon's Shadow: The History of an Image* (2003); *Presidential Doodles* (2006); and *Calvin Coolidge* (2006). A columnist for *Slate*, he has also written for the *Atlantic, Foreign Affairs,* the *New York Times,* the *New Yorker*, and the *New Republic*, of which he is a former managing and acting editor.

STEVE GREENBERG is a music executive and record producer. He has discovered and produced artists such as Joss Stone, Hanson, and the Jonas Brothers. He won a 2000 Grammy Award as producer of "Who Let the Dogs Out" by Baha Men. He is currently CEO of S-Curve Records, a New York-based music company.

EDWIN MEESE III holds the Ronald Reagan Chair in Public Policy at The Heritage Foundation, a Washington-based public policy research and education institution. He is also the chairman of Heritage's Center for Legal and Judicial Studies. During Ronald Reagan's first term, Mr. Meese served as counsellor to the president from 1981 to 1985. During Reagan's second term, Mr. Meese served as attorney general of the United States from 1985 to 1988. He was also appointed by the president as chairman of the Domestic Policy Council and the National Drug Policy Board and was a member of the National Security Council.

KIM PHILLIPS-FEIN is an assistant professor at the Gallatin School of New York University, where she teaches classes on twentieth-century American political, intellectual, and business history. She is the author of *Invisible Hands: The Making of the Conservative Movement from the New Deal to Reagan*.

BRUCE J. SCHULMAN is the William E. Huntington Professor of History at Boston University and the author of *From Cotton Belt to Sunbelt, Lyndon B. Johnson and American Liberalism*, and *The Seventies: The Great Shift in American Politics, Culture, and Society*. His latest book, co-edited with Julian Zelizer, is *Rightward Bound*.

PETER SCHWEIZER is a research fellow at the Hoover Institution, Stanford University. His books include *Reagan's War: The Epic Story of His Forty Year Struggle and Final Triumph Over Communism* and *Victory: The Reagan Administration's*

Secret Strategy That Hastened the Collapse of the Soviet Union. His written work has appeared in *Foreign Affairs,* the *New York Times, ORBIS: A Journal of World Affairs,* and *National Review.*

GIL TROY is professor of History at McGill University in Montreal. A native of Queens, New York, he is the author of six books on American history, including *Leading from the Center: Why Moderates Make the Best Presidents, Morning in America: How Ronald Reagan Invented the 1980s,* and, most recently, *The Reagan Revolution: A Very Short Introduction* (2009).

LAUREN F. WINNER is an assistant professor at Duke Divinity School. Her study of religion in colonial Virginia, *A Cheerful and Comfortable Faith,* is forthcoming.

TIMELINE

1980

- "Miracle on Ice": U.S. Hockey Team Defeats U.S.S.R. (Feb. 22, 1980), then Defeats Finland (Feb. 24, 1980) to Win a Gold Medal during the 1980 Winter Olympics in Lake Placid, NY
- President Carter Announces U.S. Boycott of the Summer Olympics in Moscow (March 21, 1980)
- Rescue Attempt to Free U.S. Hostages in Iran Fails (April 24, 1980)
- *Pac Man* Video Game Introduced in Japan (May 22, 1980)
- Cable News Network (CNN) Begins Broadcasting (June 1, 1980)
- Iran-Iraq War Begins (Sept. 1980)
- Ronald Reagan Elected President (Nov. 4, 1980)
- John Lennon Murdered in New York City (Dec. 8, 1980)

1981

- Television Show *Dynasty* Airs (Jan. 12, 1981)
- Iran Hostage Crisis Ends, American Hostages Released (Jan. 20, 1981)
- Assassination Attempt against President Reagan (March 30, 1981)
- First Space Shuttle Flight, STS-1, *Columbia* (April 12, 1981)
- House of Representatives Passes Reagan Budget with Deep Budget Cuts (May 8, 1981)

- Assassination attempt against Pope John Paul II (May 13, 1981)
- Centers for Disease Control and Prevention (CDC) Identifies the First Cases of AIDS (June 5, 1981)
- Prince Charles Marries Diana Spencer (July 29, 1981)
- Acquired Immune Deficiency Syndrome (AIDS) Makes Its Debut (HIV indentified in 1980; AIDS 1981)
- MTV (Music Television) Begins Broadcasting (August 1, 1981)
- President Reagan Fires 12,000 Striking Air Traffic Controllers (August 5, 1981)
- IBM Personal Computer Introduced (August 12, 1981)
- Sandra Day O'Connor Becomes First Female Supreme Court Justice (Sept. 25, 1981)

1982

- Falklands War between England and Argentina (April 1982)
- The Equal Rights Amendment Fails Ratification (June 30, 1982)
- Vietnam Veterans Memorial Dedicated (Nov. 13, 1982)
- Michael Jackson's Album *Thriller* Released (Nov. 30, 1982)
- First Jarvik-7 Artificial Heart Transplant (Dec. 2, 1982)

1983

- Compact Discs (CDs) Introduced in the United States (March 2, 1983)
- Reagan Proposes Strategic Defense Initiative (SDI) (March 23, 1983)
- Bombing of U.S. Embassy in Beirut(April 18, 1983)
- Astronaut Sally Ride Becomes First American Woman in Space (June 18, 1983)
- Korean Air Lines Flight 007 Shot Down by Soviet Fighters (Sept. 1, 1983)
- Vanessa Williams Becomes the First African-American Miss America (Sept. 17, 1983)
- Bombing of the U.S. Marine Corps Barracks in Lebanon (Oct. 23, 1983)
- United States Invades Grenada (Oct. 25, 1983)

1984

- AT&T Phone Company Divested (Jan. 1, 1984)
- Apple Macintosh Computer Introduced (Jan. 24, 1984)
- Soviet Union Announces Boycott of Summer Olympics Held in Los Angeles (May 8, 1984)

- Geraldine Ferraro Becomes the First Female Candidate for Vice President of the United States (July 12, 1984)
- "Miami Vice" Television Show Airs (Sept. 16, 1984)
- Ronald Reagan Reelected President of the United States (Nov. 6, 1984)

1985

- Mikhail Gorbachev Becomes Leader of the Soviet Union (March 11, 1985)
- Coke Introduces "New Coke" (April 23, 1985)
- Actor Rock Hudson Dies from AIDS (Oct. 2, 1985)
- Nintendo Entertainment System Introduced (Oct. 18, 1985)
- Microsoft *Windows* Operating System Introduced (Nov. 20, 1985)

1986

- First Observance of Martin Luther King, Jr., Federal Holiday (Jan. 20, 1986)
- Space Shuttle *Challenger* Accident (Jan. 28, 1986)
- United States Bombs Libya (April 14, 1986)
- Soviet Nuclear Reactor Accident at Chernobyl (April 26, 1986)
- Statue of Liberty's Centennial (July 3, 1986)
- Ronald Reagan and Mikhail Gorbachev Meet at Reykjavík Summit (Oct. 11–12, 1986)

1987

- President Reagan Takes Responsibility for Iran-Contra Scandal (March 4, 1987)
- Jim Bakker resigns from PTL Club (March 19, 1987)
- "Black Monday" Stock Market Crash (Oct. 19, 1987)
- Intermediate-Range Nuclear Forces (INF) Treaty Signed by the Soviet Union and the United States (Dec. 8, 1987)
- Oliver Stone's Movie "Wall Street" Is Released (Dec. 11, 1987)
- Federal Drug Administration Approves Use of Prozac (Dec. 29, 1987)
- Donald Trump's Book, *Trump: The Art of the Deal*, Is Published
- Tom Wolfe's Novel, *Bonfire of the Vanities*, Is Published

1988

- Bobby McFerrin Releases Hit Song "Don't Worry, Be Happy" (September 1988)

- George H. W. Bush Elected President of the United States (Nov. 8, 1988)
- Pan Am Flight 103 Terrorist Attack over Lockerbie, Scotland (Dec. 21, 1988)

1989

- Fatwa Issued against Salmon Rushdie by Iranian Leader Ayatollah Khomeini in Response to Rushdie's Novel *The Satanic Verses* (Feb. 14, 1989)
- Soviet Union Completes Withdrawal from Afghanistan (Feb. 15, 1989)
- Exxon Valdez Oil Spill (March 24, 1989)
- Protests at Tiananmen Square in China (April 14, 1989)
- The Pilot Episode for the Television Show That Would Become Known as *Seinfeld* airs (July 5, 1989)
- B-2 Stealth Bomber's Maiden Flight (July 17, 1989)
- Pete Rose Permanently Banned from Baseball (Aug. 24, 1989)
- Colin Powell Becomes Chairman of the Joint Chiefs of Staff (Oct. 1, 1989)
- Dismantling of the Berlin Wall Begins (Nov. 9, 1989)
- United States Invades Panama (Dec. 20, 1989)

LIVING IN THE EIGHTIES

INTRODUCTION

Gil Troy and Vincent J. Cannato

Once upon a time, back in 1980, when people heard about "AIDS," they thought of assistants or helpers, not a deadly disease. An "Apple" was something you ate, not something you would boot up. Windows could break but did not crash. "Trump" was a term from bridge, not the brand name of a celebrity tycoon. "Madonna" evoked feelings of spirituality rather than provoking controversy about a pop star's aggressive sexuality. The "Moonwalk" referred to the astronaut Neil Armstrong's famous first steps on the moon not the singer Michael Jackson's silky-smooth dance move. And most people thought PC meant "partly cloudy," not "personal computer" or "politically correct."

By 1990, the new meanings for these words reflected a new world. American politics were more conservative. American capitalism was more aggressive. American society was more individualistic. American culture was more indulgent. It is important to appreciate and analyze the vast social, economic, and political changes that occurred during the decade of the 1980s, placing them in historical perspective.

In the "decades derby" that so many people play when discussing the twentieth century, it is easy to caricature the 1980s as frivolous. It was indeed the decade of the difficult-to-solve Rubik's Cube and the ever-so-lovable Cabbage Patch Kids. It was a time defined by movies such as "The Big Chill," which showed how a group of baby boomers went from being idealistic Sixties hippies to self-involved Eighties "yuppies"—Young Urban Professionals, a term that would become shorthand for spoiled and self-indulgent. Those were also the years of Wall Street executives in power suits and red suspenders like Gordon Gekko in Oliver Stone's movie "Wall Street." The 1980s was also the era of arcane financial instruments such as junk bonds and the debuts of CNN, MTV, New Coke, and "E.T."—both the daily celebrity television showcase which debuted in 1981, "Entertainment Tonight," and Steven Spielberg's 1982 movie about the cuddly extraterrestrial.

But the headlines of the 1980s were about more than just trivial matters. At the start of the decade, relations between the communist world and the free world grew even tenser. Anticommunists abroad such as Pope John Paul II, Polish labor leader Lech Walesa, and British Prime Minister Margaret Thatcher were just starting to convince the world that communism might be a fleeting failure not a permanent fixture. For the United States, a decade that began with Iranian Islamic radicals holding 52 American hostages in the American embassy would also be punctuated by terrorist attacks, including a Hezbollah-backed suicide bombing of a U.S. Marine barracks in Beirut, Lebanon, in 1983, Palestinian terrorists hijacking the cruise ship the *Achille Lauro* in 1985 and throwing a wheelchair-bound American Jewish tourist named Leon Klinghoffer overboard, and Libyan intelligence agents bombing Pan Am Flight 103 over Lockerbie, Scotland, in 1988, killing 270 people, including 180 Americans.

Meanwhile, at home, Americans debated the political power of evangelical Christians such as "The Moral Majority" as well as the effectiveness of the "War on Drugs." In the wake of the economic problems of the 1970s, Americans witnessed a tremendous prosperity during the 1980s. But this was not without controversy. The decade saw a real debate over economics and capitalism, about the effectiveness and justice of tax cuts, and about how best to reduce poverty. Man-made disasters, such as the lethal poison gas leak in Bhopal, India, the Soviet nuclear accident at Chernobyl, and the Exxon Valdez oil spill that fouled the Alaska coast with millions of barrels of oil, focused the world's attention on the fragility of the environment.

Amid all of this, President Ronald Reagan would come to define the 1980s for many Americans. In his 1981 inaugural address, he tried to reorient American politics when he declared that in the present economic crisis, government was the problem and not the solution. He celebrated America's subsequent prosperity as a vindication of his free market ideology and proof of the nation's enduring greatness. And he reignited the flames of the Cold War by refusing to simply coexist with communism. During a visit to Berlin in 1987, he demanded of his Soviet rival, "Mr. Gorbachev, tear down this wall." Reagan left office in 1989, retreated from public view because of Alzheimer's in 1994, and died in

2004. Yet his legacy has shaped the debate of every subsequent presidential campaign.

Today, some see the 1980s as a Golden Age, a "Morning in America" when President Ronald Reagan, American conservatives, and baby boomer entrepreneurs revived America's economy, reoriented American politics, reformed American society, and restored Americans' faith in their country and in themselves. Others see the 1980s as a new "Gilded Age," an era that was selfish, superficial, divisive, and destructive. The financial meltdown of 2008 intensified the debate, as Democrats rushed to declare the Reagan era "over" and a failure.

Viewed in these stark terms, the debate about the 1980s often continues the cultural and political clash regarding the legacy of the 1960s. The "Golden Age" narrative is a story of recovery from the moral degradation, ideological confusion, military weakness, and political failures of the 1960s. Those who think that the United States "came back" in the 1980s see the 1960s as a time when the country was derailed. They view President Lyndon B. Johnson's Great Society programs that expanded government to fight poverty, achieve racial justice, and provide health care to the elderly and poor as a great failure, which yielded high taxes, onerous regulations, and more crime, while doing little to end poverty. They see the ethos of "sex, drugs, and rock and roll" as a blight on society that undermined morality at home and American strength abroad, especially in Vietnam.

At the same time, many critiques of the 1980s as a "Gilded Age" are tinged with nostalgia for the 1960s. For these critics, the narrative is one of "backlash," of resentful white males depriving blacks, women, and the poor of whatever gains they made during the 1960s. They see a rise in corporatism and selfishness at the expense of idealism. From this point of view, the 1960s was the time of great heroics and the 1980s was the time of great sellouts. One popular journalistic history of the decade, published in 1991, was dismissively titled *Sleepwalking Through History*.

Most of the contributors to this volume answer the either/or question of whether the 1980s was a Golden Age or a Gilded Age with a resounding "yes." Many of us argue that there were both good and bad elements, noble moments and embarrassments during the decade. Rather than arguing about whether the decade was good or bad, we should push the conversation from the political to the historical, from the polemical to the analytical, from quick, partisan judgments to a more nuanced understanding of where the country was then and where it is today.

Placing the decade of the 1980s in a greater historical perspective will help readers better understand the contemporary political and cultural divide of

America into "red states" and "blue states." The Reagan administration's reductions in taxes and regulations and its encouragement of entrepreneurial capitalism helped create the new era of economic globalization, whose problems became apparent in the 2008 subprime mortgage and credit crises. And the 1980s holds many lessons on the eternal question of what America's proper role in world affairs should be.

Trying to write the history of a decade is a daunting task. How can you capture, with any degree of authority or authenticity, what 250 million proudly individualistic Americans were thinking, doing, feeling, and experiencing at any one time? This collection is an attempt to understand America during the 1980s from many different angles. Rather than sharing one interpretive lens or one methodological focus, these essays bring together a variety of voices from different political persuasions, ideologies, and vantage points.

Our contributors are mostly historians, but we also have essays written by one of President Reagan's closest aides and by a Grammy-award winning record producer. We have Reagan critics and Reagan fans. We have people who think the 1980s were a disastrous time for America, those who think it was a glorious time, and those who see the decade's blessings and curses. Although each essay stands on its own, tracing one significant thematic strand, we also hope that all the threads together weave a rich, multidimensional tapestry that will help readers understand just what happened in America during that decade.

The collection begins with Gil Troy's essay, "Ronald Reagan's 100-Day Revolution." The tension in the title reflects the tension in the essay—any serious revolution would have to last longer than three-and-a-third months. The essay argues that most of the major changes President Reagan implemented occurred during his First Hundred Days in office, or, at best, his first eight months in office. This interpretation, then, views Ronald Reagan as relatively moderate, as someone who offered a mid-course correction, slowed down the growth of government, without delivering the massive change he originally promised, that his supporters desperately wanted, and that Democrats so intensely feared.

Ed Meese, the Counselor to the President during Reagan's first term, and Attorney General during his second term, counters the first essay by detailing the Reagan Revolution's many significant achievements. Meese's case for Reagan hinges on "three major accomplishments": turning the economy around, fighting communism effectively, and "reviv[ing] the spirit of the American people." Meese roots his analysis in the narrative of seventies crisis and eighties rebirth. He acknowledges shortcomings, too, but mostly offers a passionate defense of Reagan as a leader, and the eighties as a time of prosperity, productivity, power—and generosity, he insists, not greed.

Whereas in the essay that follows David Greenberg uncovers some of the great debates that took place in the 1980s by looking at Reagan's rivals, Joseph Crespino uncovers some of the significant social changes in the eighties by looking at Reagan's supporters. In "Ronald Reagan's South: The Tangled Roots of Modern Southern Conservatism," Crespino shows how by analyzing Reagan's southern base, we can learn more about the Sunbelt's new social and political power as millions flocked south and west. Crespino highlights a tension within the New South, between holding onto traditional racism and moving beyond it, reflected in the rise of two "Georges," Ronald Reagan's Vice President George H.W. Bush and the populist demagogic Alabama governor George Wallace. One reading of the evidence leads to a dismaying conclusion about racism underlying Reaganite conservatism. A more benign interpretation emphasizes a constructive marriage between southern progress and Reaganite centrism. Sunbelt states such as Florida, Texas, and California balanced out the traditional power of Rustbelt states such as New York, Ohio, and Michigan with a new potent demographic mix of longstanding black and white residents, mostly white snowbirds from the North, and Latinos.

David Greenberg weighs in with his essay, "The Reorientation of Liberalism in the 1980s." In some ways, this essay is positioned between Meese's and Troy's interpretations. In chronicling the confusion liberals experienced, Greenberg reinforces Meese's claim that Reagan propelled America in a dramatically different direction. But in analyzing the center-seeking syntheses that emerged among "neoliberals," Greenberg echoes Troy's analysis about a more moderate spirit among the Left and the Right spreading in the 1980s.

If Crespino found America dancing on the edge between the old and the new, between the racist past and the multicultural future, between exclusion and inclusion by looking south and to the suburbs, Vincent Cannato finds similar tensions by looking north and to the cities. Cannato rests his essay, "Bright Lights, Doomed Cities: The Rise or Fall of New York City in the 1980s?," on the tension in the period between decline and restoration and between decay and revival. Cannato looks at the decline of the cities, specifically New York, from the 1950s to the 1970s as emblematic of the broader crisis Meese and others recognize as launching the Reagan revolution. Looking at New York's Mayor Ed Koch, the Wall Street boom, the scourge of crime, and the spread of AIDS, among other factors, Cannato shows how ideologues of different stripes constructed contrasting narratives of decay and restoration. He ends by noting the irony that even as New York and other cities thrived due to their 1980s revival, politically, socially, and economically, America's future growth would be concentrated in its suburbs and exurbs.

Women, too, can construct parallel narratives of backlash and redemption for the 1980s, according to Sara Evans in "Feminism in the Eighties: Surviving the Backlash." Evans shows that even as many younger women were benefiting from feminism, they were stepping back from the movement. Fewer women were willing to engage in activist politics in the 1980s, even as they institutionalized and internalized many changes launched in the 1960s. Still, despite the growing attacks on feminism as doctrinaire, and despite the failure to change the Constitution by passing the Equal Rights Amendment, Evans shows that feminism in the 1980s remained a potent force as women became more accepted as equals as lawyers and bus drivers and as clerics and doctors.

Multiculturalism was another offshoot from the sixties that took root in the eighties, but with more mixed results than feminism. "Intellectual Affirmative Action: How Multiculturalism Became Mandatory and Mainstream in Higher Education," by Mark Brilliant, looks at the demands that higher education become more inclusive. Brilliant understands that not all change is permanent and not all fights are acrimonious. He views the debate about multiculturalism as invigorating. At the same time he notes the great irony of multiculturalism in the 1980s: as the ideals of diversity became second nature to a next generation, that generation would be more likely to demand a more cosmopolitan and less identity-based curriculum and approach.

Although when he served as California's governor Ronald Reagan happily fought the culture wars of the 1960s, as president Reagan usually tried to dodge messy debates about feminism and multiculturalism. Ultimately, Ronald Reagan built his career and shaped the 1980s on his defense of capitalism and his fight against communism. Kim Phillips-Fein looks at the package of free-enterprise ideas that Reagan imposed on the American agenda in "Reaganomics: The Rebirth of the Free Market." She concludes that although Reaganomics experienced mixed success economically, it dramatically transformed the landscape politically, ideologically, and symbolically. The argument continues about how central Reagan's policies were to the subsequent boom, and how equitably the benefits of that prosperity were distributed. Few can doubt, however, that Reagan shaped the economic and political conversation among both Democrats and Republicans well into the twenty-first century.

While Peter Schweizer believes that Reagan's anticommunism forged his commitment to free enterprise, his essay focuses on Reagan's foreign policy. In "Did Ronald Reagan Make the Berlin Wall Fall Down?" Schweizer views Reagan as a consequential president who changed the course of history. He gives Reagan credit for following a more muscular yet flexible approach to the Soviet Union, repudiating the appeasement of the 1970s, and setting the stage for the implosion of Soviet communism in the 1990s. Reagan was often less sure-footed when he left the anticommunist paradigm, Schweizer notes, as evidenced by fiascoes such as the Iran-Contra scandal, wherein Reagan's subordinates tried bargaining with Middle Eastern terrorists and funneled money illegally to Latin American guerillas. Still, Reagan's anticommunism proved essential in achieving a peaceful end to the Cold War.

This fragmentation that affected Americans, as discussed in the following essay by Bruce Schulman, affected popular music as well. Steve Greenberg demonstrates this in his essay "Where Is Graceland?: 1980s Pop Culture through Music." He shows that the decline of disco and the spread of "specialized formats" on radio initially resegregated pop music. It took the centripetal power of MTV and the marketing magic of Michael Jackson to reintegrate and reunite popular culture, for a while. Popular culture parallels many of the tensions of the Reagan years, as Americans both withdrew into their private spheres and rallied around new national icons and ideas.

In his essay "The Privatization of Everyday Life: Public Policy, Public Services, and Public Space in the 1980s," Bruce Schulman explores one of the most significant values of Reagan's free-market ideology. Schulman links Reagan's gospel of freedom and his cynicism about public bureaucracies with the growing retreat of Americans from Main Street to the mall, from authentic neighborhoods to gated communities, and from diverse, community-based interactions to sanitized class-based sanctuaries. The result, even with a nostalgia-drenched countertrend of coffee houses and farmers' markets, was a country in which citizens were more isolated from each other and less engaged politically.

Just as the 1980s' realities transformed Reaganite conservatism, evangelical Protestantism also changed. Lauren Winner's essay, "Reaganizing Religion: Changing Political and Cultural Norms among Evangelicals in Ronald Reagan's America," charts the entry of evangelicals into politics during the Carter and Reagan years. That engagement transformed the American landscape. But, she argues, the movement was subtly shaped by the Reagan Revolution as it made its own accommodations with political realities, especially by targeting abortion, which remained a politically explosive issue, rather than divorce, which more directly frayed the nation's social fabric, as a central moral dilemma.

Although there are many additional topics left to address, when taken together, these essays help push the conversation about Reagan and the 1980s beyond the dualistic "Golden Age" or "Gilded Age" question and toward an appreciation of the longstanding forces and contingent events that shaped the period. It is a vast oversimplification to call the 1980s, as some do, a decade of greed or rabid conservatism.

Despite its frequent use by historians and journalists, the term "backlash" to describe conservatism and the 1980s is unhelpful. It implies that history inexorably moves only in one direction. Any opposition to that movement is deemed a backlash, rather than a legitimate debate, criticism or alternative point of view. Labeling Reaganism or conservatism a kind of "backlash" marginalizes and denigrates, suggesting that these movements and ideas were hampering the natural forces of progressivism. Somehow, no one ever calls the New Deal a "backlash" against laissez faire capitalism. Moving beyond both the Golden Age/Gilded Age dualism and the simplistic "backlash" against liberalism idea, this collection of essays highlights the greater complexity in the interplay of ideology, politics, and social relations during this decade. Though the country did shift somewhat to the right during the 1980s, it was a modified conservatism that actually incorporated and mainstreamed many of the social and cultural revolutions of the 1960s. The powers of the presidency expanded, but the limits to how much a president could change the system also became apparent. A sense of American patriotism and optimism returned after the cynicism and pessimism of the 1960s and 1970s, but distrust in government still lingered. Much of the nation's optimism was also tinged with worry that the economic boom might be fleeting or limited to a lucky few. Still, the Age of Reagan represented the revival of military strength, economic vitality, optimism, and entrepreneurship that Americans so desperately yearned for in the 1970s.

But as many of the essays demonstrate, the Reagan Revolution may not have been the great victory that many of its supporters hoped for and many of its critics feared. Ultimately, 1960s-style liberalism continued to thrive in the 1980s as it adapted to the new realities of the era. Many once-radical social movements of the 1960s—feminism, civil rights, environmentalism, gay rights—increasingly became mainstream in the 1980s. American society became more open and more multicultural, with a greater sense of informality in dress and manners. Traditional family structure continued to witness a decline.

These essays also paint a portrait of the 1980s as a decade of dissolution, an age of fragmentation, when individualism trumped community, particularist affiliations frequently overrode national sensibilities, niche marketing became pervasive, and the traditional bonds that bound Americans weakened. The twentieth century was a centrifugal century, spinning individuals away from traditional structures, values, and allegiances. Tom Wolfe aptly labeled the 1970s as the "Me-Decade," when many Americans turned inward, becoming more concerned with making their bodies buff and their psyches strong rather than reforming their society or saving the world.

These trends continued in the 1980s. Liberalism became more rights-based with an increased emphasis on civil liberties. Conservatism became more consumption-based, anti-government, and individualistic. Despite their clashes, both liberalism and conservatism further individuated Americans, while weakening communal ties. The bigger shifts during the decade tended more toward fragmentation than cohesion. Hopefully, this collection will allow us to start looking back on the 1980s as one of the more fascinating and transformative decades in the twentieth century, a time of dramatic political, economic, and cultural shifts, which most Americans will be grappling with for years to come.

Chapter 1

RONALD REAGAN'S 100-DAY REVOLUTION

Gil Troy

Ronald Reagan's "First Hundred Days" have become central to the Reagan mythology. Supporters wistfully recall the "Reagan Revolution's" heady days, whereas critics mourn Reagan's assault on Franklin Roosevelt's New Deal and Lyndon Johnson's Great Society—both of which also benefited from a major inaugural push. In fact, Johnson and Reagan were following Roosevelt in starting their terms vigorously.

Almost daily during those first hundred days—and certainly the first sixty days—progressives awoke to headlines that sickened them. Ronald Reagan seemed to be dismantling half a century's worth of accomplishments—to great applause. "REAGAN BRINGS OPTIMISM FOR THE FUTURE, ROOTED IN VALUES OF THE PAST," the *Washington Post* declared on Inauguration Day.[1] "REAGAN CONTINUES HIS ATTACK ON U.S. SPENDING, REGULATIONS," the *Post* front page cried in January.[2] "DEEP BUDGET CUTS URGED FOR POPULAR FEDERAL PROGRAMS," it proclaimed in February.[3] By March, Reagan was ramming his program through—and enjoying public acclaim, as the *Post* announced "SUDDEN SHIFT TO GOP EMERGES IN POLLS."[4] On one Thursday, the headline above the fold said: "PRESIDENT WINS FIRST HILL VOTE ON BUDGET CUTS," while the headline below warned: "AX POSED FOR POVERTY AGENCY AND ANTI-SMOKING PROGRAM."[5]

The conservative offensive extended beyond budgetary matters into seemingly every sacred cow of the 1960s and 1970s. "REAGAN DECONTROLS

GASOLINE, CRUDE IN DEREGULATION DEBUT," readers learned.[6] "ABORTION FOES GAIN KEY FEDERAL POSTS FROM INSIDE [THE] ADMINISTRATION," the subheading explained, "THEY TARGET BIRTH CONTROL, OTHER PROGRAMS."[7] Another day, readers discovered "AFFIRMATIVE ACTION IS UNDER A NEW GUN."[8] Reporting the obvious, the *Post* confirmed by early February: "EPIC POLITICAL STRUGGLE LOOMS: OFFICIAL WASHINGTON REALIZING REFORM CRUSADE IS NOT BUSINESS AS USUAL."[9]

America's relationship with the world also seemed to have become suddenly tenser, with a new saber-rattling president in office. Speaking of the new Secretary of Defense, Caspar Weinberger, after his public debut, the *Post* proclaimed: "WEINBERGER, IN HIS FIRST MESSAGE, SAYS MISSION IS TO 'REARM AMERICA.' "[10] This assertion of military might triggered a predictable reaction as "TOP SOVIET OFFICAL SAYS U.S. PREPARING FOR A 'WORLD WAR.' "[11]

Then, Reagan's revolution stumbled as suddenly as it had soared. A mid-March Gallup poll suggested that while 59 percent of the public supported the new chief executive, "REAGAN APPROVAL RATING TRAILS EARLIER PRESIDENTS."[12] Four days later, Reagan's pollster, Richard Wirthlin, was still trying to spin the story positively by hailing Reagan's nobility, saying, "In California, as now, he attempted to immediately implement his campaign promises. This coalesces support and polarizes opposition."[13] By April—even after the popularity boost unwittingly triggered by John Hinckley's attempt to assassinate the president, news of Reaganite legislative successes mixed with headlines reporting: "IN BLOW TO REAGAN, SENATE UNIT REJECTS 1982 BUDGET PLAN" and, even more surprising, "PROSPECTS ARE GLOOMY FOR ECONOMIC PLAN, REAGAN IS TOLD."[14]

What happened? How did Ronald Reagan's instant revolution sour? And how, despite the sputtering, did the legend of the First Hundred Days grow? Ronald Reagan's presidential debut demonstrated the breadth of his vision, as well as some of the limits to his program. Critics and supporters are both half-right. The First Hundred Days showcased much of what Ronald Reagan hoped to accomplish, and marked one of his most productive political periods. But the First Hundred Days also proved the illusory nature of Reagan's mandate, the structural and ideological resistance to his plans, and Reagan's mix of symbolism and pragmatism, which popularized yet diluted conservatism.

Reagan understood American political culture's fragility following the 1960s and 1970s. When pressed, therefore, he usually chose popularity over principle and compromise over conscience. An odd ideologue, he tempered a strong, even rigid, worldview with flexibility and pragmatism. At once wheeler-dealer and political evangelist, he could settle for the proverbial half a loaf and sell it as a revolution in bread-making.

In the most intense assault on the post–New Deal status quo in a generation, the center held. But Reagan and Republicans experienced enough success to begin nudging the American political compass gradually so that the shift of a few degrees rightward resulted in a changed navigational trajectory two decades later. Due to this dramatic hundred day launch to Reagan's administration, we still live in a Reaganized America.

These defining First Hundred Days unfolded in three phases. During the first two months after his January 20 inauguration, Reagan, with his chief lieutenant David Stockman, launched the Budget Battles as the Reagan Revolution's opening salvo. By mid-March, an effective Democratic counteroffensive began to weaken the president's standing. Then, on March 30, an assassination attempt badly injured Reagan. This tragedy may have triggered the real honeymoon between the president and the people, one shaped more by Reagan's personality than his program, cementing Reagan's popularity while derailing his revolution.

Ronald Reagan ran for office seeking to renew the American center by pushing it to the right, back where he believed it belonged. Born in small-town Illinois in 1911, the tall, broad-shouldered, Midwesterner crowned with an old-fashioned Brylcreem-slick pompadour, had spent three decades as a Hollywood actor, both romanticizing and living out the American dream. He then spent nearly a decade as a conservative California governor fighting the culture wars of the sixties while living through many of the era's upheavals within his own blended family. Although coming to embody American traditionalism, he would become the first divorced president ever, plagued by rebellious children who, though grown, continued to act out against him and his second wife, Nancy. A New Deal Democrat alienated by the postwar tax burden and red tape while terrified by Communist "fifth columnists" in Hollywood and Washington, Reagan often quipped, "I never left the Democratic party, the Democratic party left me."

The oldest man ever elected president, an ideologue whose core principles rejected the conventional wisdom, Reagan was easily caricatured by critics as an aging, amateurish extremist more suited to Hollywood make-believe than Washington realpolitik. Yet Reagan understood politics as the art of the possible, sweetened by lofty dreams of the improbable. Running California from 1967 through 1975, he refused to "jump off the cliff with the flag flying if you can't get everything you want." He recalled: "If I found when I was governor that I could not get 100 percent of what I asked for, I took 80 percent"[15] Governor

Reagan's moderate abortion and welfare policies belied his fiery rhetoric. "You want a principled man, which Reagan is," the economist Milton Friedman said. "But he is not a rigidly principled man, which you don't want."[16]

Reagan was self-confident, and relentlessly, infectiously happy. A conservative crusader with a pragmatic governing record, Reagan was an amiable ideologue, an accommodating extremist. He was charming but opinionated, glib but bookish in an antiintellectual *Reader's Digest* way, rooted in the right but wooing the center.

Detractors tended to forget that Reagan had been in politics since the 1960s, serving two rather successful terms as California's governor. Tip O'Neill, the venerable Democratic Speaker of the House, would recall lecturing the president-elect at their first meeting: "You're in the big leagues now." O'Neill would record that the clueless Reagan "seemed genuinely surprised to hear that"; Reagan would remember replying that having been "the governor of one of the largest states in the union," he had been in the big leagues "for quite a while."[17] Reagan did not mind being underestimated. But Reagan did not like being insulted—and his affability, simplicity, and flexibility obscured an ambitiousness and stubbornness that brought him to the White House.

This most unlikely president was entering office during a particularly challenging time. It was not just the litany of traumas Jimmy Carter mentioned in his 1980 address once again accepting the Democratic nomination: "the civil rights revolution, the bitterness of Vietnam, the shame of Watergate, the twilight peace of nuclear terror," along with the American diplomats held hostage in Iran. Americans endured political drift, diplomatic weakness, moral upheaval, and economic disaster. Carter's "misery index" from 1976, combining inflation and unemployment, nearly doubled in four years from 12.5 to over 20. When the 1980 campaign began the annual inflation rate was 22.3 percent, the prime rate—the bellwether interest rate banks charged their best customers—was at 11.25 percent. As the inflation rate, the unemployment rate, and the divorce rate soared, Americans doubted their government and themselves. The upheavals of the 1960s, the Vietnam War protests, and the Watergate scandal had undermined faith in the country, the presidency, and particularly the scandal-tarred Republican party. In 1959, 85 percent of Americans considered their "political institutions" the source of their greatest pride in their country. By 1973, 66 percent polled were "dissatisfied" with the government—making Americans more open to the growing conservative critique of a gigantic government threatening freedom and strangling the economy.[18]

By 1980, the federal government was indeed a behemoth. The half-trillion-dollar-a-year federal budget consumed nearly 25 percent of America's gross national product. This greedy, growing leviathan, which devoured hard-working Americans' tax dollars, was also an angel of mercy feeding the hungry, housing the homeless, healing the sick—one of every two households received some form of federal, state, or local government support; 37 million individuals accepted Social Security assistance; 50 million children attended 170,000 public schools; and a quarter of a billion Americans enjoyed the use of 29,500 post offices, one million bridges, and four million miles of roads.

Ronald Reagan did not invent conservatism. His First Hundred Days became conservatism's highpoint, the golden moment when the political frustrations accumulating over decades, the proposals kicked around for years, found expression in a powerful individual. The moderate Republican senator Charles Percy, responding to Reagan's broad call to members of Congress for legislative suggestions, wrote: "The response across the country to the issues raised in your campaign this year echoes much of what I heard on domestic issues from the people of Illinois during my own re-election campaign in 1978: the American people want an end to inflation; a reduction in their tax burdens; economic opportunity free of needless and burdensome regulations; and a stable supply of energy."[19]

Reagan's White House was uniquely positioned to exploit some profound cultural changes. Theodore Roosevelt's turn-of-the-century bully pulpit had become the late twentieth century's most formidable sound stage. Franklin D. Roosevelt and John F. Kennedy had expanded, invigorated, and wired the presidency. Dominating the federal government and the media, the president became the nation's focal point. Reagan brought to this souped-up soapbox an ease with the cameras, a fluidity of formal speech, an ear for popular concerns, an instinct for mass leadership, and an appreciation for the presidency's public relations power.

In his twenty-minute Inaugural Address, Ronald Reagan tapped into that power and demonstrated those skills. Warning of the national crisis while reassuring Americans that, together, they could solve it, Reagan targeted this "longest and one of the worst sustained inflations in our national history. It distorts our economic decisions, penalizes thrift, and crushes the struggling young and the fixed-income elderly alike." Reagan then pronounced his mantra: "In this present crisis, government is not the solution to our problem; government is the problem." He insisted, "it is not my intention to do away with government. It is, rather, to make it work—work with us, not over us; to stand by our side, not ride on our back." Reagan wanted to recalibrate the relationship between the government and the people: "We are a nation that has a government—not the other way around.... It is time to check and reverse the growth of government which shows signs of having grown beyond the consent of the governed."

Reagan's realized his vision—and typified his luck. Marching from the inauguration into the President's Room of the Senate, he signed an Executive Order freezing federal civilian hiring. Reagan proclaimed: "This begins the process of restoring our economic strength and returning the Nation to prosperity."[20] Concluding the inaugural lunch in Statuary Hall, Reagan declared: "With thanks to Almighty God, I have been given a tag line, the get-off line everyone wants at the end of a toast or speech. Some 30 minutes ago, the planes bearing our prisoners left Iranian airspace and now are free of Iran. We can all drink to this one." Iran's Ayatollah Khomeini had given the old performer a great gift, symbolizing Reagan's call to "begin an era of national renewal."

With their sensitivity to the symbolic, with all their bluster not quite eliminating their worries about their fragile popular base, with the zeal of ideologues and the humility of patriots, Reagan's aides understood that this administration had to make a good first impression. They recognized that "the central thrust of the presidency will be defined during the early period." Remembering John Kennedy's failed invasion of Cuba at the Bay of Pigs and other rookie fiascoes, they also worried that "As the administration seeks to establish control of the government, it is extremely vulnerable to making big mistakes." Reagan's team would carefully monitor the first day, the first week, the first month, the first 90 days, and the first 100 days—assessing the "symbolic as well as substantive values" of the president's actions at each plateau.[21]

Overall, Reagan's team was more moderate than conservatives wished. Where "is the dash, color and controversy" in the Cabinet—"the customary concomitants of a Reagan campaign?" the columnist Patrick Buchanan wondered.[22] The only fire-and-brimstone, rabidly conservative Cabinet member was James Watt. His presence, however, as an interior secretary hostile to environmentalism was enough to taunt liberals.

Reagan would have a rocky relationship with conservatives. He was too cautious and affable to alienate them, but he played to the center, knowing that conservatives had no alternative—they were not about to defect to the party of Jimmy Carter, Jesse Jackson, Ted Kennedy, and Walter Mondale. Early in the administration, when a reporter asked one aide what the White House wanted to give to conservatives, the aide replied: "symbolism."[23]

Meanwhile, Reagan and his aides focused on the economy. On February 5, 1981, President Reagan addressed America's "economic mess" on national television. Repudiating half-a-century's worth of policy, Reagan advocated dramatic tax cuts of 10 percent per year over three years and budget cuts of $40 to $50 million in the coming fiscal year. The new president banked the future of his two-and-half-week-old administration on his revolutionary "Program for Economic

Recovery." Reagan's main number cruncher and program architect was the new Office of Management and Budget (OMB) Director, David Stockman.

Stockman's push for the OMB job had climaxed with an "admittedly alarmist" thirty-five-page memo: "On the Danger of a GOP Economic Dunkirk." This call to arms warned about burgeoning budget deficits and a grim economic outlook that could be avoided only if the Republicans slashed taxes. Cutting all the fat from the federal budget—goodies for the rich as well as for the poor— would reassure Wall Street. The revived capital markets would trigger a boom that would allow the Federal Reserve Board to limit the money supply.

Like Franklin Roosevelt, Reagan wanted to reshape America in a "First Hundred Days" blitzkrieg. To seize the initiative, Reagan wanted to unveil his budget plan a month after his inauguration. The clichés of the moment had Cabinet members vowing they would not take a "'business-as-usual' approach" and journalists saying the administration "hit the ground running."[24] David Stockman, a thirty-something ex-hippie, became the Reagan Revolution's whirling dervish, chopping decades-old governmental programs promiscuously, saving $2.6 billion in food stamps here and $6 billion in waste-treatment grants there. Even critics marveled at his 20-hour days and his encyclopedic command of arcane budget details. And Stockman wanted to be an equal opportunity budget cutter. He targeted corporate freebies such as the Export-Import Bank, as well as the welfare state's signature programs. He was as committed to cutting defense as he was education, energy, housing, and health. Only across-the-board cuts could tame the budgetary behemoth and retain credibility, he believed.

Reagan presented his "Program for Economic Recovery" to a joint-session of Congress and a national television audience of 60 million during his first address to a joint session of Congress on February 18, 1981. In a 35-minute speech interrupted by applause fifteen times, the president proposed 83 major program cuts totaling $41.4 billion for fiscal year 1982 and tax cuts totaling $53.9 billion, averaging 10 percent a year for individuals over 3 years. He also asked the Congress to cut $4.4 billion in outlays for fiscal 1981. Ignoring the naysayers who feared a budget deficit as high as $25 billion by 1984, Reagan estimated that his program would yield a $500 million surplus by 1984. In fact, the 1984 deficit would be $185.3 billion, and by 1988 the total U.S. federal debt would be $2.6 trillion.

Even in this initial call to economic arms, Reagan and Stockman acknowledged they were proposing "a substantial reduction in the *growth* of federal expenditures" only. The program also called for tax cuts, regulatory rollbacks, and a new and more effective monetary policy.[25]

Reagan tempered his conservatism with compassion, or at least the appearance thereof. Reagan's recognition of the legitimacy of "entitlements" and his vow not to dismantle the "social safety net" illustrated America's consensus in favor of the social welfare state. Whereas David Stockman, the baby boomer, did not "think people are entitled to any services,"[26] Reagan, the depression baby, did not doubt the government's central role in protecting the "truly needy." Early in February Reagan had deemed untouchable seven basic social programs serving 80 million people at an annual cost of $210 billion. By protecting Social Security's Old Age and Survivors Insurance; Medicare's health program for the elderly; the Veterans Administration disabilities program; Supplemental Security Income for the blind, disabled, and elderly poor; school lunch and breakfasts for low-income children; Head Start preschool services; and the Summer Youth Jobs Program, Reagan limited his revolution. Reagan also handcuffed himself. With entitlement programs consuming approximately 60 percent of federal expenditures, and with half of these programs subject to automatic Cost of Living Adjustments (COLAs), Reagan could only chip away at the budget with a toothpick rather than an icepick.

Stockman's revolution needed an "Iron Chancellor," not an amiable former actor. Stockman gradually realized the Reagan Revolution was merely a "metaphor," he complained in his memoirs, an empty posture ruined by the politicians.[27] In fairness, Reagan did not share Stockman's zeal for budget-cutting or confrontation. The president was most concerned with cutting taxes and regulations.

Surprisingly, as Stockman crusaded, most Democrats conceded to Reagan his mandate. On Capitol Hill, many Democrats rushed to ride what they suddenly perceived to be a popular wave. It was not just Southern Conservative "Boll Weevils," who had long been cooperating with the Republicans. Congressman Richard Gephardt's Democratic Statement of Economic Principles said, "A national consensus has developed behind slowing the growth rate of federal spending, reducing the size of government, including its maze of regulations, and providing tax relief.... Democrats will support each of these goals and will work with the new administration to achieve them."[28]

As Democrats were divided, Republicans united. Tip O'Neill would insist that the true headline of the Congressional year, and the secret of Reagan's success, was the Republicans' lockstep approach on key votes. Managing this political campaign with military precision, White House senior staffers formed the Legislative Strategy Group (LSG) to shepherd the legislation. Chaired by Richard Darman, the Chief of Staff James Baker's aggressive protégé, the LSG hounded Republicans to follow their leader. When Senator Roger Jepsen of

Iowa threatened to stray on a difficult foreign policy vote to sell the Air Force's sophisticated airborne warning and control system called AWACS to Saudi Arabia, these political enforcers brooked no dissent. "We beat his brains in," the White House political director Ed Rollins exulted, in an uncharacteristically honest but indiscreet moment.[29]

Meanwhile, the president preferred wooing congressmen with a softer touch. Reagan spent many nights calling legislators from both parties, chatting, selling his program, and assessing where they stood. Reagan took his homework seriously, checking off his list, and writing capsule summaries of each call. "Mission accomplished. He sounds like he wants to help," "RR" scrawled after congratulating Democratic senator David Boren on his fortieth birthday.[30] "He's gung ho and working all out to bring about a win for the Gramm-Latta," the budget reconciliation bill cutting taxes and boosting defense spending, Reagan reported after phoning another conservative Democrat.[31]

Contrary to his reputation and while keeping banker's hours, Reagan worked hard those first few weeks. By the end of March, after 66 days in office— forty-eight working days, Reagan noted—he had met over 400 members of Congress on a "personal basis" and had presided over fourteen Cabinet meetings, making his the most active Cabinet since Franklin Roosevelt's. He also found time for 10 meetings with mayors, governors, and state legislators, met leaders of seven foreign countries and the foreign ministers from six more, while visiting Capitol Hill twice and Canada once.[32]

Reagan's budget proposal provoked an intense power struggle between his Republican revolutionaries and Democratic defenders of the welfare state. Despite his splashy inauguration, stirring speechmaking, and dramatic posturing, despite enjoying the first Republican majority in the Senate since 1954, the president faced formidable opposition. The House of Representatives remained solidly Democratic. "Every day we will be fifty-one votes short in the House to pass the president's legislation even if all Republicans vote with us," Vice President George Bush warned Cabinet members.[33] Washington's "permanent government" of bureaucrats and media bigwigs remained overwhelmingly allied to the New Deal. And while many Americans agreed that the welfare state was broken, few agreed on just how to fix it.

Despite its Republican majority, the Senate Budget Committee skewered Stockman and other Reaganites. Prospects for passage in the House were bleaker. Reagan was running into trouble. The more specific he was about his plans, the less popular he became. For all the talk about a Reagan "mandate," Reagan entered office with the lowest popularity rating of any president-elect since polling had begun. Americans seemed more enamored with the idea of budget cuts, and with the budget cutter, than with actual budget cuts. Furthermore, Reagan's activism—so essential to the success of his administration—risked depleting his already limited political capital.

Yet the new president seemed undisturbed. He was his usual affable self, charming legislators with his Irish wit, following his carefully stage-managed public appearances, and delivering the occasional speech. On March 30, after one such address to the AFL/CIO's National Conference of the Building and Construction Trades Department, the president heard "what sounded like two or three firecrackers" as he left the Washington Hilton and entered his armored limousine.[34] White House press secretary Jim Brady, Secret Service Agent Tim McCarthy, and policeman Tom Delehanty all fell to the ground, with bullet wounds. Shot in the head, Brady would never recover fully. Once again, in a continuing and unwelcome tribute to the presidency's unique position in American life, a crazed lone gunman had shot his way into American history.

It would be months before most Americans would discover how close their president came to dying that March day. Ronald Reagan not only defeated death, the old actor rose to the occasion, tossing off quips that obscured the seriousness of his wounds and mimicked the 1940's insouciant Hollywood heroes. When one nurse held his hand, he joshed "Does Nancy know about us?" When another asked how he felt, he echoed W. C. Fields: "All in all, I'd rather be in Philadelphia." When the surgeon approached him, he quipped "I hope you're a Republican"—prompting the classy response: "Today, Mr. President, we're all Republicans."

Reagan's miraculous recovery offered a welcome bookend to John Kennedy's traumatic murder. The failed assassination of the oldest man elected president helped exorcise the defeatist spirit of the 1960s, just as the murder of the youngest man elected president helped trigger a decade of nationwide self-doubt. Reagan had already emerged as a man most Americans loved to like. His poll ratings shot up, a sense of patriotism soared, and opposition to his programs folded, for a while. By May 8, just over 100 days after the inauguration, the Democratic-controlled House of Representatives passed Reagan's budget with a comfortable sixty-vote margin. "HOUSE PASSES DEEPEST BUDGET CUT IN HISTORY," the *Los Angeles Times* proclaimed, hailing the "270–154 vote" as "A BIG VICTORY FOR PRESIDENT."[35]

The Reagan Revolution's first round reduced the personal income tax rate by almost 25 percent and dropped the capital gains tax from 28 to 20 percent, yielding an unprecedented tax reduction of $162 billion. By the summer, Reagan had eliminated $35 billion in domestic spending from the request Jimmy Carter had submitted, and defense spending had ballooned. By 1986, the defense budget would be double 1980's allocation. "We have boldly reversed the trend of government," Reagan rejoiced. "As we promised to do in 1980, we have begun to trust the people to make their own decisions, by restoring their economic independence. We have started to free the energies and initiatives of Americans in an economy committed to growth."[36]

That summer of 1981, Reaganism peaked. The Reagan legislative steam-roller continued to flatten the Democratic opposition in the Congress, passing the Kemp-Roth tax cuts on the heels of the Stockman-Weinberger mix of social program cuts and defense increases. In July, Reagan nominated Sandra Day O'Connor to be the first female Supreme Court justice in American history, demonstrating Reagan's genius for public relations and his pragmatic, centrist tendencies on social issues. In August, the president's dramatic showdown with the PATCO air traffic controller's union, wherein he fired all of the government's air traffic controllers who obeyed the union's strike call, solidified his image as a no-nonsense leader determined to repudiate his predecessors' weaknesses and liberal instincts.

By September, however, the Democrats had seized upon the "fairness" issue to counterattack. And Reagan's great legislative successes during the spring and summer allowed his rivals to blame him for the growing recession. Much of the next seven and a quarter years would be spent scrambling on the scrimmage line Reagan and his men reached initially with breakneck speed.

The attempt on Reagan's life improved the president's public standing and helped ram through his program. As a result, the many successes during his first seven months in office were more personal than political. Cashing in on his personal popularity, Reagan failed to make the sale. Polls showed that millions of Americans still doubted Reagan's supply-side magic promising tax cuts would jumpstart the economy enough to raise government revenue. Yet the assassination attempt helped pass the Reagan economic package without forcing the president to convert the public. The counterattacks, and Reagan's endorsement of "entitlements" and "the social safety net," charted the limits of his revolution. Symbols not substance, Reagan's personality not his ideology, triumphed. "It's clear the President's overall strength is greater than the sum of his strengths on individual issues," one 1986 White House memo would acknowledge. "We can never avoid this fact—only turn it to our advantage."[37]

Ronald Reagan proved no more willing than Franklin Roosevelt, John Kennedy, or Lyndon Johnson had been to demand sacrifices. The budgetary compromises Reagan continued to accept reflected the power of the Democratic House and the welfare state's entrenched power. Some called the impasse between Reagan's budget-cutting and the Democrats' "tax and spend" approach "gridlock." Others recognized it as the historic, moderating force of the American consensus, one more proof of the Framers' genius.

Still, the end of Reagan's First Hundred Days enabled most reporters to toast the new president. Roosevelt analogies, the assassination quips, and amazed references to Reagan's popularity and sang froid abounded. In perhaps the most surprising salute, the liberal, usually anti-Reagan *New York Times* White House correspondent Steven R. Weisman gushed in the Sunday *New York Times Magazine*: "With a gift for political theater, Mr. Reagan has established his goals faster, communicated a greater sense of economic urgency and come forward with more comprehensive proposals than any new President since the first 100 days of Franklin D. Roosevelt, the hero of his youth."[38]

Nevertheless, at the peak of Reagan's power two anomalies emerged that would haunt his presidency. His aura of great success would obscure certain important failures. And he would be far more popular personally than his programs were politically. The First Hundred Days, then, accounts for a significant portion of Reagan's greatest success while delineating the limits of his Revolution. That it became such a central part of his mythology reflects just how much more successful Reagan and his aides were in perpetuating the Reagan narrative rather than the Reagan program, even as it serves as a case study of the Reagan Revolution's broad vision but often limited horizons.

NOTES

1. *Washington Post*, 20 Jan. 1981, p. 9.
2. *Washington Post*, 23 Jan. 1981, p. A1.
3. *Washington Post*, 4 Feb. 1981, p. A1.
4. *Washington Post*, 1 Mar. 1981, p. A1.
5. *Washington Post*, 5 Mar. 1981, p. A1.
6. *Washington Post*, 29 Jan. 1981, p. A1.
7. *Washington Post*, 6 Mar. 1981, p. A1.
8. *Washington Post*, 27 Mar. 1981, p. A8.
9. *Washington Post*, 8 Feb. 1981, p. A1.
10. *Washington Post*, 23 Jan 1981, p. A1.
11. *Washington Post*, 22 Feb. 1981, p. A1.
12. *Washington Post*, 18 Mar. 1981, p. A3.
13. *Washington Post*, 22 Mar. 1981, p. A1.
14. *Washington Post*, 10 Apr. 1981, p. A1; *Washington Post*, 15 Apr. 1981, p. A1.
15. *The United States News & World Report*, 5 May 1980, p. 33.
16. *Fortune*, 19 May 1980, p. 79.

17. Tip O'Neill with William Novak, *Man of the House* (New York: Random House, 1987), pp. 332–33; Ronald Reagan, *An American Life* (New York: Simon & Schuster, 1990), p. 233.

18. Samuel Huntington, "The Democratic Distemper," in Nathan Glazer and Irving Kristol, eds., *The American Commonwealth 1976* (New York: Basic Books, 1976), pp. 17, 18.

19. Charles H. Percy to Ronald Reagan, 22 Dec. 1980, 005377, FG 010 Box 1, Ronald Reagan Library, Simi Valley, California.

20. Ronald Reagan Memo, 20 Jan 1981, 0711, Box 64:6, Donald T Regan MSS Library of Congress, Washington, DC.

21. Final Report of the Initial Actions Project, 29 Jan. 1981, 33, Strategic Planning Memoranda-4 (1), CFOA465, Richard S. Beal MSS, Reagan Library; Stan Ebner to Ed Meese et al., "First 90 Days Project, Rough Draft," 13 Jan. 1981, 1, Box 12,390, Richard S. Beal MSS, Reagan Library.

22. *Boston Herald American*, 4 Jan. 1981.

23. *Washington Post*, 25 Jan. 1981, p. A5.

24. Donald T. Regan, Tim McNamar, Denish Thomas to Ed Meese, Jim Baker, Max Friedersdorf, Jim Brady, 16 Feb. 1981, [not sent], "Treasury Department Economic Recovery Program," 16 Nov. 1980 to 17 Feb. 1981, Box 138:1, Donald T Regan MSS, Library of Congress, Jack W. Germond and Jules Witcover, "Reagan's Style Dulls His Image as President," *Washington Star*, 25 Mar. 1981.

25. "America's New Beginning: A Program for Economic Recovery," p. 2, 18 Feb. 1981, OA 2991, Edwin A. Meese MSS, Ronald Reagan Library.

26. William Safire, *Safire's New Political Dictionary* (New York: Random House, 1993), p. 220.

27. David Stockman, *The Triumph of Politics* (New York: Harper & Row, 1986), p. 11.

28. Joseph Kraft, "The 'Republicrat' Debate," *Washington Post*, 12 Apr. 1981.

29. Ed Rollins, *Bare Knuckles and Back Rooms* (New York: Broadway Books, 1996), p. 103.

30. Max L. Friedersdorf and Powell A. Moore [to Ronald Reagan], 21 Apr. 1981, PR 007–02, President's Handwriting File, IV:1, Ronald Reagan Library.

31. Max L. Friedersdorf [to Ronald Reagan], Ronald Reagan comment, 23–26 Apr. 1981, PR 007–02, Box 1, President's Handwriting File, IV, Ronald Reagan Library.

32. James Baker to Ronald Reagan, 26 Mar. 1981, "Preparation for Washington Post Interview," Box 1, PR 016, 00058155, Ronald Reagan Library.

33. Terrel H. Bell, *The Thirteenth Man* (New York: Free Press, 1988), p. 19.

34. Reagan, *American Life*, p. 259.

35. *Los Angeles Times*, 8 May 1981, p. 1.

36. Ronald Reagan to Wendell Bailey, 9 Sept. 1981, M.B. Oglesby, Jr., MSS OA 8618, Box 3, Ronald Reagan Library.

37. William B. Lacy to Mitchell E. Daniels, 13 Mar. 1986, 396197, Box 42, FG 001, Ronald Reagan Library.

38. Steven R. Weisman, "A Test of the Man and the Presidency," *New York Times Magazine*, 26 Apr. 1981.

Chapter 2

AN INSIDER'S LOOK
AT THE REAGAN LEGACY

Edwin Meese III

A NATION IN TROUBLE

In January of 1981, when Ronald Reagan was inaugurated as president, the United States was in the midst of serious trouble. In almost every area of public policy—the economy, energy, national security, our position of leadership in world affairs, crime, and drug abuse—major problems existed that had grown worse during the latter years of the 1970s.

On the economic front, the nation faced its most serious crisis since the Great Depression of the 1930s. Inflation and unemployment had been steadily on the rise—contradicting the standard Keynesian view of a tradeoff between these economic evils. The Consumer Price Index had risen at a rate of 12.5 percent in 1980, after rising 13 percent in 1979. Joblessness in the second half of 1980 had risen to 7.5 percent and was still climbing. Interest rates were in double digits, topping out at 21.5 percent by the end of 1980, thus making borrowing for construction or capital investments in businesses almost impossible. Taxes on the average citizen were high and rising, so that the combination of high taxes and high inflation caused the real wages of American workers to plunge by 9 percent in just the two-year period 1979–1981, offsetting nearly two decades of growth and reducing real wages to their 1962 level.

Adding to the nation's woes were the petroleum and natural gas shortages of 1978–1979, which saw people shivering for lack of fuel supplies and enduring huge gas lines at service stations in many areas of the country.

America's foreign affairs were, if anything, even worse. Fifty-two Americans were being held hostage at our embassy in Iran, which had been taken over by mobs as a result of the Islamic revolution in that country. Elsewhere, the forces of communism were making inroads in most corridors of the globe. America's citizens, allies, and security interests seemed everywhere in danger.

In the later 1970s, the roster of countries taken over by Marxist revolution was long and ominous: Vietnam, Laos, Cambodia, Angola, Mozambique, Ethiopia, and more. In the final years of the Carter presidency, the Soviets invaded Afghanistan, Marxist-Leninist regimes took power in Nicaragua and Grenada, while El Salvador was being threatened by a similar fate. Combined with Castro's Cuba, this meant that the communist menace reached into the Western Hemisphere.

Likewise, in Europe, the oppression of the Soviet Union and its Warsaw Pact allies continued in the captive nations of Czechoslovakia, Hungary, Poland, Latvia, Lithuania, Estonia, and others.

While these threats to American national security and to the freedom of the Western world persisted, the country's national security capabilities had dramatically decreased. Over the prior decade, the share of federal dollars going to military preparedness had been in a state of free-fall. In 1961, when John Kennedy was president, defense comprised almost exactly 50 percent of the federal budget. In the ensuing years this fraction steadily declined so that by 1981, when Reagan came to office, it was down to 23.2 percent—less than half the budget share of almost two decades before.

This curtailment of relative spending for defense was due to the surging budgets for social welfare that began with the "Great Society" of Lyndon Johnson and accelerated in the 1970s. The Soviets were in the meantime devoting even greater resources to their own strategic arsenal, not to mention the billions they were spending to encourage revolution around the globe.

This reduction in defense spending meant that outlays for long-term military development were relentlessly contracted. Modernization of strategic weapons, including an aging bomber force, had been indefinitely postponed. Minuteman Missiles were state of the art in 1960, but by 1980 lagged far behind the Soviets' offensive weapons. U.S. naval forces had been cut in half. And pay raises for the military were put off, and then put off again.

The decline of American defenses and the disparity between the military efforts of the United States and the USSR affected not only our national security capability, but also our position of world leadership. There was a widespread consensus, not only at home, but in foreign capitals, that the defenses of the United States were inadequate to protect its people, to protect its national interests, and to fulfill its treaty obligations. Some claimed that the United States was neither a credible deterrent to its adversaries nor a reliable ally to its friends.

PROBLEMS AT HOME

Although the foreign affairs and national security situation was grave, the threat to domestic peace and safety in communities across the country was equally serious. Between 1960 and 1980 the number of serious crimes committed in the United States increased a frightening 322 percent. Crime rates for all major offenses had reached historical highs. At the same time, however, the percentage of serious criminals being sent to prison had steadily decreased. Those who did receive prison sentences served exceedingly short terms. As a result, a disproportionate number of new crimes was committed by a relatively small group of serious habitual offenders who engaged in criminal acts repeatedly. This lenient approach to criminal justice, at the expense of law abiding citizens who were the victims of crime, was the result of liberal theories of penology, which stressed the rehabilitation of criminals rather than the protection of society.

Directly related to the increase in crime was a dramatic increase in drug abuse during the period 1960 to the peak years of 1979 and 1980. The use of illicit drugs had become common on college campuses, among high school students, and even in the military. This widespread scourge of narcotics trafficking and abuse brought with it an associated toll in crime and death, as well as the ruined lives of many of the addicted.

As the above summary suggests, the prospects facing the United States at the beginning of the 1980s could scarcely have been worse. Nor did the authorities in the nation's capital apparently have any strategy to improve the situation. There appeared to be a vacuum of both leadership and new ideas. The people were told, in essence, that they would have to learn to accept these conditions on a permanent basis. They should learn to do with less gasoline; submit to the ever-rising burden of taxation and the slowdown of the economy; sit by idly while Marxists forces took over one country after another; and hope that through agreements with the Soviets we could persuade them, by appealing to their "charitable instincts," not to exploit our growing weakness.

Too many pundits at that time proclaimed that the days of capitalism had peaked and that socialism was the wave of the future. Many contended that the democratic governments of the West would have to live side by side with the Soviet-dominated Iron Curtain nations in a state of perpetual tension. Furthermore, some even contended that there was a moral equivalence between the governments of free peoples and the totalitarianism of the Marxist nations.

CONTENDING WITH CRISIS

This was the situation that Ronald Reagan faced in January 1981. His preparation to take on the new responsibilities had been extensive. As governor of California he had headed a state that, if it were a nation, would have been the seventh largest economy in the world. Furthermore, he had initiated during the campaigns of 1976 and 1980 a series of ideas and strategies to solve the problems facing the nation. He had developed these plans through consultation with several hundred experts from throughout America on a variety of domestic and foreign policy issues. These advisors, many of whom continued on into the administration, included former Cabinet members of previous administrations, prominent academic experts, Nobel Laureates, and successful leaders in government, business, labor, and the academic world.

Recognizing that a strong economy was essential to success both at home and abroad, President Reagan submitted to Congress a four-point economic program:

- A budget reform program to cut the rate of growth in federal spending;
- A series of proposals to reduce personal income tax rates by 10 percent a year, for all taxpayers, over three years and to create jobs by accelerating depreciation for business investment in plants and equipment;
- A far-reaching program of regulatory relief; and
- In cooperation with the Federal Reserve Board, a new commitment to a monetary policy that would restore a stable currency and healthy financial markets.

The key to economic revitalization was the reduction of tax rates. When Reagan became president, the top marginal rate on individual income was 70 percent. As a result of the tax-rate reductions of 1981 and then a tax reform program enacted in 1986, when Reagan left office, that top rate was 28 percent.

The net effect was to restore incentives to work, produce, save, and invest. With dramatically lower marginal rates and extra dollars of purchasing power, both individuals and businesses worked harder and produced more. With sub-stantially lower inflation, individuals were not so rapidly pushed into higher tax brackets and were thus less tempted to divert resources from investment to tax-and-inflation shelters. And businesses were better able to recover their investment in the capital investment that increased productivity. Likewise, dire predictions of massive revenue loss because of the tax rate reduction did not materialize.

With the closing of some "loopholes" in the 1986 Tax Act, and because the taxes were raised on a broader base, tax receipts actually increased from $517 billion to $1.03 trillion during the decade of the 1980s, nearly doubling this form of revenue to the federal treasury.

REBUILDING THE ARMED FORCES

Simultaneously, while addressing the economic problems, President Reagan also began to rebuild the nation's military capabilities. In this he was greatly aided by the sound advice of Secretary of Defense Caspar Weinberger, who had previous experience in a prior administration as Director of the Office of Management and Budget. Weinberger presented detailed plans to upgrade both strategic and conventional defense capabilities. Although making only modest increases in defense spending as a share of the federal budget (23.2% in 1981 to a high of 28.1% in 1987, followed by a reduction to 23.9% in 1990), funds were provided to modernize the strategic triad, acquire new ballistic missiles, begin replacing the aging B-52 aircraft with new stealth planes, rebuild the navy, upgrade tactical weapons systems, and adjust pay and living conditions to improve recruiting, morale, and reenlistment rates within the armed forces.

Particularly important was the latter effort. In the years following the Vietnam War, the antimilitary spirit that dominated some areas of public opin-ion during and after the war caused a deterioration in recruiting and in the quality of personnel in the military services. The result was a series of discipline problems, difficulty in recruiting, and a lack of pride in the uniform—both among some in the military and among too many in the civilian population. Some military commanders even directed their personnel not to wear their uni-forms off-post, for fear of being insulted and otherwise badly treated by anti-military civilians.

Ronald Reagan set out to change the military, both internally and in terms of civilian attitudes. In addition to improvements in pay and living conditions, he began to rebuild respect for the military and pride among its members. In his messages to the country he discussed the importance of military strength and applauded the men and women who served their country. He followed these words by personal example. He brought back Marines, in full dress uniform, to man the entrances to the White House. He visited military posts and bases and spent time talking with the service members and their families. He went to the Pentagon to personally award the Medal of Honor to an Army Master Sergeant, who had won this award during the Vietnam War, but had never been officially presented with the decoration. This combination of material and inspirational attention made a dramatic change in the morale of the armed forces and restored the viability of the all-volunteer armed forces, which had been in doubt during the latter part of the 1970s.

FROM ARMS CONTROL TO ARMS REDUCTION

Of all the difficulties President Reagan had to deal with in refurbishing our defenses, none was more complicated than "arms control." The president had very definite ideas about arms control, based on two guiding principles: (1) the security of the United States must be protected from any possible attack by keeping our defenses strong and by properly utilizing our technology; and (2) the idea of nuclear war and the reliance upon nuclear weapons was abhorrent and should be repudiated.

Reagan had often said that a "nuclear war could never be won and should never be fought." Toward this end, he deplored the strategy that existed when he arrived in office, known as "mutual assured destruction" (MAD). Under this theory each side in the Cold War could blow the other to smithereens and therefore neither, supposedly, would dare launch an attack. A "balance of terror" was supposed to ensure the peace. This theory dictated that each side could have sufficient offensive weapons to wreak destruction on the other, but neither could have defenses that would deter the carnage. This was the basis of the anti-ballistic missile (ABM) treaty of 1972.

Although the United States limited its building of strategic weapons and scrupulously obeyed the ABM treaty, the Soviet Union continued its rapid buildup of offensive nuclear weapons and also cheated on the AMB treaty by working on components of a ballistic missile defense system. This raised the specter of a preemptive strike by Moscow, with enough strategic weapons left, and a potential ballistic missile defense system, to nullify any American effort at retaliation. This was known as the "window of vulnerability" that concerned

Ronald Reagan and U.S. defense experts. As a result, President Reagan directed that the United States begin development of the Strategic Defense Initiative (SDI), a system of defenses against ballistic missiles, which he believed—when fully developed—would make nuclear weapons obsolete. Although a difficult technological challenge, work on the SDI has continued to this date, and recent tests on its components have been successful.

CONTAINING THE SOVIET UNION

Ronald Reagan had studied the communists since the 1940's, when as president of the Screen Actors Guild he led his union and other portions of the movie industry in defeating domestic communists, who were attempting to take over the motion picture industry for use as a propaganda vehicle. Decades of studying communism, including its international manifestations, led him to believe that the theory of "détente," which was our formal policy response to the Soviet Union during the 1970s, was ineffective and self-defeating. The Soviets had continued their aggression around the world and continued to be a threat to the free world. Therefore, upon taking office, Ronald Reagan initiated a new strategy for dealing with worldwide Marxism.

In addition to rebuilding our own military capabilities, he initiated strategic efforts to deal with the USSR, which became known as the "Reagan Doctrine." First, he took on the Soviet Union and international communism on a moral plane. He refused to accept the so-called moral equivalence theory between the communist regimes and the democratic governments of free people. It was in this sense that he referred to the USSR as an "evil empire." Second, Reagan warned the Soviet Union that any further attempts at aggression, such as the invasion of Afghanistan and the efforts taking place in Angola and El Salvador, would be resisted by the United States and the free nations of the world. Third, he began a process of rolling back prior Soviet aggression by supporting the freedom fighters in Poland, Afghanistan, Angola, and Nicaragua.

Reagan presented his strategy to the world in his historic June 1982 speech to the British Parliament in which he proclaimed that the free world would "transcend communism" and would "consign Marxism-Leninism to the ash heap of history." It culminated in his famous 1987 challenge to Mikhail Gorbachev, then general secretary of the communist party and leader of the Soviet Union: "Mr. Gorbachev...tear down this [Berlin] wall!"

DEALING WITH CRIME AND DRUGS

Upon taking office, President Reagan recognized the tremendous problems of crime and drugs that were facing the American people. At the same time he appreciated the limited constitutional role of the federal government, since the police power belonged to the states and to local governments. He did feel, however, that the federal government had some role in stemming the tide of crime. Accordingly, he directed Attorney General William French Smith to convene a bipartisan national task force on crime control. It was headed by James Thompson, governor of Illinois, and Griffin Bell, a former federal appeals judge who had been attorney general in the prior Carter administration.

This task force traveled throughout the United States, interviewing chiefs of police, sheriffs, state and local public officials, crime victims, and others who had knowledge of the public safety difficulties pervading the nation. The almost unanimous request from local police executives was for the federal government to make a greater effort in dealing with the problem of illegal drugs.

This was an appropriate federal role, since it was the international and interstate trafficking in drugs that was at the heart of the problem. Accordingly, the president took the recommendations of the Task Force and developed a five-part national strategy for the control of drug trafficking and drug abuse: (1) expanded international cooperation to deal with the production and trafficking in illicit drugs; (2) strengthened domestic law enforcement efforts against drug dealers; (3) increased education and prevention efforts to deter the initial use of drugs, particularly among young people; (4) expanded programs for the treatment of drug abuse and the rehabilitation of drug offenders; and (5) continued research to better understand the incentives for drug use, the addicting properties of these substances, and additional means of preventing and treating drug abuse.

This strategy was augmented by the personal efforts of President Reagan and First Lady Nancy Reagan, who led a nationwide campaign against the dangers of drug abuse and which enlisted the cooperation of the news media, schools and colleges, the entertainment industry, and a variety of citizen organizations that emphasized the cost in both lives and material resources attributed to the scourge of drugs.

COMMUNICATING WITH THE PEOPLE

An important part of Ronald Reagan's efforts to deal with the substantive problems that he had inherited was his continuing practice of speaking directly to the American people. He recognized that the preceding decade had been a time in which many citizens had lost confidence in their country and its institutions and had been persuaded by pessimistic pundits that our "best days were over" and that the nation faced a future of diminished progress and success. For too many people the sense of pride in the country, the "can do" spirit, and the appreciation of freedom that had characterized our country before and during World War II had been replaced in the 1970s by a bleak view of the future and what some termed a "national identity crisis."

Ronald Reagan dealt with this problem by frequently addressing the American people on television and by explaining the reasons for his measures to improve our national condition, as well as his confidence in the ability of the American people to rise above crisis and to regain their traditional optimism. He was often called "the great communicator," but he always contended that it was not his greatness that was effective but the ideas that he was communicating. This effort to restore the self-confidence of the American people and their faith in the traditions and institutions of the country was an important part of the national recovery during the 1980s.

ASSESSING THE RESULTS

By the end of Ronald Reagan's two terms, a major change was seen in the direction of the public policy of the United States. Prior to his election, America had seen a succession of presidencies cut short by tragedy or turmoil. The assassination of John Kennedy, the Vietnam upheaval that forced the withdrawal of Lyndon Johnson, the Watergate-driven resignation of Richard Nixon, the brief tenure of Gerald Ford, and the erratic term of Jimmy Carter seemed to define the burdens and limits of the office. Prior to 1981, it was widely assumed that the job of president had gotten too big and complicated for any one person to handle.

In all respects, the Reagan era overturned such thinking. He was the first American president since Eisenhower to complete two full terms in office. He had strategies for dealing with our domestic and foreign challenges and his success in carrying them forward, despite a vast array of obstacles, produced a series of significant results.

In economic matters, Reagan demonstrated his faith in the free market and proved that reducing the rate of federal taxation, regulatory reform, and slowing the growth of federal spending could spur the forces of recovery and stimulate market growth, thus bettering the lot of all Americans.

The results were significant: inflation as expressed by the Consumer Price Index showed the rate of increase fall from several digits in 1979–1980 to an average rate of 3.3 percent in 1981–1986, the lowest level since the early 1960s. Along with the decrease in inflation, interest rates dropped dramatically as well.

The Reagan policies contributed to recovery in three ways: first, by leaving more purchasing power in the hands of private citizens, due to a reduction in their taxes; second, by cutting marginal tax rates on extra dollars of income, encouraging additional investment, work, and entrepreneurial risks; and third, by helping to slow the rate of increase in government spending. Because of lower tax and inflation rates American citizens were able to keep more dollars of their income, and those dollars were depreciating less rapidly in terms of purchasing power.

As a result, for the first time in a decade, the average citizen had a substantial increase in disposable real income, rising from $9722 in 1980 (expressed in constant 1982 dollars) to $11,793—more than $2000 higher than it had been when Reagan was elected. The economic growth of the Reagan era was also reflected in the rise of the stock market: the Dow Jones industrial average went from 776 in 1982 to nearly 3000 by the end of the decade. This was matched by corresponding growth, not only in personal incomes, but also in jobs, output, and productivity. Some 20 million new jobs were created and this became one of the longest and most dynamic economic expansions in American history, and by far the most substantial in a time of peace. Likewise the real median income rose by 11.5% from a low of $27,320 in 1982 to a high of $30,468 in 1989, an important boost in household income that resulted from increasing worker productivity and an expanding economy.

Despite claims of Reagan detractors that the 1980s were a "decade of greed," the truth is totally different. By every measure, the decade of the 1980s was actually a period of unusual generosity on the part of Americans. The annual rate of growth in total real giving in the 1980s was nearly 55% higher than in the previous twenty-five years. The annual compound growth rate of per capita giving over the 9 years 1980 through 1989 was double the average annual increase during the twenty-five years prior to the decade of the 1980s.

Another indication that all segments of the economy benefited from the Reagan economic policies is reflected in the shares of total federal taxes paid by all families before and after the tax rate reductions. In 1988 the most affluent quintile of tax paying families paid a higher percentage of the total tax burden than in 1980. By contrast, all other quintiles, lowest through the forth, had a reduction in the share of federal tax paid by families in those categories. The share of total federal taxes paid by the highest 1 percent of earning families had increased by over 23 percent from 1980 to 1988. By 1988, the average tax burden of the top 1 percent of families was 240 times the average tax burden of the lowest quintile.

FREEDOM, SECURITY, AND WORLD LEADERSHIP

The rebuilding of America's defense capabilities and the strategy of dealing with the Soviet Union resulted in the end of the Cold War, with the West and the forces of freedom winning. After forty-five years of tension, the imminent threat of nuclear warfare was effectively ended.

Through the "Reagan Doctrine," the United States nurtured anticommunist resistance forces in Poland, Angola, Afghanistan, and Nicaragua. This was a prelude to the implosion of the Soviet Union in 1991, which freed the captive nations and expanded the number of democracies throughout the globe. The buildup of the armed forces—which had convinced the Soviet Union that it could not prevail in an armed conflict with the West—also provided the finest military force in history; this force was subsequently available when it became necessary for the United States to lead a coalition of nations in repelling Iraq, which had invaded Kuwait in 1991. The pioneering efforts for ballistic missile defense—The Strategic Defense Initiative—provided hope for a future means of achieving Reagan's dream of making nuclear weapons obsolete.

The economic success within the United States and the use of free market principles provided the formula for economic growth throughout the world, particularly to the emerging democracies that were beginning, following the end of the Cold War. Reagan's personal leadership became apparent as he and Margaret Thatcher, then prime minister of Great Britain, became dominant figures in the annual meetings of the seven leading industrialized nations, as well as in the diplomatic efforts that took place between such events.

This combination of economic, diplomatic, military, and philosophical success undergirded the restoration of America's position of leadership in the world. Both at home and abroad there was a new respect for the traditions and capabilities of our Republic, and many nations fashioned their new Constitutions in a manner similar to that of the United States, hoping to emulate its concepts of ordered liberty.

Not only was the nation protected from the threat of external attack, but domestic security was also improved. The new strategies and expanded national leadership in the effort against drug trafficking and drug abuse produced remarkable results. During the ten-year period between 1982 (the beginning of the Reagan five-point strategy) and 1992, drug abuse in the United States was reduced by over 50 percent. This had an impact on crime as well, as the crime rate throughout the country decreased from its 1980 high. There is no question that other important factors contributed to this downturn in criminal activity. New policies among the states, which sent serious habitual offenders to prison for longer periods of time, and improved police methods, such as the computer-assisted crime deterrent strategies in New York City and elsewhere, had a significant effect on the crime situation. But it was also evident that decreased drug activity was an important factor in obtaining safer streets and communities, and in having fewer young people initiated into a life of drug abuse and crime.

DISAPPOINTMENT AMIDST PROGRESS

Despite the numerous accomplishments of the Reagan Era, not everything went right. At the end of his term as president, Reagan stated that his greatest disappointment was his failure to reduce the size and cost of the federal government. Although tax revenues during the 1980s increased by 99.4%, federal spending increased still more—growing by 112%.

Part of this was due to the way the federal fiscal machinery operates, essentially being on autopilot, with huge increases built into the very structure of the budget. These increases were primarily in the social welfare area, including social security, Medicare, and Medicaid. But even in the so-called discretionary spending, there were increases because of the habit of Congress—particularly the House of Representatives, which was controlled during the entire 8 years by Democratic leadership—of holding up the appropriate spending bills until after the beginning of the next fiscal year, and then presenting them to the president in a single omnibus budget act. The president then had no option except to sign the budget in order to keep the government operating, since the new spending year had already begun. Therefore budget deficits existed during the Reagan years, which were particularly high between 1983 and 1986. Finally, in 1985, President Reagan was able to obtain adoption of the Gramm-Rudman-Hollings Budget Act, which moved to enact a series of mandatory deficit reductions to be reached through automatic cuts, if targets were not met by statutory deadlines. While Gramm-Rudman limits could be and were evaded by the Congress, the limits acted as a general restraint on the spending impulse, and as a result, deficits declined markedly during the last three budgets attributed to President Reagan. Despite the budget problems discussed above, President Reagan was able to hold the annual real domestic spending increases to a much lower level than any other president since World War II.

IRAN-CONTRA

One of the most serious episodes that threatened the Reagan presidency was the so-called Iran-Contra Affair. Actually this matter grew from two legitimate policy actions. One was the attempt to open communications with moderate elements within the Iranian government and to obtain their aid in locating American hostages who had been kidnapped by terrorist groups in Lebanon. The other was the support given by the Reagan administration to the Freedom Fighters seeking to liberate Nicaragua from its Marxist regime. The problem occurred when overzealous members of the National Security Council staff diverted funds derived from weapons sales that were part of the Iranian Initiative and redirected them to provide financial support to the Nicaraguan Freedom Fighters. Such a diversion was unauthorized and wrong, and provided political adversaries with a weapon to attack the president. Ultimately, numerous investigations revealed that Reagan knew nothing about the diversion until it was discovered by a member of his Cabinet. By his immediate action in revealing the facts about the misconduct to Congress and the public, firing those responsible, and taking steps to ensure that such wrongdoing could not be repeated in the future, Reagan was able to minimize the potential political damage and maintain the confidence of the American people.

THE LEGACY OF RONALD REAGAN

Ronald Reagan will be best remembered for his three major accomplishments as president: First, he led the country out of the worst economic conditions since the Great Depression of the 1930s and instituted policies that began the longest period of peacetime economic growth and prosperity in U.S. history. Second, he developed a new strategy of victory over communism and set in motion the forces that led to the end of the Cold War, with the West winning, and the implosion of the Soviet Union. Third, he revived the spirit of the American people and restored their confidence in their nation and themselves.

But in addition, Reagan's presidency is also a legacy of great personal qualities: leadership, courage, and cheerfulness. Despite fierce opposition by his political opponents and many in the news media, Reagan persevered in his objectives, continually showed good humor and civility, and took the high road by forcefully presenting his views to the American public, rather than engaging in mudslinging battles with his adversaries.

The era of the Reagan presidency presaged one of the most remarkable expansions of liberty and democracy in the history of man. Blessed with unquenchable optimism about the creative power of the human spirit, Ronald Reagan proved that freedom works, not only for the people of this land, but for those anywhere who have suffered from governmental oppression and subjugation. As he himself put it at the end of his term in office, "We came to change the nation, and we changed the world."

Chapter 3

RONALD REAGAN'S SOUTH: THE TANGLED ROOTS OF MODERN SOUTHERN CONSERVATISM

Joseph Crespino

In August 1980, Ronald Reagan's first campaign stop after winning the Republican Party presidential nomination was at the Neshoba County Fair in Philadelphia, Mississippi. Addressing a crowd of over 15,000 enthusiastic supporters, Reagan invoked the "states' rights" mantra that had sustained a generation of southern segregationists.[1] Just 16 years earlier, the discovery of three murdered civil rights workers in Neshoba County had horrified the nation. Reports on the men's disappearance and the federal manhunt to find them revealed a white population in Mississippi dramatically out of step with the rest of America.

Reagan's Neshoba County appearance made for a powerful symbol. From one view, it represented another stop in an on-going Republican electoral strategy that dated back to 1964. Sixteen years earlier the only states that Goldwater won outside of Arizona were the five states of the Deep South. Only four elections later, his ideological successor swept every southern state except for Jimmy Carter's home state of Georgia. In between, southern racial populists such as George Wallace pioneered a politics of white backlash that became the channel for an emerging Republican operation across the region. GOP officials in Mississippi knew this strategy well. A year before Reagan's appearance, when asked where a Republican nominee should visit in the state, the Mississippi national committeeman recommended the Neshoba County Fair. Any Republican nominee would have to do well among "the George Wallace–inclined voters," he reasoned. The Neshoba County Fair, the traditional hill county spot for Mississippi stump-speaking, was the place to do it.[2]

As intriguing as this political folklore is, Reagan's visit to Neshoba County obscures as much as it reveals about the nature of the southern Republican Party in the 1980s. By that decade long-term trends had shifted the region's dominant political culture away from the Black Belt, areas in the Deep South with the richest agricultural land, the largest percentage of African Americans, and home to the powerful planter elite. This included developments such as the in-migration of outsiders to the region, the growth of urban and suburbanized spaces, the rise of the Sunbelt economy, and the growing convergence of southern and national standards of living. These were broad social and economic changes that did not always translate into electoral victories. Only in the 1980s did Republican success in presidential elections begin to filter to local elections across the region. Still, the GOP's dominance in terms of presidential politics was remarkable in the 1980s: Republicans carried 32 of 33 state presidential elections in the South during the decade. The great accomplishment of Ronald Reagan was his ability to convince thousands of long-standing conservative white Democrats to abandon their traditional party allegiance and elect not only Republican presidents, but also Republican members of congress, governors, and state representatives.[3]

Scholars have debated the best way to explain the change in southern partisanship in the post–World War II period. Did the road to the Republican South lead through the urban and suburbanized spaces created by the dramatic economic modernization in the postwar period? Or was a place like Neshoba County, with its history of racial antagonism and violence, more important in understanding how modern Republican success was built upon the GOP's ability to tap into white southerners' resentment of the civil rights movement? It is a question of no small importance. Conservative white southerners have played a vital role in the electoral success of the conservative-dominated Republican Party. Examining the roots of this partisan shift is important not just in understanding modern southern politics, but also in recounting the origins and success of Ronald Reagan's America.

The three and a half decades following the end of World War II were a period of remarkable change in the American South. As late as 1938, Franklin Roosevelt famously declared the South the nation's "number one economic problem." The region remained mired in a low-wage agricultural economy that made its citizens some of the poorest, most destitute Americans. The system of sharecropping that had emerged in the aftermath of emancipation as a peculiarly southern compromise between wage labor and slavery intensified agricultural poverty and created disincentives toward mechanization and agricultural modernization. Socially, the system of legalized separation and the systemic political exclusion of African Americans created a southern caste system that encouraged massive African American migration out of the region and fed the national perception of white racism as a particularly southern phenomenon.[4]

In the half century that followed Roosevelt's declaration, the South experienced an economic and social revolution. The United States as a whole experienced unprecedented economic expansion, yet the South still managed to narrow the gap between the region and the nation in any number of economic indicators. The South went from being the nation's number one economic problem to an important link in the Sunbelt, which connected the former states of the Confederacy from Texas westward to California. These states were home to the most dynamic growth areas in the country. Since 1964, every elected American president has hailed from a Sunbelt state.

But the South's role in the Sunbelt obscures the low-wage jobs that typified industrialization in nonmetropolitan areas of the South. Intense poverty continued to plague the region, particularly in the Black Belt and Appalachia.[5] Perhaps the most striking continuity from the 1930s to the 1980s South was the almost militant social conservatism of the region's white population. White southerners had been among the most enthusiastic supporters of Franklin Roosevelt's New Deal, because the region was in desperate need of the assistance the Democrats offered. Most white southerners were economic progressives in the 1930s, but there were also many who quickly soured on the idea of an expansionistic, modern federal state. The 1937 "Conservative Manifesto," which represented the first significant break within the New Deal coalition over the future of Roosevelt's economic reforms, was organized and inspired by southern Democrats. According to David Kennedy, the statement represented "a kind of founding charter for modern American conservatism."[6] By the late 1940s, as the national Democratic Party increasingly identified with a progressive civil rights position, southern whites were on their way out of the Democratic Party. The defection was slowed by the fact that they had no particular place to go in national politics for another two decades, but the unraveling of the Solid South had begun.

The question is when and how did these white conservative Democrats end up as Republicans. One way to reframe the issue is to ask which George was more important, George Wallace or George H.W. Bush? Cases can be made for both as a representative forerunner of Republican politics in the region. George Wallace, the four-time Democratic governor of Alabama and four-time presidential candidate, was the quintessential figure of the white South's "massive resistance" to the civil rights movement. This was an ironic development given that early in his career Wallace was an economic populist and racial moderate, positions that grew out of the New Deal politics of the desperately poor South. But Wallace made a Faustian bargain after he lost the race for governor in 1958. His opponent, John Patterson, portrayed Wallace as soft on segregation, by far the most significant issue in Alabama politics in the late 1950s. Wallace, the story goes, vowed to friends and associates that he would never be "out-niggered" again. Wallace won the governorship in 1962 as a hard-line segregationist. The following year, he became a national symbol of segregationist resistance during his infamous stand in the schoolhouse door, blocking African American students from registering at the University of Alabama.

Throughout the 1960s, Wallace never missed an opportunity to defend southern home rule in the face of what he argued was a meddlesome, all-powerful federal government, dominated by liberal do-gooders who ignored the concerns of everyday Americans. His entry into the Democratic presidential primary in 1964 uncovered a white working-class backlash against liberal civil rights reforms, a constituency that he united with white Deep South voters in his 1968 presidential run as a third-party candidate. Wallace's presence in the campaign siphoned off conservative support for the Republican candidate Richard Nixon. Wallace ran even stronger in 1972 before an assassination attempt effectively ended his national political career. In the process, however, Wallace pioneered a set of populist, antiliberal positions that grew naturally out of his role as the most talented and ingenious leader of southern massive resistance. Wallace's pioneering work among "forgotten Americans" both inside and outside the South blazed the trail for populist conservative politicians in the Republican Party.[7]

The career of a new breed of southern Republican politicians suggests a different trajectory of modern southern Republicanism. George H.W. Bush, the Connecticut-born son of a U.S. senator who moved to Texas to make his fortune in the oil business, is a good example. In his first foray into national politics, Bush ran a hard-edged campaign in 1964 for the U.S. Senate in Texas against a liberal Democrat. He adopted many of the right-wing positions that had helped Barry Goldwater rally conservative activists and win the Republican presidential nomination that year. Bush lost that election. He later expressed regret to his minister in Houston over how he had conducted the campaign. Two years later, Bush won a House seat from a Houston district that was 90 percent white by advocating "modern Republicanism." He served two terms before again losing a Senate race. From there Bush's political career oscillated around appointed party positions in Washington, but his mixed success in Texas state politics

reflected the slow but steady progress of Republican candidates in the traditionally Democratic South. Bush embodied many of the characteristics of the new
southern Republican voter. He was a white-collar professional, college-educated
and affluent, a migrant to the economically booming suburban Sunbelt. Bush's
position on racial issues reflected Sunbelt moderation. He came out strongly
against the Civil Rights Act in his 1964 campaign, but his moderate leanings
soon came to the fore. He won 35 percent of the black and Hispanic vote in
his 1966 campaign (up from 3 percent statewide in 1964). In his first term in
the House, he took a controversial stand in favor of open-housing legislation,
which attempted to break down racially segregated neighborhoods.[8]

Wallace and Bush's political careers present two different trajectories for
understanding Republican politics in the South. Wallace's career highlighted
the continuity both in southern politics and in white racial attitudes from the
Jim Crow era to the 1980s. Wallace himself never became a Republican. Late
in his political career, he would win election as Alabama's governor and return
to the economic populism and racial moderation that characterized his early
career. Even so, Wallace's ability in the 1960s and early 1970s to translate white
racial populism in the South into a broader conservative rejection of liberal
social and political reforms paved the way for Republican success in the region.
As Democrats clearly aligned themselves with the forces of change in the South,
white conservative southerners fled the Democratic Party and became Republicans largely on the basis of racial politics. The great success of the modern
Republican Party has been in masking this racist reaction in the color-blind
language of conservative ideology.

The George Wallace road to the Republican South, however, raises at least
three interpretive problems. First, the notion that white racist reactionaries of
the 1960s, in effect, found their redemption in the conservative politics of the
Republican Party in the 1980s overstates the success of southern massive resistance politicians. The idea is rooted in an ironic, tail-wagging-the-dog formulation: instead of the South becoming more like the rest of the nation, in fact,
the nation was "southernized." But this analysis ignores important southern
breakthroughs. Just look at the signature issue of southern massive resistance—
school desegregation. Massive resistance leaders predicted that 50 to 100 years
would pass before whites would attend school with blacks in southern public
schools (George Wallace's formulation in his 1962 inaugural speech was stark-
est of all: "Segregation today. Segregation tomorrow. Segregation forever").
Certainly, school desegregation did not flow easily or immediately from the
Supreme Court's decision in Brown v. Board of Education, and a small but significant number of southern whites left the public schools for private, all-white

academies rather than attend desegregated public schools. Still, by the early 1970s, public schools in Deep South states that had seen the fiercest, most unified resistance from white politicians were among the most fully integrated schools in the nation. The number of southern black students in majority white schools reached its high point in the 1980s.[9]

In the longer view, the massive resistance of the white South—despite all of its bluster—was notable for its relative ineffectiveness. This leads to a second critique: the attention given to the gothic politics of resistance in the South have often obscured the significant history of white racism outside of the region. Metropolitan historians of the North and West have shown how central white racism was in fights over housing, jobs, and civil rights in the post-World War II period.[10] White Americans—whether in California or New York, Michigan or Massachusetts—did not need George Wallace to tell them what was wrong with the liberal wing of the Democratic Party. The large migration of southern African Americans into overcrowded urban areas had been exacerbating racial tensions in American cities since the 1940s. This had a slow-burn effect, one that laid the groundwork for the eventual defection of white ethnic working class Americans—"Reagan Democrats" to use the term that developed in the 1980s—out of the Democratic Party.

Finally, interpretations that connect the era of massive resistance with the Republican policies of the 1980s fail to appreciate the dramatic changes in both the legal status of African Americans and the political economy of the South. These changes certainly did not erase racial inequality but they did transform its dynamics.[11] Important legal and legislative developments fundamentally transformed the antidemocratic, white supremacist regimes that dominated southern politics in the rough century following emancipation. In *Smith v. Allwright* (1944), the Supreme Court outlawed the white primary, which had allowed the southern Democratic Party to act as a private organization, excluding African Americans from political participation. In 1962, the Supreme Court's decision in *Baker v. Carr* broke the back of the rural, Black Belt conservatives who had dominated southern state legislatures since the late nineteenth century. Reapportioned state legislatures shifted political power away from rural districts to urban and suburban districts. Equally important, the 1965 Voting Rights Act abolished the systematic exclusion of the Jim Crow South and became the basis for a southern black political leadership that transformed Democratic Party politics in the region by the 1980s. The struggle against recalcitrant southern whites to dilute black voting strength, though heated, was largely successful. In the 1980s, the former bastions of Deep South recalcitrance like Louisiana, Alabama, and Mississippi led the nation in the number of black elected officials.[12]

The shift in power away from the rural Blackbelt to metropolitan areas of the Sunbelt explains a lot about Republican Party growth in the South. In fact, two political scientists have argued recently that the story of economic modernization in the South—and an associated politics of class, not race—best explain the shift in partisan identification among southern whites. Most of the Republican representatives from the South in the 1980s came from white majority districts in upper South areas in which racial politics were not as polarized. It was the peripheral south—not the Deep South districts that George Wallace won when he ran in 1968—that first began to regularly send Republican representatives to Congress and that was the most consistent source of Republican Party growth.[13]

But the problem with the George Wallace versus George Bush formulation is that it treats race and class as mutually exclusive categories. It obscures how economic and social change combined in contributing to Republican ascendancy in the region. Southern suburbs were fed by an expanding white-collar middle class, yet suburbanization in the South, as across the nation, was hardly a nonracialized historical development. No southern metropolitan area offers clearer evidence on this score than Atlanta, the unofficial capital of the modern Sunbelt South. Atlanta was hailed by no less of an authority than President Kennedy for being the first major southern city to voluntarily desegregate its schools. High-profile boycotts and sit-ins in the early 1960s forced the city's business elite to broker desegregation agreements. A progressive Atlanta business community held a dinner honoring hometown hero Martin Luther King after he won the Nobel Peace Prize, and Mayor William B. Hartsfield coined the phrase that would become shorthand for the business community's pro-growth, racially moderate ethos—Atlanta: The City Too Busy To Hate.

Yet the racial moderation of Atlanta's business and civic boosters masked widespread conflict over the desegregation of schools, neighborhoods, and public accommodations in the city. The white flight that took place in that city was both literal and metaphoric. White city dwellers fled racially diversifying neighborhoods for lily-white suburbs north of city. But, more broadly, white Atlantans fled the public sphere for a private one, whether that meant schools, clubs, or public services. Thus, the intensely privatized, antigovernment ideology of conservative whites living in the Atlanta suburbs cannot be divorced from the racial divisions that had characterized urban politics in Atlanta. By the 1980s, suburbanites in Atlanta or in similar suburbs throughout the Sunbelt may have projected an image of racial innocence compared to urban working-class whites or to other southern whites in the rural Deep South, but it was innocence born of amnesia. Whites had moved to the suburbs, in part at least, to escape the racial politics of the cities. Their racial conservatism, however, could be seen in virulent suburban politics that fought to protect the privileged racial and class makeup of their communities. In suburban communities north of Atlanta, antiannexation campaigns, fights against the extension of public transit into the suburbs, and the nearly all-white public school system all testified to how deeply the protection of white privilege remained a part of suburban Sunbelt politics.[14]

White flight either in Atlanta or in other cities should not be reduced to the individual racism of white urban dwellers. The phenomenon can be traced backed to federal housing policies initiated in the 1930s that created economic incentives toward suburban development and contributed directly to the segregated landscape of metropolitan America. Urban renewal programs in the postwar period also had the unintended effect of leaving behind benighted urban landscapes. And the difficult task of desegregating urban school districts placed pressures on families that went beyond the mere antipathy that many white parents felt about having their children in school with blacks. The concept of the neighborhood school that would provide a safe and familiar environment in which their children could learn became an ideal that white parents could realize in the suburbs, particularly after the Supreme Court's 1974 decision in *Milliken v. Bradley* that outlawed desegregation plans bridging the cities and the suburbs.[15]

In this sense, suburbanization in the Sunbelt and the political changes it encompassed were hardly regional phenomenon. By the end of the 1970s, as one historian has pointed out, more than two-thirds of voters in 11 southern states lived in metropolitan regions, "where residential patterns of race and class mirrored the prevailing trends throughout the nation."[16] The new suburban communities of the Sunbelt pioneered a set of political arguments about race and rights that would resonate far outside the region. From this view, it was not the southern strategies of Republican politicians that were important so much as suburban ones. A broad, bipartisan consensus of white middle-class and upper-class homeowners emerged in the 1960s and 1970s that protected suburban interests over those of underserved and underresourced urban areas with high percentages of minority population. Whites in the Sunbelt suburbs pioneered a "colorblind conservatism" that became the basis of modern Republican politics. This political identity developed not from top-down political strategies of Republican Party elites—as the older "southern strategy" thesis held—but out of grass-roots political struggles at the local level, such as fights over busing, public transportation, taxation, and municipal annexation.

For all that was new about the conservative colorblindness of the Sunbelt by the 1980s, however, it is important to remember that conservative uses of colorblind arguments have a longer history. In the 1960s, southern segregationists in the Deep South—at least the most successful ones—increasingly shied away from racially explicit language to defend their conservative positions, either in the courts or in the court of public opinion. The language of states' rights was, after all, a "colorblind" argument—only it was language that by the 1960s the majority of Americans recognized as a mere cover for white racism. What was new about the 1980s was which Americans were using colorblind conservative arguments and where those Americans lived. By the 1980s a critical number of Americans bought the argument that suburban whites had made: the de facto racial segregation of the suburbs *was* different from the de jure segregation that had existed in the Jim Crow South.

The focus on the suburbanization of the Sunbelt provides a common ground in which arguments over a changing southern political economy and white racism can merge. But the focus on the Sunbelt suburbs has not adequately accounted for one of the most notable and important developments in the 1980s in both southern and national politics—namely, the growing influence of conservative religious voters in the Republican Party. This has not merely been a southern phenomenon, of course, yet many of the leaders of the religious right have come from the South and much of the character of the movement has derived from southern-influenced evangelical churches—many of which, incidentally, have been founded on the nondenominational, mega-church model in developing suburban areas.

As much as Republicans have benefited from the support of evangelicals, the rise of religious activists within the Republican Party was a source of tension in Republican state organizations in the 1980s. Traditional country club and business elites that had dominated the southern GOP since the 1960s sometimes clashed with new evangelicals who were increasingly setting the agenda for southern Republican organizations.[17] No matter how much conservative businessmen chafed at the increasing prominence of preachers and religious activists, conservative Christians offered a powerful critique of liberal forces in the Democratic Party. Racial politics were implicated in this critique in subtle but important ways.

The best example is the case of tax policy for racially discriminatory private schools, an issue of enormous public controversy during Ronald Reagan's first administration. In 1982, the Reagan administration reversed a decades-old policy established by the Nixon administration to deny tax exemptions to racially discriminatory private schools. Whether this decision came as a political favor to southern segregationist supporters or from more arcane legal considerations in the Justice Department is a source of some debate.[18] The upshot, however, was that the decision created a storm of protest. The *New York Times*, for example, dubbed the policy reversal an example of "Tax-Exempt Hate." Though the administration quickly reversed course, the logic of the decision led Reagan's Justice Department to abandon the government's case against Bob Jones University, a fundamentalist school in South Carolina that had sued the government to have its tax exemptions reinstituted as part of the First Amendment's protection of religious freedom (the school had a policy banning interracial dating that it maintained derived from religious beliefs).

The Nixon administration's initial decision to deny tax exemptions to racially discriminatory private schools grew directly out of the struggle to desegregate recalcitrant all-white public schools. In the late 1960s, private schools sprang up across the South in response to public school desegregation. In the early 1970s, the Internal Revenue Service (IRS) amended the order to include private schools that claimed a religious affiliation, and thus sought protection under the First Amendment protections of freedom of religion. Over the course of the 1970s, it became very difficult for the IRS to distinguish between white flight private academies, many of them founded in rural areas and small towns that essentially reconstituted the all-white public school that had previously existed, and small, sectarian church schools founded by expanding suburban churches in the metropolitan South or by smaller denominations with a pedagogy centered around conservative theological education. The latter were part of a growing national trend in the 1970s and 1980s toward religious education.

The issue came to a head in 1978. The Carter administration, determined to crack down on southern segregation academies that were flying below the radar of IRS enforcement, created new guidelines that included a numerical formula for determining whether schools had sufficient minority enrollment. The new policy created a storm of protest among religious groups, the most vocal of which were the advocates of small church schools. Republican Party activists who had been trying to draw evangelical and fundamentalist voters into the GOP for years seized on the issue. Conservative Republican lawmakers in the House passed laws banning the IRS from denying the tax exemptions. The issue even factored into the 1980 presidential election. The Republican Party platform carried a provision pledging to halt the Carter administration's "unconstitutional regulatory vendetta" against Christian schools. Ronald Reagan gave a speech at Bob Jones University criticizing racial quotas. Reporters characterized it as one of the warmest receptions Reagan received during the 1980 campaign.[19]

Ronald Reagan took personal offense at accusations that he was advocating racist policies. Reagan often told the story of inviting home two African American teammates from his college football team because they could not find local accommodations. But in this instance, as in others, Reagan's approach to race was, as Gil Troy has written, "more anecdotal than theoretical, more scattershot than systematic."[20] The anecdote was that some church schools had complained that IRS bureaucrats were hassling them over enrollment issues and, in the process, violating the principle of the separation of church and state. The reality, however, was much more complex. In the end, however, the church school issue—at least according to conservative activists themselves—was the key in bringing conservative Christian voters into the Republican fold.[21] It helps explain one of the most remarkable developments in the 1980 presidential election: that year, conservative evangelicals voted in greater numbers for a divorced Hollywood actor than for a devout southern Baptist who spoke openly and earnestly of his personal relationship with Jesus Christ.

The controversy over tax exemptions showed how civil rights enforcement efforts in the 1980s helped spur modern evangelical politics in the South. It also showed the odd way that Ronald Reagan and his supporters had come to remember the 1960s.[22] Even top-ranking officials in the Reagan administration did not recall how central the tax policy against racist private schools had been in the fight to desegregate southern schools. Dramatic struggles over race and rights in the 1960s seemed by the 1980s to be framed in more ambiguous terms. The tax policy seemed representative of other liberal projects of the 1960s that were now viewed with suspicion. Conservative Republicans saw the 1960s as a time when liberal elites ran wild, threatening basic principles of constitutional government and sneering at the traditional values of everyday Americans. It was easy to forget that the decade was also a time in which the nation had finally addressed a democratic system in the South that was fundamentally broken and in which the country had finally pushed the principle of equality under the law closer toward reality than mere rhetoric. This was an accomplishment that most patriots in Ronald Reagan's South were slow to recognize.

NOTES

1. *Clarion-Ledger*, Aug. 8, 1980, 1; *New York Times*, Aug. 4, 1980, 11; *WP*, Aug. 4, 1980, p. 3 (all newspaper references refer to the first section unless otherwise noted).

2. Michael L. Retzer to Ben Cotten, Dec. 6, 1979, box 85-5: Presidential campaign, 1980, Mississippi Republican Party Papers, Mitchell Memorial Library, Mississippi State University.

3. Earl Black and Merle Black, *The Rise of Southern Republicans* (Cambridge, Mass.: Harvard University Press, 2002), p. 174.

4. George B. Tindall, *The Emergence of the New South, 1913–1945* (Baton Rouge: Louisiana State University Press, 1967); Pete Daniels, *Breaking the Land: The Transformation of the Cotton, Tobacco, and Rice Cultures Since 1880* (Urbana: University of Illinois Press, 1985); Numan Bartley, *The New South, 1945–1980* (Baton Rouge: Louisiana State University Press, 1995); Gavin Wright, *Old South, New South: Revolutions in the Southern Economy Since the Civil War* (New York: Basic Books, 1986).

5. Bruce Schulman, *From Cotton Belt to Sunbelt: Federal Policy, Economic Development, and the Transformation of the South, 1938–1980* (New York: Oxford University Press, 1991); James C. Cobb, *The Selling of the South: The Southern Crusade for Industrial Development, 1936–1990* (Urbana: University of Illinois Press, 1993); Philip Scranton, ed., *The Second Wave: Southern Industrialization from the 1940s to the 1970s* (Athens: University of Georgia Press, 2001).

6. John Robert Moore, "Josiah W. Bailey and the 'Conservative Manifesto' of 1937," *Journal of Southern History* 31, no. 1 (1965): 21–39; David M. Kennedy, *Freedom From Fear: The American People in Depression and War, 1929–1945* (New York: Oxford University Press, 1999), p. 340.

7. Dan T. Carter, *The Politics of Rage: George Wallace, the Origins of the New Conservatism, and the Transformation of American Politics* (Baton Rouge: Louisiana University Press, 1995); Dan T. Carter, *From George Wallace to Newt Gingrich: Race in the Conservative Counterrevolution, 1963–1994* (Baton Rouge: Louisiana University Press, 1996); Glenn Feldman, ed., *Before Brown: Civil Rights and White Backlash in the Modern South* (Tuscaloosa, Ala.: University of Alabama Press, 2004), pp. 268–310.

8. Tom Wicker, *George Herbert Walker Bush* (New York: Viking, 2004); Herbert S. Parmet, *George Bush: The Life of a Lone Star Yankee* (New York: Scribner, 1997).

9. The two best works on southern massive resistance—Numan Bartley, *The Rise of Massive Resistance*, and Neil McMillen, *The Citzens' Council*—both end their histories in 1964, and thus fail to capture how fully the program of massive resistance was repudiated at the national level. On southern school desegregation compared to the rest of the country, see Gary Orfield, *Public School Desegregation in the United States, 1968–1980* (Washington, D.C.: Joint Center for Political Studies, 1983). Since the late 1980s, however, public schools have undergone a process of "resegregation"; for more on this development, see John Charles Boger and Gary Orfield, *School Resegregation: Must the South Turn Back?* (Chapel Hill: University of North Carolina Press, 2006).

10. Arnold R. Hirsch, *Making the Second Ghetto: Race and Housing in Chicago, 1940–1960* (New York: Cambridge University Press, 1983); Jonathan Reider, *Canarsie: The Jews and Italians of Brooklyn Against Liberalism* (Cambridge, Mass.: Harvard University Press, 1985); Thomas Sugrue, *The Origins of the Suburban Crisis: Race and Inequality in Postwar Detroit* (Princeton: Princeton University Press, 1996); John McGreevy, *Parish Boundaries: The Catholic Encounter With Race in the Twentieth Century Urban North* (Chicago: University of

Chicago Press, 1996); Robert Self, *American Babylon: Race and the Struggle for Postwar Oakland* (Princeton: Princeton University Press, 2003).

11. Historians who emphasize continuity in white southerners' racial attitudes have to be mindful of Barbara Fields's warning: "A historian looking for continuity in attitudes is likely to find it regardless of the set of attitudes selected, provided he is sufficiently imaginative in his construction of what constitutes evidence for the existence of an attitude." Barbara Fields, "Ideology and Race in American History," in *Region, Race, and Reconstruction: Essays in Honor of C. Vann Woodward*, J. Morgan Kousser and James M. McPherson, eds. (New York: Oxford University Press, 1982), p. 155.

12. Matthew D. McCubbins and Thomas Schwartz, "Congress, the Courts, and Public Policy: Consequences of the One Man, One Vote Rule," *American Journal of Political Science* 32, no. 2 (1988): 388–415; Steven Lawson, *In Pursuit of Power: Southern Blacks and Electoral Politics, 1965–1982* (New York: Columbia University Press, 1985); Frank Parker, *Black Votes Count: Political Empowerment in Mississippi After 1965* (Chapel Hill: University of North Carolina Press, 1990); for conservative Supreme Court rulings on voting rights that threatened the gains won during the Second Reconstruction, see J. Morgan Kousser, *Colorblind Injustice: Minority Voting Rights and the Undoing of the Second Reconstruction* (Chapel Hill: University of North Carolina Press, 1999).

13. Byron E. Shafer and Richard Johnston, *The End of Southern Exceptionalism: Class, Race, and Partisan Change in the Postwar South* (Cambridge, Mass.: Harvard University Press, 2006).

14. Kevin Kruse, *White Flight: Atlanta and the Making of Modern Conservatism* (Princeton: Princeton University Press, 2005). Also see Ronald Bayor, *Race and the Shaping of Twentieth Century Atlanta* (Chapel Hill: University of North Carolina Press, 1996).

15. Matthew Lassiter, *The Silent Majority: Suburban Politics in the Sunbelt South* (Princeton: Princeton University Press, 2005). Also see Kevin M. Kruse and Thomas J. Sugrue, *The New Suburban History* (Chicago: University of Chicago Press, 2006).

16. Lassiter, *The Silent Majority*, p. 15.

17. *Washington Post*, May 18, 1986, 1. Also see the *Washington Post* series "Dixie Rising: Changing Politics of the South," May 18–23, 1986.

18. For example, contrast Dan Carter's account of the controversy, which highlights the letter that Mississippi Republican Trent Lott sent to Reagan urging him to reverse the policy, with David Whitman's review of the conservative legal culture of the Reagan Justice Department. Whitman argues that fairly abstract considerations of constitutional law had more to do with the policy reversal than did the desire to placate southern segregationist supporters. Carter, *From George Wallace to Newt Gingrich*, pp. 56–57; David Whitman, "Ronald Reagan and Tax Exemptions For Racist Schools," case #609.0, Case Studies in Public Policy and Management, John F. Kennedy School of Government.

19. Joseph Crespino, *In Search of Another Country: Mississippi and the Conservative Counterrevolution* (Princeton: Princeton University Press, 2007), pp. 237–66.

20. Gil Troy, *Morning in America: How Ronald Reagan Invented the 1980s* (Princeton: Princeton University Press, 2005), pp. 89–90.

21. Michael Cromartie, ed., *No Longer Exiles: The Religious New Right In American Politics* (Washington: Ethics and Public Policy Center, 1993), p. 26; Godfrey Hodgson, *The World Turned Right Side Up: A History of the Conservative Ascendancy in America* (New York: Houghton Mifflin, 1996), pp. 176–77.

22. For more on the memory of the civil rights movement and its political uses, see Jacquelyn Dowd Hall, "The Long Civil Rights Movement and the Political Uses of the Past," *Journal of American History* 91, no. 4 (2005): 1233–63.

Chapter 4

THE REORIENTATION
OF LIBERALISM IN THE 1980S

David Greenberg

LIBERALISM EMBATTLED

For most of the twentieth century, liberalism reigned as the dominant ideology in American political life. Despite periods of conservative retrenchment in the 1920s and 1950s and radical agitation in the 1930s and 1960s, the first two-thirds of the last century represented a heyday for the liberal creed. Mid-century observers deemed liberalism the nation's consensus philosophy and considered the Democrats—the primary instrument of liberalism—the nation's majority party.

Although rooted in an older doctrine of individual rights and distrust of state power, liberalism in its twentieth-century form—and especially after the New Deal—posited an active federal government. In the journalist Herbert Croly's classic formulation from the Progressive Era, modern liberalism used state power to advance individual freedom and used Hamiltonian means to reach Jeffersonian ends. Thus, although twentieth-century liberals guarded fiercely against governmental intrusions on civil liberties, they otherwise enlisted a strong state to tackle the challenges of a complex, industrial mass society. Modern liberalism, though basically capitalist in its economics, called on the federal government to shield workers and consumers from predatory corporate power, to fine-tune economic policy in pursuit of high employment, and to weave a safety net for the poor and the weak. Liberals backed affirmative measures to ensure equality for blacks, other minorities, and women. Although antiimperialist in their foreign policy, most liberals nonetheless believed that America's strength and power conferred on it a duty to play a leading role in global affairs.

In the 1960s and 1970s these assumptions came under attack. Both the New Left and the New Right took aim at the policies and theoretical underpinnings of liberalism. Liberalism seemed to be reaching the limits of what it could attain with broad public backing. The policies that had undergirded economic growth in the postwar years proved powerless after 1973 to combat stagflation. The social programs that constituted Lyndon Johnson's Great Society, while reducing poverty and raising living standards, did not stanch the spread of social maladies such as divorce, out-of-wedlock births, drug use, and violent crime. The civil rights movement, after securing basic rights for black Americans and inspiring efforts to do likewise for women, gays, and other groups, fell from favor when it urged more aggressive measures to guarantee not just political and legal but also economic and social equality. The Vietnam War, finally, undermined the credibility of an interventionist foreign policy, leaving many Democrats leery of wielding American power abroad.

These developments produced a dire situation for the Democratic party, which hemorrhaged support in the 1970s and 1980s from key constituencies—notably Catholics, blue-collar workers, white southerners, and the intellectuals known as neoconservatives. These voters, wrote the political analysts Thomas and Mary Edsall, began "focusing their anger on two pillars of the Democratic party: domestic government spending and the concept of collective social responsibility."[1] Americans turned against both federal social programs and the taxes that paid for them. Liberalism's broadened notions of rights and equality—in particular its sensitivities to the demands of minority groups—made many white voters, especially men, skeptical of its stands on issues such as crime, education, and welfare. Many also came to view the Democrats' post-Vietnam isolationist tendencies as signs of weakness on defense. Lastly, the postwar liberals' reliance on technocratic experts—from academic social scientists to Supreme Court judges—to devise and revise policy made many Americans feel that their government wasn't accountable to them anymore.

All these discontents culminated in the November 1980 election of Ronald Reagan, the most conservative president since before the New Deal. Although Reagan's share of the popular vote barely cleared 50 percent, he won a stunning 44 states and 489 electoral votes, while the Democratic incumbent, Jimmy Carter, won just 41 percent of the vote, the lowest for an incumbent since Herbert Hoover in 1932. (John Anderson, a Republican congressman from

Illinois running as an independent, garnered 7 percent.) Reagan also led the Republicans to a surprise take-over of the Senate for the first time since 1955 and to gains in the House of Representatives. For the balance of the century, no traditionally liberal candidate would win the presidency.

A sea change had occurred, as many analysts were quick to grasp. "Unless they recover their partisan energies and intellectual vigor, the Democrats could enter a long historical passage of declining influence and relevance," warned Lance Morrow of *Time* magazine in 1980, "becoming the political equivalent of some of the decaying cities of the Northeast, once flourishingly productive, the exuberant places where the modern Democratic Party originated."[2] Similar refrains would be heard for the rest of the decade.

Recognizing this crisis of liberalism, left-of-center scholars, journalists, politicians, and voters in the 1980s engaged in a collective reassessment of their philosophy and policies, seeking to adapt to changing times and win back the "Reagan Democrats." Although the reassessment was less than wholly successful—Democrats would not regain the White House until 1992—it did produce a partial revision of liberalism that Arkansas Governor Bill Clinton would espouse in his presidential campaign and embody as president. The story of how liberalism changed in the 1980s thus represents an important and neglected element of the political culture in a decade largely dominated by Reagan and conservatism.

RUSSIANS AND REAGANOMICS

It took time for the reconsideration of liberalism to begin in earnest. When Reagan assumed office, many Democrats doubted that his victory represented a triumph for the conservatism he championed. Jimmy Carter's failures in economic management and in foreign affairs—notably the debacle of the Iranian hostage crisis—allowed some on the left to comfort themselves that in electing Reagan voters had simply been seeking change. They ascribed Reagan success not to the appeal of his beliefs but to his optimism, his speaking skills, or his image-makers.

This critique had a limited validity. Into the 1980s and beyond, the public supported basic liberal goals such as racial and sexual equality, the government provision of health care, worker protection, and similar goods, and even newer, more expansive notions of freedom emerging from the 1960s. Reagan himself tacitly accepted the triumph of liberalism in countless ways. He made a point of naming a woman (Sandra Day O'Connor) to the Supreme Court;

he used progressive rhetoric to justify his policies, as when he described a tax bill as "the best antipoverty measure"; and he shelved or scaled back plans to dismantle Social Security and similar programs.[3] Polls, moreover, showed that Americans remained, as the opinion analysts Hadley Cantril and Lloyd Free had put it some years earlier, "ideologically conservative" but "operationally liberal"—responsive to antitax and small-government rhetoric but still keenly desirous of government services.[4]

Yet despite the quiet persistence of liberalism in these ways, the ascent of conservative ideas could not be denied. Reagan made smaller government and lower taxes and an aggressive anti-Soviet foreign policy his main goals, and although his manner of pursuing them provoked widespread concern, liberals failed to offer compelling responses. Their difficulty in defining themselves in the early 1980s revealed how much hard work lay ahead for them.

On economics, Reagan's positions were far from impregnable. At the start of his presidency, a majority of the public opposed his plan to slash taxes levied on the wealthy and cut programs such as job training, Food Stamps, and Medicare. But Reagan helped his cause with two nationally televised speeches in February 1981, and a failed attempt on his life in March boosted his popularity. A caucus of conservative Southern Democrats dubbed the "boll weevils"—named, pejoratively, after the parasitic insects that feed off the South's cotton crop—rallied behind his budget overhaul; key Democratic committee chairmen, fearing rising antitax sentiment, also agreed to compromise with the president. Eventually, the Democrats offered their own tax cuts, creating a bidding war in which each side sweetened the budget package with goodies for its favored constituencies such as the oil and savings-and-loan industries. In the spring of 1981, large majorities in both houses of Congress passed Reagan's plan. And although "Reaganomics" continued to attract much skepticism—especially after a major recession the following year—by 1984 prosperity was returning, inflation had fallen dramatically, and Reagan's policies were receiving credit.

Foreign affairs told a similar story: Reagan took controversial stands that might have hurt him, but liberals failed to capitalize on his weaknesses. Upon assuming office, Reagan sought to dispel the national feelings of shame and vulnerability resulting from Carter's failure to free the American hostages in Iran. The new president redoubled defense spending, abandoned nuclear arms control talks with the Soviet Union, and engaged in bellicose rhetoric reminiscent of the truly dangerous years of the Cold War. These moves revived long-dormant fears of a nuclear showdown and cast Reagan as a potentially dangerous war-monger. But Democrats, chastened by Vietnam, articulated no muscular foreign policy vision of their own. The foreign policy idea in vogue was a nuclear freeze between the superpowers—a sensible enough prescription if it could be enforced, but one that stood little hope of implementation and mainly reinforced its advocates' image as weak or naive about defense.[5]

FIRST RESPONDERS: THE FAILED PROMISE OF NEOLIBERALISM

The first significant group that sought to reshape liberalism in the face of these challenges was a cadre of Democrats known as "neoliberals."[6] The neoliberal movement was in some sense a stage in the development of the 1960s New Left, and it shared the earlier campaign's self-conscious generational rebelliousness, including its parricidal thrusts against New Deal liberalism—though, of course, the attacks now came from the right, not the left. "We are not a bunch of little Hubert Humphreys," declared one of its leaders, Colorado Senator Gary Hart, scorning a giant of midcentury liberalism. Neoliberalism's leading lights were, notably, mostly baby boomers: elected officials such as Hart, Bill Bradley of New Jersey, Michael Dukakis of Massachusetts, and Bruce Babbitt of Arizona; journalists centered at the *Washington Monthly*, edited by Charlie Peters, and *The New Republic*, edited by Michael Kinsley; and academics such as economist Lester Thurow of MIT and public policy analyst Robert Reich of Harvard's Kennedy School of Government.[7]

Neoliberals focused mainly on political economy. Like other liberals, they wanted to maintain a strong safety net and even to use government for other positive goods. They agreed with Reagan on the need to prune bureaucracy and to rejuvenate capitalism. In the 1950s and 1960s, when prosperity seemed widespread and long-lasting, Democratic leaders had come to focus on economic fairness, arguing for greater public benefits, a more redistributive tax code, and, later, during hard times, wage and price controls. In contrast, neoliberals, reacting to the stagnation of the 1970s, concluded that the assumptions underpinning the New Deal and Great Society no longer held. They emphasized the ways in which the economy would likely be changing in the future with the globalization of commerce. "Much of the thrust of the 1980 Democratic platform," wrote Massachusetts Senator Paul Tsongas, a leading neoliberal, "reflected the realities of the 1930s and 1960s, not those of the decade ahead."[8]

As the neoliberals saw it, the nationally rooted, industrial manufacturing economy of the mid-twentieth century was yielding to a global, postindustrial framework centered on the high-tech, information, and service sectors. No longer could Democrats rely on Keynesian policies, support for unions, and taxes on corporations and the rich to satisfy the needs of a growing middle-class base. On the contrary, stagflation, energy crises, and international competition were destroying job opportunities and depressing wages. Shuttered factories, decaying cities, and mounting despair told the story.

Rejecting the return to a largely unfettered capitalism urged by Reaganites, neoliberals emphasized cultivating growth, not redistributing it. To this end, they prescribed a new gospel of efficiency. They favored investment in education and research and development and took aim at groups long allied with liberalism—government bureaucrats, unions, public-interest lawyers, and pro-regulation lobbyists—whose goals seemed to clash with the prime goal of an increasing gross national product. Extending this critique beyond economics, neoliberals further sought to expose what they considered the unjustifiable costs of many of the Democrats' traditional sympathies, such as for teachers' unions, strict regulations on business, and entitlement programs such as Social Security and Medicare that largely served the middle class.

Some neoliberals, furthermore, wanted the United States to develop an "industrial policy," as Japan had recently done. Advocated in various forms by Thurow, Reich, business consultant Ira Magaziner, and investment banker Felix Rohatyn, industrial policies sought to target up-and-coming sectors of the economy for receiving government funds, thus helping the United States to gain a global advantage in those fields. Technology in particular enchanted neoliberals—earning them the nickname "Atari Democrats," after the popular home videogame system—who expected that money channeled into research and development would foster innovation that would solve tough problems such as environmental degradation and spiraling military spending while reviving the economy. To be sure, these ideas were controversial even within neoliberal ranks; many considered such a federal plan to be antithetical both to their free-market focus and to their preference for devolving power from the federal government to the states.[9]

Neoliberalism never succeeded as an overall program. It was a creature of the 1980s, and the Democrats who supported it didn't gain power until its moment had passed. More basically, it never resolved its own internal contradictions, of which the confusion over industrial policy was but one. Some neoliberals, for example, advocated free trade—the traditional Democratic position—arguing that technology was connecting once-isolated economies and allowing goods, capital, and services to cross borders more easily. Others, seeing competition with Japan and Germany as a direct threat, turned protectionist. What was more, neoliberalism's demonization of experts and bureaucrats clashed with its technocratic strains. Torn by such divisions, neoliberalism could offer suggestive ideas for policy innovation but no clear strategy for governance, and it never found much of a constituency beyond the Washington policy shops.

Nonetheless, the movement's heady talk of the future and its precocious appreciation of the changes being wrought by globalization forced progressives to realize that as economic conditions changed, their views had to change as well. Neoliberal proposals for military, legal, and education reform won a respectful hearing and would return in different forms. Most important, by gaining a foothold in public policy debates, neoliberals demonstrated the possibility of questioning liberal orthodoxies without endorsing Reaganite positions—and made it possible for liberalism in the 1990s to plausibly reclaim its historical position as the ideology of economic growth.

1984: HART, JACKSON, MONDALE, AND CUOMO

The fate of neoliberalism could be seen in the ballyhooed but unsuccessful 1984 presidential primary campaign of its first major standard-bearer, Gary Hart. Boldly challenging the presumptive Democratic nominee, Walter F. Mondale of Minnesota—Carter's vice president and a mainstream liberal—Hart hoped to rebuild a progressive majority by reaching the college students, professionals, and upscale independent voters drawn to John Anderson's candidacy in 1980. To that end, the forty-eight-year-old senator touted a program of generational change and "new ideas," arguing, as he had for years, that traditional liberalism was dead. (Hart had titled the stump speech of his 1974 Senate race "The End of the New Deal.") Undergirding his campaign were neoliberal planks such as military reform, tax simplification, privately funded accounts for worker retraining, and government-brokered labor compacts that would foster innovation while protecting jobs.[10]

Whether voters liked these new ideas or just the idea of newness, they gave Hart an upset victory in the New Hampshire primary in February 1984, in which he won 37 percent of the vote to Mondale's 28 percent. Victories in Maine, Vermont, and Wyoming followed.[11] Mondale, already suffering from charges that he was unexciting, untelegenic, and unoriginal, was further tagged by Hart as beholden to "special interests"—a term coined to denote corporate powers but now applied to union workers, blacks, women, and other traditionally powerless groups that tended to support Mondale. The effectiveness of Hart's attack underscored the fact that Mondale's brand of liberalism—long associated with equality and justice—had become linked with elite favoritism toward minorities.

For all of Hart's talk of newness, however, he and Mondale differed little on most issues. They had almost identical voting records. It took little more than a stinging barb in a key primary-season debate—"Where's the beef?" Mondale asked of Hart's vaunted "new ideas"—for the former vice president to regain momentum and sew up the nomination. Yet Mondale, though victorious, emerged from the primaries bruised. Hart's challenge forced the vice president to belittle neoliberal ideas, and his advisers feared that embracing them for the fall campaign against Reagan would make Mondale seem not only inconsistent but also, as one aide put it, "like a trend-minded Atari Democrat with whom our party's main constituencies have nothing in common." Making matters worse, a second primary challenge, from the radical black minister Jesse Jackson, had led Mondale to make intensive overtures to the party's left-wing activists, thereby accentuating worries that he stood for a fusty, hidebound ideology—and ensuring that the "special interest" bugaboo would return in the fall. Tellingly, the Democratic party issued a platform that finessed policy differences through vague language. "What I'm hoping to do," said New York Representative Geraldine A. Ferraro, the platform committee chair, "is to bring forth a product that does not endorse specific legislation."[12]

Mondale's selection of Ferraro as the first female vice presidential running mate, though winning him plaudits at first for its boldness, wound up reinforcing his image as captive to interest groups. Before selecting her, Mondale had conspicuously interviewed a host of possible running mates, including blacks, Hispanics, and women. Feminist groups had even threatened a walk-out from the convention if he chose a man.[13] Thus, despite Ferraro's manifest qualifications for the job, observers derided her selection as an act of tokenism—even though the purported "minority" group at issue actually represented a majority of the electorate.

Vanquishing Reagan in 1984 was, in any event, a long-shot. A year earlier, with the recession's effects lingering, Mondale had led the incumbent in hypothetical head-to-head contests. By the fall of 1984, however, the president was riding high as the economy bounced back and the Olympics, held in Los Angeles, sparked a blaze of jingoism. For a fleeting moment at the Democratic convention, a winning synthesis for the Democrats seemed within reach—though, tellingly, it came not from Mondale but from New York Governor Mario Cuomo. In an eloquent, spellbinding keynote, Cuomo described Reagan's America as "more a 'Tale of Two Cities' than...a 'shining city on a hill,'" a country offering material comfort to some but tolerating deepening distress for many more. With his metaphor of the nation as a family, in which burdens had to be shared, Cuomo struck a balance between a principled commitment to venerable liberal concerns and the focus on community and reciprocity pre-scribed by reformers.[14]

Cuomo's address made many Democrats wish he were their nominee. But the actual nominee's speech—and his subsequent campaign—convinced few Reagan Democrats that the party had indeed fashioned, as Mondale claimed, "a new realism." Mondale dutifully insisted that liberals now understood "that government must be as well-managed as it is well-meaning,...that a healthy, growing private economy is the key to the future," but his invocations of the now-distant New Deal reflected his vain hopes of putting Humpty Dumpty together again.[15] He revealed himself, one liberal analyst wrote, to be more a "curator of a tradition" than a visionary.[16] He lost to Reagan in every state but one.

THE VALUES SOLUTION

Mondale's 1984 rout renewed efforts to reorient the Democratic party. But where in the early 1980s economics-minded neoliberals had led the charge, this time southern conservatives seized the initiative. Their main vehicle was the Democratic Leadership Council (DLC), a caucus formed in 1985 by sev-eral of the party's more conservative officials, including Sam Nunn of Georgia and Chuck Robb of Virginia. The DLC's members and the neoliberals were not wholly discrete; in fact, they overlapped, and casual observers sometimes failed to distinguish between them. The DLC, moreover, adopted several key neo-liberal assumptions—about the challenge of global competitiveness, the need for more efficient government and market-friendly policies, and the pursuit of economic growth over fairness.

But the focus of the southerners' new push wasn't by and large techno-cratic, and it didn't seek primarily to court the upscale voters pursued by neo-liberals. DLC Democrats targeted, rather, the more numerous working-class Reagan Democrats who had come to view their former party as too permissive on a host of values-laden social issues. These voters—who had provided the key to Democratic victories in years past—believed that welfare had become too generous, public education too progressive, crime policies too lenient, drug policies too indulgent, and busing and affirmative action too preferential toward blacks. By reasserting traditional values of patriotism, religion, work, discipline, and responsibility—as well as smaller government and a more hawk-ish defense policy—the self-styled "New Democrats" of the DLC hoped to win back these voters.

The DLC fast became a lightning rod for controversy. Its cultivation of wealthy donors and business-friendly policies drew fire from mainstream liberals such as Arthur Schlesinger Jr., who faulted the organization for "worshipping at the shrine of the free market." Its Hart-like attacks on the party's allegiance to "special interests" prompted left-wing Democrats to warn that blacks, union workers, and other hard-pressed Americans were being abandoned. Indeed, it was on racial issues that the DLC strayed most from liberal traditions. Its leaders weren't segregationists or even necessarily hostile to black aspirations; many relied on biracial support to get elected. Their natural sympathies, however, lay with white Southern men, and their worldview contained trace elements of the philosophy of their fathers, for whom white supremacy and segregation were facts of life. The key issues on which they broke with liberalism—welfare, crime, affirmative action—were more than a little racially inflected, and their stands on these issues, along with the DLC's southern nucleus and its dearth of prominent black members, troubled civil rights liberals. Jesse Jackson publicly warred with the DLC, branding it "Democrats for the Leisure Class," a moniker that stuck.[17]

The DLC's inability to transcend its regionalism or accommodate the aspirations of African Americans kept it from unifying the Democratic party. But like the neoliberal movement, the DLC contributed to liberalism's eventual revival—mainly through its populistic emphasis on what had come to be called "values," which gained support from many quarters. Not long after the DLC's formation, Democratic party chairman Paul Kirk, a former aide to Massachusetts Senator Edward M. Kennedy, put forward a party platform that emphasized the Democrats' commitment to families, to entrepreneurship, and to a strong anti-Soviet stand. A few years later, Representative Barney Frank of Massachusetts, a quintessential northeastern liberal, called on Democrats to surmount their unease about using a language of morality—about proclaiming their patriotism or condemning criminals—lest they be seen as succoring conservative efforts. Although policy disagreements among Democrats remained significant—Frank, for example, denounced the DLC for pushing policies that strayed too far from liberal principles—liberals came to agree broadly on the centrality of values to politics.

THE COMMUNITARIAN CHALLENGE

Related to the DLC's emphasis on values, as well as to the neoliberals' critique of interest-group liberalism and stress of a common good, was a backlash against what many progressives saw as an excessive focus on individual rights. Sometimes called communitarianism, this critique of liberalism argued that the privileging of rights meant neglecting social responsibilities. Drawing on traditions of civic republicanism, communitarianism called for liberals to bolster "civil society" and place greater weight on the needs of communities and of society as a whole.

Communitarianism emerged as a critique of the liberal individualism that dominated postwar American life. At a philosophical level, the theorist John Rawls best articulated those dominant ideas, arguing that in a liberal society, rights had to be paramount. Rejecting an older liberal vision of utilitarianism—which required that the rights of some be sacrificed to maximize the common good—Rawls wrote that "each person possesses an inviolability founded on justice that even the welfare of society as a whole cannot override."[18] Rawls's philosophy also explained how such a belief in the primacy of rights could be reconciled with the commitment to the welfare state and the redistributive economics established by the New Deal that most liberals shared. Although most fully expressed by academic theorists like Rawls, this synthesis of rights-based individualism and egalitarianism held sway far beyond the academy; it was evident in popular statements of liberalism, whether by intellectuals such as economist John Kenneth Galbraith and historian Arthur Schlesinger Jr., by opinion journalists, or by ordinary citizens.

In the 1970s and 1980s—again in a kind of generational challenge—younger scholars and social critics challenged the dominance of Rawlsian liberalism. Like the neoliberal politicians who were their rough contemporaries (and with whom their group overlapped), these scholars had come of age under the influence of the student movement of the 1960s, which emphasized the needs of the community. Lamenting an atomized society of cars, televisions, and workplaces detached from home life, they found fault not just in the material conditions of suburban culture but also in the assumptions that enabled such anomie by valuing individual rights and prerogatives over common goods and community obligations. In the formulation of the political theorist Michael Sandel, Rawls had it backward: the common "good" in fact should be prior to the individual "right."[19] In more extreme language, the Catholic legal theorist Mary Ann Glendon charged that "an intemperate rhetoric of personal liberty"—what she called "rights talk"—was "corrod[ing] the social foundations on which individual freedom and security ultimately rest."[20]

Certainly, "rights talk" had proliferated since World War II, and especially since the 1960s. Economically, liberalism's embrace of Keynesianism and consumerism had moved it away from the quasisocialistic reform visions of the early twentieth century and toward a view of purchasing as a right and an expression of personal freedom. Liberalism's support for minority or downtrodden groups had also come to rest on a philosophy of equal rights; following the lead of the civil rights movements of the 1960s, social and ethnic groups ranging from Asians and Latinos to the handicapped to, eventually, homosexuals and even transsexuals all claimed entitlement to the same benefits that other Americans enjoyed. Finally, on issues of personal autonomy, liberals' support for the freedom to make choices unimpeded by the state led them to defend such policies as fair procedures for accused criminals, greater ease in obtaining divorce and abortion, and fewer restrictions on speech, expression, and even victimless behavior such as drug use. In all of these cases, communitarians of one sort or another argued that the liberal position undermined the greater social good.

In response to the communitarian critique, many liberals acknowledged that the primacy they placed on rights sometimes exacerbated these problems in modern American life. But, as with the question of values, the growing consensus extolling the virtues of civil society didn't translate into clear policy decisions. Liberals remained loath, for example, to advocate school prayer or impose obstacles on divorce, and other communitarian prescriptions, such as the provision of more extensive health care and day care, already enjoyed favor on the left, albeit on individualist grounds. Nonetheless, communitarianism, like neoliberalism and the DLC's social populism, offered language and concepts that challenged and helped to modify the dominant liberal assumptions of the time.

REAGAN'S SECOND TERM: A DOSE OF PRAGMATISM

Although discussions of civil society and values increasingly informed liberal discussions during Reagan's second term, as a practical matter liberal politicians were mainly reacting to events shaped by the White House. And as the president ran into political trouble in his second term, many Democrats waited to advance any new ideological visions. They reverted to the (false) hope that mere disenchantment with Reagan and the Republicans would return them to the White House and majority status.

They had several reasons for optimism. First, incidents of corruption and criminality among the president's closest aides, already significant in his first term, became epidemic in his second. Among those indicted, convicted of crimes, or forced to resign under clouds of scandal were Reagan's top aides Michael Deaver and Lyn Nofziger and Cabinet Secretaries James Watt, Edwin Meese, Caspar Weinberger, and Samuel Pierce. By one count, some 138 officials were implicated in official wrongdoing.[21] In the most serious of these scandals, the Iran-contra affair, Reagan officials violated their own policy by selling arms to Iran in exchange for the release of American hostages and then used the proceeds to illegally fund the *contras* fighting the Marxist Sandinista government in Nicaragua. These scandals led Democrats to imagine that the public would restore them to power out of a desire to clean house, as it had after Watergate.

A second ray of hope for liberals came in 1987. The stock market crashed in October, and though it rebounded, wealthier as well as poorer Americans began to worry about instabilities in the economy. Also tainting Reaganomics was the skyrocketing federal debt. Reagan had pledged to balance the budget, but by his second term the annual deficit and the total debt had reached historic peaks, calling the Republicans' economic stewardship into question. Moreover, the mounting shortfalls appeared to moot the debates over taxes and spending that had hurt the Democrats for years, underscoring instead the need for pragmatic leadership on fiscal issues. In 1987 Democrats even took the lead in resurrecting the Gramm-Rudman-Hollings bill to mandate balanced budgets—a traditionally conservative stand.

Liberals also took heart in 1987 from the decisive rejection of Reagan's ultra-conservative nominee for the Supreme Court, Judge Robert Bork. If a majority of the public still faulted liberalism as too permissive, they had no wish to roll back the social and cultural freedoms gained since the 1960s. Bork said plainly, for example, that he didn't believe married couples had a right to use birth control—a stand at odds with that of most Americans, and one that showed how much cultural norms had evolved.

Finally, the rise to power of Mikhail Gorbachev in the Soviet Union and Reagan's adoption of a more conciliatory foreign policy, including new limits on nuclear arms, eased fears about a catastrophic war. Though the Democrats and Republicans would fight over the credit for this shift, it certainly meant that the Cold War would not loom large in future presidential campaigns, eliminating an area in which Democrats had fared poorly with the public.

Collectively, these developments boded well for Democrats. In 1986 the party regained control of the Senate for the first time since 1980 and picked up seats in the House as well. Younger and independent voters returned to the fold. And Republican party rifts seemingly healed by Reagan—between neoconservatives and paleoconservatives, between libertarians and Christian moralists—now reemerged. "If there was a Reagan Revolution," declared the retiring House Speaker, "Tip" O'Neill, "it's over."[22]

But the 1986 victory couldn't erase the ongoing differences within the party about how, if at all, liberalism should change. "Democrats still haven't defined what they want to be when they grow up," said the political scientist Erwin C. Hargrove after the 1986 victory.[23] The Democrats fared relatively well in advancing their goals in the last years of Reagan's term. In 1987 the president signed and the Senate ratified the first arms-control treaty with the Soviet Union since 1972, and on the domestic front the 1987 budget was, according to the progressive journalist Robert Kuttner, "from a liberal viewpoint...by far the best of the Reagan budgets," with modest increases for certain programs such as Head Start, which provided early education for the poor.[24]

But the 1988 presidential campaign suggested liberalism was still, in basic ways, adrift. The Democrats' nominee that year was Michael Dukakis of Massachusetts, a son of Greek immigrants, a Harvard law school graduate, and a skilled, manifestly intelligent manager. Though remembered as a "Massachusetts liberal," Dukakis wasn't the traditional Democrat in the field. That title belonged to the bespectacled, bow-tied Senator Paul Simon of Illinois, who ran as a proud, unreconstructed New Dealer, while Jesse Jackson again staked out the far left, and Tennessee Senator Al Gore carried the DLC banner. Dukakis, though a mainstream liberal on civil rights and liberties, promised a technocratic, neoliberal efficiency. He pointed to the "Massachusetts miracle" of an economic recovery based on computer, communications, and health care industries that occurred on his watch. He claimed in his speech to the Democratic convention that the fall election would turn on competence, not ideology, and he studiously avoided affiliating himself with the liberal tradition. This approach evoked the Democrats' avoidance of a policy-heavy platform in 1984. It too proved futile.

Although Dukakis led his rival, Vice President George Bush, Sr., by 17 points in opinion polls at the end of the Democratic convention, he faltered in the fall campaign. Bush not only ran a viciously negative campaign, but also cannily steered the debate into a tangle of "wedge issues" such as race, crime, patriotism, and defense, on which swing voters reliably leaned Republican. Believing his intelligence and competence to be self-evidently superior to Bush's, Dukakis never enunciated an ideological vision and declined to defend liberalism when Bush assailed it. Although the Democrat found a populist pitch as Election Day neared and gained ground, it was too little and too late.[25]

Although Dukakis's passionless cerebral style, like Mondale's blandness, brought blame upon the candidate himself, many liberals continued to call for a more thoroughgoing overhaul of the party's outlook. In 1989 the DLC, continuing to press its case, founded a think tank called the Progressive Policy Institute. Under its aegis, Bill Galston, a communitarian professor, and Elaine Kamarck, a policy analyst, issued a monograph called "The Politics of Evasion" that decried the effort to blame the Democrats' recent losses on the personal qualities of candidates, the news media, poor fundraising efforts, or other factors besides their actual ideas. Galston and Kamarck urged a new commitment to a strong foreign policy, a progressive economic policy that united the middle and lower classes, and "above all...a clear understanding of an identification with the social values of moral sentiments of average Americans," particularly "hard work, equal opportunity," and a strict intolerance of crime.[26]

BILL CLINTON: THE NEW LIBERAL SYNTHESIS

As the Bush presidency dawned, Democrats faced a dilemma much like that of 1981 and 1985—only if anything they were more demoralized, since Bush had been a weaker candidate than Reagan, and Dukakis had labored to escape the stigma now associated with liberalism, to no avail. But the last years of the 1980s showed that if conservatism hadn't cracked up, it wasn't all it was cracked up to be either. Apart from his widely praised handling of the 1991 Gulf War, Bush struggled throughout his presidency, not least because the after-effects of many of Reagan's policies were now becoming clear: a costly bail-out of the deregulated savings-and-loan institutions; the continued stagnation of wages and widening gaps in income and wealth; and a continuing surge in crime, divorce, and other social ills. Moreover, Bush, a wealthy businessman born to a blue-blood family who had spent most of his career focused on foreign policy, seemed to feel little urgency about the recession that struck toward the end of his term.

The sluggish state of the economy and the public appetite for change both contributed to Bush's failure to win reelection in 1992. But equally important was the reformed liberalism of the Democratic candidate, Governor Bill Clinton of Arkansas—the first major leader to articulate a persuasive new liberal synthesis. Though sometimes erroneously portrayed as a creature of the DLC and a "centrist," Clinton was no garden-variety southern moderate and certainly not a conservative like Sam Nunn. The DLC was a vehicle for Clinton's aspirations, not the other way around. The organization, after all, was just one of many groups—the black community, the nation's governors, the intellectuals, the liberal interest groups, and others—whose support Clinton marshaled en route to his victory and whose ideas he drew upon.

Indeed, while taking up the DLC's call for a populistic stress on values and the communitarian talk of social responsibility, Clinton also availed himself of pragmatic, neoliberal ideas—Reich and Magaziner were key advisers—about investment, globalization, and governmental efficiency. He wedded these, moreover, to two traditional, mainstream liberal ideas: an emphasis on economic fairness and a conscious appeal to black voters. On economics, Clinton stiffened his market orientation with a proud populism, stressing the need for a bottom-up coalition of the working and middle classes and calling for Keynesian economic stimulation, jobs programs, and progressive taxation. And although he picked fights with Jesse Jackson to prove that he was bona fide to certain white constituencies, and took a moderate stance on crime (pro-death penalty) and welfare (time limits and work requirements), Clinton also appealed to blacks by highlighting, in a Southern idiom familiar to many of them, the common plight of the black and white lower middle classes. The rare national politician young enough in 1992 to have come of age during the Civil Rights movement, he painted himself as a son of the new South, a white man who not only wasn't hostile to black equality but whose interracial friendships dated to childhood and whose sympathy for African American grievances ran bone-deep. Above all, Clinton put meat on the bones of his rhetoric with policies that both liberals and conservatives could endorse, such as a crack-down on "deadbeat dads" who defaulted on welfare payments—a position that carried a whiff of law-and-order populism while signaling that he wasn't about to scapegoat "welfare queens" as Reagan had.

Clinton was undeniably a liberal—but not in the caricatured sense of the term that came into common parlance in the 1990s. No 1960s flower child or bleeding-heart big spender, he remained attached to the premises of the New Deal and the Great Society—using government to promote growth, economic fairness, and racial equality. At the same time, his southern, working-class upbringing made it natural for him to incorporate DLC-style prescriptions about attending to middle-class values, while his years in elite universities (Georgetown, Oxford, and Yale) and policy circles made him hospitable to neoliberal ideas about the changing global economy. Sometimes, to be sure, his attempted compromises crashed spectacularly—as with his 1994 plan for health care reform, a textbook "New Democrat" idea that prescribed market mechanisms to provide universal coverage that Congress roundly rejected. But on the whole his administration oversaw an impressive array of achievements that, although sometimes disappointing the left with their moderate elements, remained decidedly within a liberal tradition.

Clinton's popularity and reelection suggested a robustness in his brand of revamped liberalism. Although the term "liberal" remained rhetorically lethal into the 1990s—the trend toward using the synonym "progressive," begun in the 1980s, caught hold—the philosophy's core ideas displayed a renewed vigor. In 1996 the journalist E. J. Dionne foresaw "the coming of a second progressive era."[27] Two years later the sociologist Alan Wolfe found in a survey of middle-class communities that for all the claims of resurgent traditionalism, Americans largely accepted the post-1960s values of toleration and diversity.[28] In 1999 the historian Sean Wilentz proclaimed, "Liberalism is back—maybe not in name, but in spirit and in substance.... From voter surveys to the floors of Congress, we see abundant evidence that Americans are embracing sensible activist government."[29] These judgments reflected a recognition that prosperity, relative peace in the world, and a drop in social maladies such as crime and welfare dependency had restored a measure of faith in venerable liberal tenets such as cultural toleration and activist government.

In the years after his presidency, however, it would become clear that Clinton's presidency hadn't settled the reconsiderations of liberalism begun in the 1980s. On the one hand, Democrats and liberals were faring far better than they had two decades earlier. Al Gore's strong showing—some would say expropriated victory—in the 2000 presidential election, and Massachusetts Senator John F. Kerry's near-victory in 2004 showed that a Clintonian synthesis could still unite traditional liberals with independents and Reagan Democrats. On the other hand, from 2002 to 2007 the Republicans controlled all three branches of government, and conservative news media and electoral constituencies wielded new power. What was more, al-Qaeda's attacks on the United States on September 11, 2001, in effect commencing the war on terrorism, placed at the top of the public agenda the one set of issues on which liberals of the 1980s and 1990s had not done enough rethinking: foreign policy. In this area, a post-Vietnam political dynamic quickly returned, with most conservatives urging an aggressive international stance and most liberals—especially after the 2003 invasion of Iraq turned into a fiasco—favoring a more restrained or cooperative use of American power.

In the early years of the twenty-first century, then, liberals debated questions similar to those first hashed out in the 1980s. Were they too attached to a post-Vietnam worldview, or did the Iraq War vindicate the left's aversion to military interventions? Should Democrats espouse a market-oriented neoliberal economic policy that accommodated itself to globalization or a labor-friendly protectionism? Should they preach traditional values such as religion and patriotism or sing from the hymnbook of toleration and diversity? Should the definitions of rights be inexorably expanded, even to embrace the right of gays and lesbians to marry? The critiques of mainstream left-wing thought offered in the 1980s by neoliberals, DLC moderates, and communitarians certainly helped to forge a new breed of liberalism for the 1990s. But whether that new philosophy would have the appeal and the cohesion to long endure remained an open question.

NOTES

1. Thomas and Mary Edsall, *Chain Reaction: The Impact of Race, Rights, and Taxes on American Politics* (New York: W.W. Norton, 1991), p. 136.

2. Lance Morrow, "Is There Life After Disaster?," *Time*, November 17, 1980.

3. *New York Times*, October 23, 1986, p. D16.

4. Lloyd A. Free and Hadley Cantril, *The Political Beliefs of Americans: A Study of Public Opinion* (New Brunswick, NJ: Rutgers University Press, 1967).

5. James T. Patterson, *Restless Giant: The United States from Watergate to Bush vs. Gore* (New York: Oxford University Press, 2005), p. 200.

6. On neoliberalism see Randall Rothenberg, *The Neoliberals: Creation of the New American Politics* (New York: Simon & Schuster, 1984); and Charles Peters and Phillip Keisling, eds., *A New Road for America: The Neoliberal Movement* (Lanham, Md.: Madison Books, 1985).

7. Hart quoted in Steven M. Gillon, *The Democrats' Dilemma: Walter F. Mondale and the Liberal Legacy* (New York: Columbia University Press, 1992), p. 153.

8. Paul Tsongas, *The Road from Here* (New York: Knopf, 1981), p. xiii.

9. Rothenberg, pp. 221–35.

10. Gary Hart, *Right from the Start: A Chronicle of the McGovern Campaign* (New York: Times Books, 1973); Sidney Blumenthal, "Hart's Big Chill," *The New Republic*, January 23, 1984, pp. 17–23.

11. Gillon, pp. 338–41.

12. "The Differences That Are Dividing the Democrats," *Business Week*, June 4, 1984, p. 72.

13. Edsall and Edsall, p. 204.

14. *New York Times*, July 17, 1984, p. A16.

15. *New York Times*, July 20, 1984, p. A12.

16. Sidney Blumenthal, "The Passing of the Passé," *The New Republic*, December 3, 1984, p. 10.

17. Kenneth S. Baer, *Reinventing Democrats: The Politics of Liberalism from Reagan to Clinton* (Lawrence: University Press of Kansas, 2000), p. 81.

18. John Rawls, *A Theory of Justice* (New York: Oxford University Press, 1971), p. 3.

19. Michael J. Sandel, *Liberalism and the Limits of Justice* (Cambridge, UK: Cambridge University Press, 1982), p. 1.

20. Mary Ann Glendon, *Rights Talk: The Impoverishment of Political Discourse* (New York: Free Press, 1991), p. x.

21. Haynes Johnson, *Sleepwalking Through History: America in the Reagan Years* (New York: Norton, 1991), p. 184.

22. O'Neill quoted in *New York Times*, November 6, 1986, p. A1.

23. Hargrove quoted in Richard Fly and Howard Gleckman, "Can the Democrats Put It All Together?" *Business Week*, November 17, 1986, p. 60.

24. Robert Kuttner, "Reaganism, Liberalism, and the Democrats," in Sidney Blumenthal and Thomas Byrne Edsall, eds., *The Reagan Legacy* (New York: Pantheon Books, 1988), p. 119.

25. On the 1988 campaign, see Jack Germond and Jules Witcover, *Whose Broad Stripes and Bright Stars?: The Trivial Pursuit of the Presidency, 1988* (New York: Warner Books, 1989); and Sidney Blumenthal, *Pledging Allegiance: The Last Campaign of the Cold War* (New York: Harper Collins, 1990).

26. William Galston and Elaine Kamarck, *The Politics of Evasion: Democrats and the Presidency* (Washington, D.C.: Progressive Policy Institute, 1989), pp. 2, 18.

27. E. J. Dionne, *They Only Look Dead: Why Progressives Will Dominate the Next Political Era* (New York: Simon & Schuster, 1996), p. 11.

28. Alan Wolfe, *One Nation, After All* (New York: Viking, 1998).

29. Sean Wilentz, "For Voters, the '60s Never Died," *New York Times*, November 16, 1999, p. A27. See also John B. Judis and Ruy Teixeira, *The Emerging Democratic Majority* (New York: Scribner, 2002); Robert Reich, *Reason: Why Liberals Will Win the Battle for America* (New York: Knopf, 2004).

Chapter 5

BRIGHT LIGHTS, DOOMED CITIES: THE RISE OR FALL OF NEW YORK CITY IN THE 1980S?

Vincent J. Cannato

Sherman McCoy calls himself the "Master of the Universe." And why not? Not yet 40 years old, he is making a million dollars a year as a bond trader on Wall Street, with all of the perks attending to his status—a Park Avenue co-op apartment, a devoted wife, a child in private school, and a mistress holed up in a rent-controlled love nest. McCoy is the prototypical "Yuppie" of the era, a beneficiary of the Reagan boom that revived Wall Street. McCoy's New York was one of prosperity and glitz. The city looks good from McCoy's perch.

The protagonist of Tom Wolfe's 1987 satire *Bonfire of the Vanities*, McCoy soon finds out that 1980s New York had a dark side as well.[1] A colleague of McCoy's advises him: "If you want to live in New York, you've got to insulate, insulate, insulate." What he means is that you had to be insulated from "the other" and the social problems associated with it. McCoy's world soon comes crashing down after the car he is in accidentally runs down a black teenager and he flees the scene. The whole city does not have enough insulation to protect him now.

McCoy's downfall allows Wolfe to present New York in the 1980s in all of its complexities and contradictions. Wolfe saw a "money fever" enveloping the city, which not only afflicted McCoy and his friends, but also had its counterpart in the drug culture of the city's ghettos. Peeling away this "money fever," Wolfe found a dreary vacuousness under the glitzy veneer of McCoy's social class, as well as a grim desolation on so many city streets. The preening, narcissistic McCoy finds his counterpart in the preening, demagogic, inner-city preacher Reverend Bacon.[2]

McCoy's New York was a city rising from the malaise and gloom that had dogged the nation since the 1970s. But it was also a city whose social fabric seemed to be fraying. The city's economy was purring; prosperity was in the air. A city that had nearly gone bankrupt a decade earlier now seemed to be on the rebound. Or was it?

As the essays in this collection show, interpretations of the 1980s vary widely and often mirror the political divisions of the period. Defenders of the Reagan years see the 1980s as a period of restoration—of traditional values, of military power, of national self-confidence, and of economic and entrepreneurial strength. The Reagan restoration was meant to set the country right after the tumultuous 1960s, post–Vietnam War weakness, and economic malaise.[3]

Critics of the 1980s see a funhouse-mirror image of this vision—a time of greed and economic materialism, military waste and jingoistic belligerence, growing inequality, a lack of concern for the poor, and a rolling back of gains for the rights of minorities and women.[4]

These narratives rely heavily on the idea of "decline" and "decay." As Wolfe so dramatically demonstrated, in no place does the duality of "decline/restoration" and "decay/revival" play itself out more clearly than in New York City. During the decade, New York City managed to pull itself out of the depths of the fiscal crisis and begin to rebuild a city left in tatters from neglect, vandalism, and mismanagement. But it was often two steps forward and one step back as serious fiscal, economic, and social problems persisted.

The "urban crisis" of the post-1945 period is defined by middle-class flight to the suburbs, deindustrialization of the urban economy, and rising crime and poverty rates. Concurrently, economic and political power slowly and steadily shifted away from the old industrial northeastern cities and toward the Sunbelt. Things became so bad that in 1980, President Jimmy Carter's Commission for a National Agenda for the Eighties, created to come up with an agenda for a second Carter term that never came to be, advised the nation to accept the "inevitable decline" of northeastern and midwestern cities.[5]

From 1950 to 1990, these cities saw a precipitous decline in population: Chicago, 23 percent; Baltimore, 23 percent; Boston 28 percent; Detroit, 44 percent; Cleveland, 45 percent; and St. Louis, 54 percent. New York's population dropped less than 10 percent during that time, but it was dramatically transformed. An estimated two million lower-income Puerto Ricans and black migrants from the South replaced an equal number of middle-class whites who left for the suburbs.

In New York, the decline was palpable. Saul Bellow's 1970 novel *Mr. Sammler's Planet* is a pessimistic tale of New York, where "you could smell collapse. You could see the suicidal impulses of civilization pushing strongly....New York makes one think about the collapse of civilization, about Sodom and Gomorrah, the end of the world." Though John Lindsay was elected mayor in 1965 to bring Camelot to Gotham, he left office after 8 years of political, social, racial, and economic crises. Lindsay's "Fun City" had become "Fear City."[6]

By the early 1970s, the drumbeat of doom continued. A Ford Foundation report found "a general deterioration of the city environment, visible and palpable in streets, subways, the air and the water around New York." Architect Robert A. M. Stern argued that "New York teetered on the brink of collapse. It had lost its economic clout; worse still, many American seemed to regard the city...as the embodiment of all that was wrong with modern life." Movies of the 1970s, like *Midnight Cowboy, Taxi Driver, The Warriors*, and *Death Wish*, portrayed New York as a tabloid drama of crime, disorder, and all-around seediness.[7]

Along with the social decay, came economic and fiscal problems. Between 1969 and 1975, the city's economy shrunk by 11 percent while government spending grew by 30 percent. Beginning in 1969, the city began to hemorrhage jobs, and its economy never really recovered. In the mid-1960s, New York had been home to 25 percent of all *Fortune 500* companies; two decades later that figure was just 10 percent.[8]

To cover the revenue shortfall, the city tinkered with accounting scams and borrowed money for operating purposes from capital funds, thereby neglecting improvements in the city's infrastructure. Banks happily lent more and more money, overlooking the shoddy accounting and the economic realities of the city.

The city's nadir came in 1975 when the financial capital of America came within inches of declaring bankruptcy. Banks refused to lend the city more money. Two state-created agencies—the Emergency Financial Control Board and the Municipal Assistance Corporation (MAC)—took over operations of the city's budget, union contracts, and finances. The price the city paid was not only the loss of control of the city's books to independent agencies, but also deep cuts in social programs, parks, and libraries. City government was shrunk through layoffs, and municipal unions were forced to give back some of their earlier gains. On top of this, the city's population declined by 800,000 during the decade.[9]

In 1977, New York City elected a new mayor to deal with this wreckage. Ed Koch would serve as mayor of New York from 1978 to 1989. An ebullient and

abrasive presence, Koch embodies many of the political changes and contradictions of the era. His trademark phrase—"How'm I Doin'"—reminded many
of "some mad combination of a Lindy's waiter, Coney Island barker, Catskill
comedian, irritated school principal, and eccentric uncle."[10]

His political career straddled the fault line of postwar American politics.
A son of the Jewish lower-middle class, Koch grew up in New York and Newark.
He served in the army during World War II, became a lawyer, and in the 1950s
moved to Manhattan's Greenwich Village. There he became involved in local
politics through the reform Village Independent Democrats, which challenged
the local Democratic machine.

In keeping with the neighborhood's bohemian reputation, Koch was a
reliable and loud liberal voice, criticizing the Vietnam War and defending gay
rights, eventually winning election to Congress in 1968. But his political evolution continued. In the early 1970s, he became a leading critic of the city's plan
to build high-rise, low-income public housing in the largely Jewish, middle-
class neighborhood of Forest Hills.

In 1977, Koch won the Democratic nomination for mayor over left-wing
congresswoman Bella Abzug by portraying himself as a defender of law enforcement and supporter of the death penalty. He distanced himself from his liberal
past and became the voice of outer-borough white ethnics disenchanted with
liberalism. In Koch's own words, he had become "a liberal with sanity."[11]

Koch also made clear that he believed the old social welfare system was an
impossible arrangement in post–fiscal crisis New York. "We can't spend what we
don't have," Koch reminded New Yorkers. In his early years in office, he worked
to trim the budget, restore the city's credit rating, and bring fiscal stability back
to the city.[12]

Much of New York's renaissance, which began in the mid-1990s, was built
on the foundation of the 1980s. The city's fiscal stability was hard won. Koch
kept spending well below inflation in the late 1970s and early 1980s. In fact,
spending actually declined in constant dollars. Between 1975 and 1981, New
York had shed nearly 40,000 city government jobs. Basic services, already
strained, continued to take a hit. But the sacrifices paid off. By 1981, the city
had balanced its budget and saw its credit rating rise. The city was now poised
to take advantage of a renewed national economy.

Ironically, largely liberal New York City profited from Ronald Reagan's economic policies, such as tax cuts and deregulation. In the resulting economic
boom, Wall Street took off and drove the city's economic engine until the 1987
crash. Although a Democrat, Koch meshed well with Republican economic
policy, arguing that "the main job of city government is to create a climate in

which private business can expand in the city and not to provide jobs on the public payroll."[13]

The city also benefited from changes in the global economy. On the one hand, the deindustrialization of American cities had hurt New York, which lost 300,000 manufacturing jobs between 1967 and 1977 (and another 180,000 between 1977 and 1989); overall, the city lost 600,000 jobs between 1969 and 1977. Yet the international economy also had a need for highly specialized—and highly paid—jobs. In the 1980s, New York became a "global city," a clearing-house for the new economy and again began creating jobs, not in manufacturing but in financial services and the broader service sector, such as law, accounting, management, and computers. The city gained more than 400,000 jobs in the 1980s, although it was not until the late 1990s that employment would again reach the levels of 1969. The "post-industrial revolution" had arrived.[14]

The stock market boom filled the city's coffers and led to a real-estate boom. From 1981 to 1986, Manhattan saw nearly 45 million square feet of new commercial real estate. No man more represented the 1980s New York boom than real-estate magnate Donald Trump, whose glitzy, gilded buildings (always with his name prominently displayed) embodied the era. His 1987 book, *Trump: The Art of the Deal*, made him a symbol of Reagan-era entrepreneurship for not just New York, but for the entire nation.

As the city's economy came to life, so did other parts of the city. One example was the city's subways, which had hit rock bottom in the late 1970s. Crime was rampant, a large homeless population lived underground, and graffiti scarred nearly every inch of subway cars. Even worse, the subways were not safe. Years of delayed maintenance left a crumbling infrastructure and obsolete technology. A subway derailment or collision occurred every 15 days. New leadership of the subway system, as well as an infusion of funds from a booming economy, led to the beginning of a major overhaul of the system. The 1980s marked a turnaround in the fortunes of the New York's mass transit system.[15]

Public parks had taken a beating during the 1960s and 1970s due to greater use by citizens, increased vandalism, and fewer resources. Nowhere was this more apparent than in the city's crown jewel—Central Park. In an era of tight budgets, New York City began to turn to the private sector to meet some of its basic needs. In 1980, the Central Park Conservancy took over operations of the park. This public–private partnership raised tens of millions of dollars for the repair and restoration of Central Park. Although it was years before results were seen, the foundations were set in the 1980s.[16]

Similar changes occurred a little farther south in Bryant Park. Once a tiny jewel in midtown Manhattan behind the New York Public Library, by the 1970s Bryant Park had become a haven for drug dealers. The Bryant Park Restoration Corporation, another public–private partnership, raised money for park maintenance and rebuilding and experimented with ways to make the park more user-friendly.

Public–private partnerships were extended to other parts of the city that had deteriorated by the early 1980s. The Grand Central Partnership was formed in 1985 to restore the famous train terminal and the area surrounding it. The work in Bryant Park and Grand Central Terminal introduced the concept of Business Improvement Districts (BIDs). Local businesses would pool money to clean the streets and even hire private security. By 2005, the city had 51 BIDs. The results were largely positive, though critics complained about the increasing "privatization" of public spaces.

These public–private partnerships were in keeping with certain themes being sounded by the Reagan administration in Washington, which believed that the private sector was more efficient than sluggish government bureaucracies. This was put to the test in New York Harbor, where Reagan's Interior Department partnered with the private Statue of Liberty–Ellis Island Foundation to raise money for the restoration of those two historic monuments. The unveiling of the newly refurbished Statue of Liberty took place on July 4, 1986, in a grand, celebrity-studded patriotic Fourth of July gala. It was a great symbolic event that celebrated a renovated statue, a rejuvenated city, and a nation on the rebound. As F. Ross Holland, who had been deeply involved in the Foundation, put it, the fundraising and celebration were important "in lifting the American people out of the Vietnam syndrome and making them once again feel good about themselves as a people."[17]

The 1980s also saw a revival of the city's housing stock, which had taken a beating through neglect and arson since the 1960s, when the city lost an estimated 200,000 units of housing. When Ronald Reagan wanted to highlight the urban crisis during his 1980 presidential campaign, he traveled to Charlotte Street in the South Bronx. What had once been a stable working-class community with brick apartment buildings and stores was now a complete ruin. Reagan later recalled the scene: "You have to see it to believe it. It looks like a bombed-out city—great, gaunt skeletons of buildings. Windows smashed out...there are whole blocks of land that are left bare, just bulldozed down flat." Another observer described Charlotte Street as a place where wild dogs "roamed the streets, tearing in and out of buildings and through the trash that covered the sidewalks and the streets.... Fires burned everywhere." The South Bronx had become a national symbol of urban decay.[18]

By the 1980s, private, nonprofit groups such as the business-led New York City Housing Partnership and Brooklyn's church-based Nehemiah Project helped build new homes in low-income and working-class neighborhoods. The Koch administration also committed $4.2 billion in city money to rebuild and rehabilitate city housing. These programs helped rejuvenate city neighborhoods. By the end of the 1980s, the once-empty blocks of Charlotte Street were now the site of new single-family homes.[19]

New urban residents also made an impact on 1980s New York and other large cities. Due to the liberalization of America's immigration laws in 1965, the 1980s saw an influx of immigrants as it had not seen in over 60 years. Previous waves of immigration had come almost exclusively from Europe, but the new immigrants hailed from China, the Dominican Republic, the Soviet Union, Guyana, India, Jamaica, Haiti, and Colombia. New York received more than 800,000 immigrants in the 1980s. By 1990, 28 percent of New Yorkers were foreign born, a trend that would continue and intensify. From 1990 to 1994, there were 563,000 new arrivals and by 1998, more than 37 percent of New Yorkers were foreign born.[20]

Rather than a drain on the city, immigrants brought much-needed energy to a city reeling from numerous crises. These newcomers were ambitious and entrepreneurial, pumping vitality into the city's economy and neighborhoods. The Korean corner market, the East Indian taxicab driver, the Jamaican nurse, the Chinese garment worker, and the Dominican bodega owner all became city staples. The largest parade in the city was no longer the St. Patrick's Day parade but Brooklyn's West Indian Carnival.

Another group of new urbanites involved upwardly mobile professionals, attracted to high-paying jobs in the city, who began to rediscover the brownstones in neighborhoods such as the Upper West Side of Manhattan and Park Slope, Brooklyn. As these people—who soon came to be known by the acronym Yuppies (young, urban professionals)—began to rehabilitate their new homes, property values soared, expensive restaurants and shops followed, and the neighborhoods turned upscale—a process known as gentrification.

Other areas of the city were also being transformed. In downtown Manhattan, South Street Seaport opened in 1983. Once the home of early-nineteenth-century counting houses for the city's merchants, the area was revitalized by developer/planner James Rouse. The old merchant buildings were renovated, but most of the area was turned into an upscale outdoor mall to attract tourists.

This was a trend repeated in cities across the nation, and many of the new downtown retail centers were developed by Rouse. Boston's historic Faneuil Hall, which opened in the late 1970s, was one of the earliest such projects. More than 100 similar developments were opened across the country, with most, such as South Street Seaport and Rouse's Harborplace in downtown Baltimore, opening in the 1980s. One year after President Carter's Commission for a National Agenda for the Eighties was telling Americans to forget about the dying cities of the northeast and midwest, Rouse was on the cover of *Time* magazine with the accompanying headline: "Cities Are Fun!"[21]

New York City had made great progress throughout the 1980s, rising up from the depths of the fiscal crisis. Yet progress in certain areas of city life coexisted with continuing and worsening social problems.

One of the newest of these was also the most mysterious—at least at first. In July 1981, the *New York Times* ran an article entitled "Rare Cancer Seen in 41 Homosexuals." At the time, few knew what caused this disease or how it was transmitted. Eventually, the disease acquired a name: AIDS (acquired immune deficiency syndrome). New York, followed by San Francisco, was the city most affected by the new disease. By the late 1980s, it was estimated that 50 percent of all gay men in New York were infected with AIDS, as were 75 percent of intravenous drug users. In 1982, there were 30 reported deaths from AIDS. By 1989, there were over 4000 deaths a year and the number was rising.[22]

The birthplace of the modern gay-rights movement was the Stonewall riot in Greenwich Village in 1969. Yet it was the tragedy of the AIDS crisis that brought a greater visibility—and, eventually, sympathy—to the gay community. In 1981, the Gay Men's Health Crisis was formed in playwright Larry Kramer's Fifth Avenue apartment. By 1983, the organization was becoming a political force in the city with 12 paid staffers, 500 volunteers, and a budget of almost one million dollars. Its efforts to mobilize the gay community soon paid political dividends. By 1986, the city had outlawed discrimination against gays in housing and employment.

A more radical gay-rights group was created in 1987. The AIDS Coalition to Unleash Power (ACT-UP) harkened back to the radical politics of the 1960s. ACT-UP thrived on confrontation, relying on street protests and street theater. It stenciled its motto—"Silence = Death"—on sidewalks across the city. It staged "die-ins" on Wall Street to publicize the AIDS crisis. And in its most controversial move, it took on New York's Catholic Church, disrupting a Sunday mass at St. Patrick's Cathedral in December 1989. Protestors lay down in the aisles of the church and handcuffed themselves to pews.

The AIDS crisis struck not only at the city's gay community, but also at its African American and Hispanic communities. The crisis led to "safe sex" campaigns that changed sexual behavior for heterosexuals, as well as homosexuals, and tempered some of the freewheeling sexual expressions prevalent during the 1970s.

The late 1980s brought another insidious disruption of city life: crack, a "cheap, short-acting, and potent smokable version of cocaine." While snorting cocaine had become fashionable among the middle and upper-middle class during the late 1970s, crack users were often low-income minorities. Some now argue that the media inflated the problems associated with crack by exaggerating its addictive qualities and hyping the prevalence of "crack babies," born to addicted mothers who would suffer debilitating mental and physical problems. However, there is no disputing that crack helped fuel crime, as drug dealers fought increasingly violent gun battles over turf. In addition, one study found that 31 percent of all murder victims in New York City during 1990 and 1991 had cocaine in their systems.[23]

Crime had increased steadily during the 1960s, plateauing in the mid-1970s. Though crime declined somewhat in the early 1980s, it came back again with a vengeance in the late 1980s. From 1985 to 1990, murders increased by over 60 percent from 1384 to 2245, an all-time high. (By contrast, there were 572 murders in 2004.) Other violent crimes increased as well.

As the streets became less safe, they also became populated with more homeless individuals. New Yorkers debated whether the homeless were a social menace or victims of an insensitive and unequal society. Few debated the damage to the city's image and its social fabric caused by panhandlers, aggressive squeegee-wielding window washers, and poor huddled masses sleeping on sidewalk grates.

Certain crimes during the 1980s took on special significance. In 1984, a nerdy electronics worker named Bernard Goetz shot four African American teenagers in the subway after they asked him for money. The "Subway Vigilante" became a national hero to some, a real-life Charles Bronson who stood up to criminals making life in New York more dangerous. To others, he was a violent racist. Goetz was acquitted of the shooting, claiming self-defense, though he was convicted of gun possession. But the case exposed the still-uncivil state of New York's civil society. As Goetz explained his actions: "I was a monster, but I wasn't a monster until several years alone in New York."

Two other cases further exposed the wide chasm between black and white New Yorkers. In December 1986, three black men found themselves at a pizzeria in the Howard Beach section of Queens after their car broke down. A group of white youths chased the three men. One escaped, one was beaten, and one, Michael Griffith, died when he ran onto a highway and was hit by a car. Blacks called the attack a lynching, although others claimed it was just a street fight. The incident brought Al Sharpton, an inner-city preacher, to the city's attention as he organized marches and pressed the case in the media. Sharpton, a bombastic racial demagogue, only fueled the racial fires burning in the city. (He was Tom Wolfe's model for Rev. Bacon.) Three of the whites charged in the attacks were convicted for their role in Griffith's death. Three years later, a similar incident occurred in Bensonhurst, Brooklyn, as a group of whites killed a young black man named Yusef Hawkins.

Race, class, and crime were again intertwined in an infamous case that made headlines across the city and the nation. On an April night in 1989, a twenty-nine-year-old female investment banker went for a jog in Central Park after work. Before the night was over, the woman who came to be known as the "Central Park Jogger" would be beaten, raped, and left for dead. Police later arrested a group of five teenagers and charged them in the attack. They had been out that night robbing and attacking parkgoers, a practice the police termed "wilding," which became yet another symbol of a city in chaos.

The random and violent nature of the attack sent shock waves throughout a city whose collective nerves were already frayed. The story played across the nation, reinforcing the idea of the dangers of New York. That the victim was a middle-class white woman and the accused attackers were black and Hispanic teenagers only increased tensions. All five teenagers were convicted. The woman eventually recovered, although she suffered some permanent physical and emotional trauma. Fourteen years later, in a far different city, she went public for the first time with her story, while prosecutors released the five attackers, claiming that new evidence exonerated them. Just what exactly happened to Trisha Meili, the "Central Park Jogger," on that April night is still a mystery.[24]

Finally, scandals marred the Koch administration in the mid-1980s. Although Koch was not personally corrupt, some of his political allies found themselves in the middle of an influence-peddling scandal. It was the city's biggest corruption scandal since the 1940s. Democratic Queens Borough President Donald Manes (who committed suicide before being indicted), Bronx Democratic leader Stanley Friedman, and Geoffrey Lindenauer, the deputy director of the city's Parking Violations Bureau, were accused of fraud and bribery. (Both Friedman and Lindenauer were convicted.) Government officials were not the only ones skirting the law in 1980s New York. Stockbroker Ivan Boesky was arrested and convicted as part of an insider-trading scandal on Wall Street, tarring the economic boom of the 1980s.[25]

After three terms, the city was growing fatigued with Mayor Koch. Brought down by scandal and poor relations with the black community, he was narrowly defeated in the 1989 Democratic primary by David Dinkins, who became the city's first African American mayor by putting together a coalition of minorities and liberal whites.

Alongside the social problems of the 1980s, New York's recovering economy still displayed some underlying weaknesses. Although the economy was good at creating both high-income and low-income jobs, middle-income jobs were harder to find as the city's manufacturing sector continued to weaken. Meanwhile, concerns about poverty led to a new policy debate about the urban "underclass," those trapped in poverty for the long term by economic and/or cultural factors.

In addition, economist Matthew Drennan noted a paradox about the 1980s: although New York City had become "a smaller, poorer, and in some respects less economically important part of the region and nation, it has also remained dominant in some booming economic activities often linked to the international economy." The city continued to lose middle-class residents and jobs to its prosperous suburbs, yet at the same time it created more high-paying jobs commanding the heights of the global world of finance. The city's economy in the 1980s was thus one of "simultaneous decay and growth."[26]

Such weaknesses became more apparent after the 1987 stock market crash. Flush with money from the Wall Street boom, Koch had by then abandoned his earlier fiscal prudence and increased city spending at rates difficult to sustain in leaner years. Over the next six years, New York lost 300,000 private sector jobs, bringing it back to where it had been after the 1975 fiscal crisis. Yet the city's public-sector rolls continued to grow. Koch's successor David Dinkins made the problem worse by raising taxes during the 1991 recession. New York's economy seemed to again be sputtering.

A dark mood fell over the city. Lou Reed, whose music had defined the edgier side of New York life since the mid-1960s, came out with a new album in 1989 entitled *New York*. It was a grim litany of the social problems faced by the city; the album's single was the decidedly downbeat "Dirty Blvd." Another song, "Hold On," contained such lyrics: "There's blacks with knives and whites with guns fighting in Howard Beach. There's no such thing as human rights when you walk the New York streets.... There's a rampaging rage rising up like a plague of bloody vials washing up on the beach.... The haves and have-nots are bleeding in the tub. That's New York's future not mine. Oh you better hold on—something's happening here."[27]

New York Review of Books editor Jason Epstein wrote a long lament to what he saw as a dying city. He saw only economic decline for New York, whose last hope was a massive federal bailout. Barring that, "there is probably nothing left to do but join the majority of New Yorkers who are already planning to leave. For in the absence of countervailing pressure from a growing economy, Bushwick [a low-income Brooklyn community] and similar neighborhoods will expand until there is nothing else left."[28]

From the vantage point of a much different New York in 2005, journalist Sam Roberts has called 1990 "The Year New York Lived Really Dangerously." Roberts captured the mood of the city that year when "unglued New Yorkers in every neighborhood not only palpably feared for their personal safety, but even worried whether the problems that were bedeviling the city could ever be fixed—whether Mr. Koch's early success in recovering from the fiscal crisis was an aberration and whether New York had, in fact, become ungovernable."[29]

As if to prove that racial strife could happen under a black mayor as easily as under a white mayor, the city suffered days of tension when violence broke out in 1991 in the Crown Heights section of Brooklyn between Jews and blacks. The clash began when an Orthodox Jewish driver hit and killed a young black child playing in the street. The riots that followed took the lives of two more people and the city's slow response further exposed social and racial divisions and undermined the mayoralty of Mayor Dinkins.

New Yorkers were again in a sour mood; the successes of the 1980s were drowned out by economic recession, crime, and racial tensions. A 1993 poll found that 62 percent of New Yorkers believed that life had gotten worse since 1989.[30]

New York was ready for a change. In 1993, it elected a former prosecutor, Republican Rudolph Giuliani, as the city's 107th mayor. Backed by a similar political coalition that had supported Koch, Giuliani governed for 8 years as a conservative on fiscal issues, crime, and welfare. Many of the policies under-taken in the 1980s paved the way for a positive transformation of New York in the mid-1990s. Optimism and resiliency would soon elbow out warnings of decline. The most popular television show in America during much of the 1990s was *Seinfeld*, about four neurotic singles living in a gentrified New York City. Sherman McCoy would hardly have recognized the place.[31]

Novelist Saul Bellow wrote that "what is barely hinted in other cities is condensed and enlarged in New York." The city serves as a microcosm of the great changes sweeping America during the 1980s and beyond, in particular the effects of the postindustrial, global economy and the dominance of right-of-center politics.

For many, the changes that began after the fiscal crisis were positive. A growing economy created a more culturally vibrant and fiscally sound city.

New York's future would be a dynamic, free-market system rather than a stagnant European-style social-welfare system. Meanwhile, conservative policies helped reduce crime and restore public order.

Others were less sanguine about these changes. They believed that economic and political changes tore at the city's social safety net and allowed private capital too much power. Labor unions grew weaker even as economic insecurity and inequality worsened.[32]

Depending on your perspective or ideology, it is possible to construct a narrative of decline or restoration. Much as in the nation as a whole, tremendous progress in 1980s New York occurred at the same time that deep social problems continued to fester.

Yet by the mid-1990s, New York City had clearly rebounded from the "decline" of 1987–1993. Crime declined dramatically, while the city's economy continued to take advantage of trends in the global economy and a booming stock market. The trends that began in the 1980s—from immigration to BIDs to gentrification—continued to transform New York.

Yet there was another irony at work. Cities such as New York may have been brought back from the brink, but whatever their successes they could not stop the continued growth in the nation's suburbs and exurbs. It is doubtful that American cities, even New York, will ever regain the economic and political power they once had. That may be the ultimate tale of this era.

NOTES

1. Tom Wolfe, *Bonfire of the Vanities* (New York: Farrar Straus Giroux, 1987). For other fictional examples of successful New Yorkers brought down by the darker side of the 1980s city, see Jay McInerney, *Bright Lights, Big City* (New York: Vintage Books, 1984) and Oliver Stone's 1987 movie *Wall Street*.

2. See Tom Wolfe's 1988 speech, "Fact and Fiction in the New York of the Eighties." http://www.manhattan-institute.org/html/wl1988.htm.

3. For positive works on the Reagan years, see Dinesh D'Souza, *Ronald Reagan: How an Ordinary Man Became an Extraordinary Leader* (New York: Free Press, 1997); John Ehrman, *The Eighties: America in the Age of Reagan* (New Haven: Yale University Press, 2005); and Peggy Noonan, *What I Saw at the Revolution: A Political Life in the Reagan Era* (New York: Random House, 1990).

4. For negative views on the Reagan years, see Barbara Ehrenreich, *The Worst Years of Our Lives: Irreverent Notes from a Decade of Greed* (New York: Pantheon, 1990) and Haynes Johnson, *Sleepwalking Through History: America in the Reagan Years* (New York: W.W. Norton & Co., 1991).

5. *Washington Post*, December 26, 1980; Edward D. Berkowitz, *Something Happened: A Political and Cultural Overview of the Seventies* (New York: Columbia University Press, 2006). On deindustrialization, see Jefferson Cowie and Joseph Heathcott (eds.), *Beyond the Ruins: The Meanings of Deindustrialization* (Ithaca, NY: ILR Press, 2003) and Barry Bluestone and Bennett Harrison, *The Deindustrialization of America: Plant Closings, Abandonment and the Dismantling of Basic Industry* (New York: Basic Books, 1982).

6. Saul Bellow, *Mr. Sammler's Planet* (New York: Viking Press, 1970).

7. Vincent J. Cannato, *The Ungovernable City: John Lindsay and His Struggle to Save New York* (New York: Basic Books, 2001).

8. Martin Shefter (ed.), *Capital of the American Century: The National and International Influence of New York City* (New York: Russell Sage Foundation, 1993).

9. On the fiscal crisis, see Martin Shefter, *Political Crisis/Fiscal Crisis: The Collapse and Revival of New York City* (New York: Basic Books, 1985) and Ken Auletta, *The Streets Were Paved With Gold* (New York: Random House, 1979).

10. Pete Hamill, "Personality with a Point," in Michael Goodwin (ed.), *New York Comes Back: The Mayoralty of Edward I. Koch* (New York: powerHouse Books, 2005).

11. Duncan Currie, "A 'Liberal With Sanity,'" *The Weekly Standard*, August 31, 2004.

12. On Koch's political coalition, see John Mollenkopf, *A Phoenix in the Ashes: The Rise and Fall of the Koch Coalition in New York Politics* (Princeton: Princeton University Press, 1992).

13. Quoted in Fred Siegel, "Ground Zero for Big Government," *The American Enterprise*, June 2002.

14. Charles Brecher and Raymond D. Horton, *Power Failure: New York City Politics and Policy since 1960* (New York: Oxford University Press, 1993), p. 7; Saskia Sassen, *The Global City: New York, London, Tokyo*, 2nd ed. (Princeton: Princeton University Press, 2001).

15. Michael Lombardi, "How New York Averted Near Collapse," *International Railway Journal*, June 2005.

16. Roy Rosenzweig and Elizabeth Blackmar, *The Park and the People: A History of Central Park* (New York: Henry Holt and Company, 1994), pp. 505–30.

17. F. Ross Holland, *Idealists, Scoundrels, and the Lady: An Insider's View of the Statue of Liberty-Ellis Island Project* (Urbana: University of Illinois Press, 1993), p. 98. For a decidedly more negative take on the festivities, see Jacob Weisberg, "Gross National Production," *The New Republic*, June 23, 1986.

18. *New York Times*, August 6, 1980; "The Carter-Reagan Presidential Debate," October 28, 1980, http://www.debates.org/pages/trans80b.html; Jill Jonnes, *South Bronx Rising: The Rise, Fall, and Resurrection of an American City* (New York: Fordham University Press, 2002), p. xxiii.

19. Howard Husock, "New Frontiers in Affordable Housing," *City Journal*, Spring 1993.

20. Nancy Foner, *From Ellis Island to JFK: New York's Two Great Waves of Immigration* (New Haven: Yale University Press, 2000).

21. "He Digs Downtown," *Time*, August 24, 1981. See also Bernard J. Frieden and Lynne B. Sagalyn, *Downtown, Inc.: How American Rebuilds Cities* (Cambridge, Mass.: The MIT Press, 1989).

22. Charles Kaiser, *The Gay Metropolis, 1940–1996* (New York: Houghton Mifflin Company, 1997), pp. 279–83; Kenneth T. Jackson (ed.), *The Encyclopedia of New York City* (New Haven: Yale University Press, 1995), p. 11.

23. Jack Shafer, "Crack Then, Meth Now: What the Press Didn't Learn from the Last Drug Panic, *Slate*, August 23, 2005; Craig Reinarman and Harry G. Levine (eds.), *Crack In America: Demon Drugs and Social Justice* (Berkeley: University of California Press, 1997); Kenneth Tardiff et al., "Homicide in New York City: Cocaine Use and Firearms," *The Journal of the American Medical Association*, 272, no. 1 (1994): 43–46.

24. Trisha Meili, *I Am the Central Park Jogger: A Story of Hope and Possibility* (New York: Scribner, 2003).

25. Jack Newfield and Wayne Barrett, *City for Sale: Ed Koch and the Betrayal of New York* (New York: Harper & Row Publishers, 1988).

26. Matthew P. Drennan, "The Decline and Rise of the New York Economy," in John Hull Mollenkopf and Manuel Castells (eds.), *Dual City: Restructuring New York* (New York: Russell Sage Foundation, 1991).

27. Lou Reed, "Anarchy in the Streets," *New York Times*, May 10, 1989.

28. Jason Epstein, "The Tragical History of New York," *New York Review of Books*, April 9, 1992.

29. *New York Times*, May 15, 2005.

30. *New York Times*, October 8, 1993.

31. On Giuliani's mayoralty, see Fred Siegel, *The Prince of the City: Giuliani, New York, and the Genius of American Life* (San Francisco: Encounter Books, 2005).

32. For a pessimistic take on post–fiscal crisis New York, see Joshua B. Freeman, *Working-Class New York* (New York: The New Press, 2000), especially chapters 16–18.

Chapter 6

FEMINISM IN THE 1980S: SURVIVING THE BACKLASH

Sara M. Evans

In the 1980s, feminism was out of fashion with most young women. Like flappers in the 1920s, these women looked on feminists of the previous decade as old hat, stodgy, and unpleasantly angry. Paula Kamen, writing for the University of Illinois student newspaper in 1988, soon understood "that taking a stand on anything even remotely construed as a women's issue aroused strange and strong suspicions." When she subsequently interviewed more than 100 female peers, she found that the word "feminist" conjured for them caricatures of "bra-burning, hairy-legged, Amazon, castrating, militant-almost-anti-feminine" women. She attributed these stereotypes in part to the sense that young feminists were almost invisible in the 1980s. "During our 'coming of age' years from 1980 to 1990, young feminists didn't seem to exist."[1] The new freedoms younger women experienced were to be explored in highly individualistic ways. Yet, in fact, they were in the middle of a revolution—something more like the eye of the storm than its aftermath.

The new surge of feminism just a decade earlier had seemed invincible, growing by leaps and bounds after 1970, ticking off legal and judicial victories that shattered traditional modes of discrimination in education, jobs, sports, and reproductive rights. Women took to the streets by the tens of thousands, founded day care centers and health clinics, wrote passionately for an ever growing number of journals and newspapers, and demanded admission to professions and blue collar occupations alike. When Congress passed the Equal

Rights Amendment (ERA) in 1972 stating that "Equality of Rights under the law shall not be denied or abridged by the United States or any state on account of sex" and sent it to the states for ratification, it seemed that centuries of legal and culturally sanctioned inequality were crumbling.

Yet in 1980, the ERA languished four states short of ratification despite an extended deadline, and by 1982 it was dead. The ERA had become the symbolic focus of the polarization that reshaped the American political landscape, culminating in Ronald Reagan's 1980 campaign that drew heavily on the perception that women who wanted equality and reproductive autonomy were "antifamily," that affirmative action constituted special privilege, and that the increasing visibility of women in every dimension of public life was deeply unsettling. For the most part, the story of feminism in the 1980s has been told as one of decline in the face of backlash, but these stressful times also proved the resilience of a movement that was far from over.

In the opening years of the decade, backlash appeared to dominate. The Reagan administration was overtly antagonistic to most of the women's rights initiatives that had made some headway in the 1970s, and the political atmosphere of the 1980s authorized more open expressions of hostility toward women and minorities. Battles to eliminate language demeaning or belittling to women, for example, that seemed to have been won in the 1970s, turned out to be only partially achieved. Growing violence against abortion clinics accompanied an increase in hate crimes (violence or threats of violence against minorities and homosexuals), and a greater tolerance for overt expressions of prejudice. Perhaps because the economic boom of those years did not affect everyone—and in fact squeezed many in the middle as major industries "downsized"—women and minorities were basically offered up as scapegoats.

Defeat of the ERA removed the most effective mobilizing issue for national women's rights organizations, and they lost many members. They persisted, however, while government funding cuts, combined with membership losses, destroyed many smaller feminist groups.[2] Popular media in the early 1980s discussed the "death of feminism" or, more kindly, "postfeminism."[3] *Elle* wrote, in 1986, that the new generation of women "no longer needs to examine the whys and hows of sexism.... All those ideals that were once held as absolute truths—sexual liberation, the women's movement, true equality—have been debunked or debased."[4]

Choices cheered as liberating in the 1970s evoked criticism and dire warnings in the 1980s. In 1973, *Newsweek* had praised the emergence of singleness: "Within just eight years, singlehood has emerged as an intensely ritualized—and newly respectable—style of American life. It is finally becoming possible to be both single and whole."[5] By the mid-1980s, another cover story in the same magazine warned single women that they may have missed their opportunities to marry: "For years bright young women single-mindedly pursued their careers, assuming that when it was time for a husband they could pencil one in. They were wrong."[6] This warning was based on a poorly researched, unpublished study that inspired numerous cover stories and TV special reports in which single women (but not men) emoted about their loneliness and lost opportunities.

Similarly, popular media deplored the toll on women trying to succeed *both* as professionals *and* as housewives, two full-time jobs. Numerous articles profiled women who dropped out of high-powered, high-paying jobs to have time with their children.[7] In 1986, *Fortune* magazine published a cover article on "Why Women are Bailing Out" of successful careers.[8] Such coverage laid the groundwork for Felice M. Schwartz's idea, promulgated in the *Harvard Business Review* in 1989, that businesses should offer a separate career track for women (later dubbed the "mommy track"), on the grounds that most women are "career-and-family" oriented rather than "career primary."[9] The next year, however, a study of fifty women who left Fortune 500 companies after more than five years found that most blamed the "glass ceiling" (a popular metaphor for their limited advancement opportunities) rather than a lack of "family friendly benefits."[10]

Empowered by the Republican administration, conservatives relentlessly criticized women's work outside the home, blocking most legislation designed to ameliorate the strains of work and family life while turning the blame for those very stresses back on feminism itself. Opposing state subsidies for female-headed households, for example, right-wing pundit George Gilder charged that proponents of such measures "want to ratify the female-headed family as the norm in America. They do not want to subsidize families; they want to subsidize feminism.... The female headed families of today create an unending chain of burdens for tomorrow as their children disrupt classrooms, fill the jails, throng the welfare rolls, and gather as bitter petitioners and leftist agitators seeking to capture for themselves the bounty produced by stable families." Political commentator E. J. Dionne, Jr., pointed out that "feminism had the misfortune of gaining ground in the period when the American economy suffered from its most severe shocks since the Great Depression." As a result, women entered the labor force in two "parallel streams," one highly educated and eager to seize new opportunities and the other forced into work by a declining economy and falling male wages. The latter, of course, ended up in service jobs that were not particularly fulfilling.[11] Considering their resistance to equal pay and affirmative action, it is ironic that conservatives cast feminists as antimale and antifamily "dress for success" professionals who ignored ordinary women's challenges.[12] The lack of public mobilization on feminist issues meant that stereotypes like these went relatively uncontested in the popular culture and, as a result, they governed the perceptions of most young people in the 1980s, both male and female.

The virulent, even vicious, opposition to feminism in the 1980s, however, was less a death knell than an indicator of the fact that feminism had become a powerful force in American society and culture, reworking the shape and mission of numerous mainstream organizations as well as the nature of public life. Backlash, despite its apparent pervasiveness, was not the dominant reality of the 1980s. Indeed, the new hostility to change reflected the fact that whether as working professionals or homeless "bag ladies," women had become omnipresent in public life. Though often still tokens in terms of total numbers, they were there nonetheless—in corporate board rooms, on highway crews, at truck stops (driving trucks!), in courtrooms (as judges and lawyers, and also as the accused), in the pulpit, and in combat fatigues. The simple appearance of a woman in a position of authority no longer provoked disbelief. Furthermore, the joint impact of the feminist and civil rights movements meant that many of these newly visible women were women of color.

What the backlash accomplished, however, was to make feminists more invisible in the media and even to themselves. The result was that thousands of women were creating new patterns with few models and little support. Young professional women, for example, were on their own as they struggled to resolve the conflicting demands of careers and motherhood. At home they juggled time schedules and day care providers, while at work they discovered that new barriers appeared in the form of increased resistance to advancement as they moved through the ranks. Earlier feminist demands for a reevaluation of work and family to enable *both* parents to raise children actively without jeopardizing their careers were unknown to young women struggling to fit their lives into a mold designed for workers with traditional wives.

The media preyed on the anxieties of women living out new life patterns without familiar models. Despite overwhelming evidence of working women's satisfaction and mental health, whether married or not, many unmarried women began to believe they *should* be lonely and panic-stricken. Similarly, married women's changing work patterns provided fodder for divisive coverage. In a 1982 story entitled "Women vs. Women," *Ladies Home Journal* announced a "New Cold War Between Housewives and Working Mothers." Anyone reading the entire story found pleas for communication and understanding, but the large type framed a different message: "During the 1970s there was a lot of talk about 'sisterhood.'...In practice, however, the events of the last decade may have done more to divide us than to bring us together."[13]

Despite its decreased visibility, however, feminism persisted in the 1980s flowing into new institutional channels. Adjustment to a changed political context required creative responses. For example, in 1982, Ellen Malcolm, a former organizer for Common Cause and press secretary for the National Women's Political Caucus, gained a new perspective on one of the root problems facing women candidates when Harriet Woods, a veteran city and state politician in Missouri, had trouble raising money for her Senate campaign. "We have to have a man for the job," leaders told her. Woods lost by less than 1 percent of the vote.

Malcolm decided to found a new kind of feminist political action group to support pro-choice women candidates in the Democratic Party. She took the acronym EMILY from her belief that "early money is like yeast." Women's increased participation in the labor force, she reasoned, meant that they had—perhaps for the first time—resources to invest in the political process. At the same time, few women could make the large contributions most political fundraising sought. EMILY's list would increase women's contributions in targeted ways. An heir to one of IBM's founders, Malcolm had the money to launch her initiative.

EMILY's List enjoyed some success in the 1980s. It contributed $250,000 to Barbara Mikulski's 1986 Senate campaign ($1 out of every $5 she raised), and claimed that her victory vindicated the strategy. Between 1986 and 1990 EMILY's List helped elect seven Democratic women to the U.S. House: Nita Lowey (NY), Jolene Unsoeld (WA), Jill Long (IN), Patsy Mink (HI), Rosa DeLauro (CT), Maxine Waters (CA), and DC delegate Eleanor Holmes Norton. In 1990 it supported Ann Richards (TX) and Barbara Roberts (OR) in their successful gubernatorial campaigns.[14] By 1990, the 3500 members of EMILY's List donated $1.5 million to 14 candidates.

Women's leadership also continued to grow among community-level activists. Poor and working-class women brought new issues and definitions of public life into the political arena that countered the 1980s conservative ethos. Community-level activism increased the number of female officeholders too. In 1969, only 3.5 percent of state elected officials were women; by 1983, women held 13 percent of elected state offices. In municipal governments, the proportion of women grew from about 10 percent in 1975 to 23 percent in 1988.[15]

The momentum of women's growing public participation swept into an amazing array of institutions. In 1981, President Reagan named Sandra Day

O'Connor to the United States Supreme Court. In 1984, the Democratic Party nominated Congresswoman Geraldine Ferraro for vice president. West Point graduated its thousandth woman. The Episcopal Church elected an African American, the Reverend Barbara C. Harris, as its first woman bishop in 1989. The first woman astronaut, Sally K. Ride, traveled into space in 1983 aboard the shuttle Challenger. Indeed, on closer examination, the shock waves of changes initiated in the 1970s continued to transform the American mainstream from athletics and the military to religious and educational institutions. The force of backlash captured the media, but it could not turn back a tidal wave of change.

Women's athletics, for example, continued to trace a profound, if incomplete, revolution. The 1972 passage of Title IX of the Education Amendments required educational institutions receiving federal support to treat women equally, whether in the classroom or athletics. This momentous change reshaped young women's lives in the 1980s. In 1971, only 300,000 girls participated in intercollegiate sports, but as a result of Title IX, by 1992 that number had grown to more than two million girls. Young women could no longer even imagine the restraints their mothers had faced on the playing field. Female athletes seemed "normal." During the 1988 Olympics in Seoul, South Korea, Americans cheered as African American track stars Jackie Joyner-Kersee and Florence Griffith Joyner set world records.

The observable change in athletic participation modified the backlash. Few openly dared to argue that women should not compete or that an athletic body was, by definition, mannish. But when the NCAA realized that it could not reverse Title IX, it brought women's athletics under its control. The result was a dramatic loss in female leadership for women's sports, as most schools merged men's and women's athletic programs under male leadership. When coaches for women's teams began receiving better salaries, higher status male coaches displaced almost half the women coaches. Men's programs routinely received twice the scholarship money and three times the operating funds that women's programs did.[16]

In the case of women in the military, gains occurred despite the fact that the ERA's defeat in 1982 had rested, in part, on arguments that it would expose women to unacceptable physical stresses and dangers on the battlefield. By the 1991 Gulf War, women constituted 11 percent of the armed forces, and many, though supposedly not "in combat," served within range of enemy fire. Women flew helicopters, reconnaissance planes, in-flight fueling tankers, strategic transport, and medical airlifts. Two women were taken as prisoners of war and fifteen women died.[17]

Although changes in areas such as athletics and the military were more embodied than ideological, feminist ideas continued to flourish within religious and educational institutions. Religious institutions, for example, not only witnessed a rising number of female leaders, they also wrestled with feminist theology. Many denominations ordained their first female clergy in the 1970s. By the 1980s, seminaries were filled with women, and major denominations embarked on inclusive language revisions of liturgies and hymnals. "Mankind" and "brotherhood" gave way to "humankind" or "people of faith." Congregations experimented with feminine images of God.[18]

Catholic women who pressed in the 1970s for women's ordination turned in the 1980s to building a grassroots network of women who shared liturgy and rituals, celebrated life-cycle events (puberty, menopause, divorce), and wrestled with theological inquiry, calling themselves Women Church. Theologian Mary Hunt proclaimed "a new baptism—a baptism into a Church which acknowledges that it is guilty of sexism, heterosexism, racism and classism."[19] This radical challenge, however, was at once exhilarating and painful: "The Roman Catholic Church is our history and our heritage. It is our spiritual and religious 'home,' an integral and essential aspect of our identity. It is also the source of our greatest pain and alienation for, as women, we are both invisible and insignificant to this church we call 'ours.'"[20] The church hierarchy responded to the visible threat of feminist activism with targeted assertions of authority. Several nuns who had become elected officials, for example, were forced to give up politics or resign from the Church. Swift discipline was meted out to ninety-seven Catholic scholars, social activists, priests, and nuns who signed an October 1984 ad in the *New York Times* asserting a "diversity of opinions regarding abortion" among committed Catholics and calling for "candid and respectful discussion on this diversity of opinion within the church."[20]

Throughout the 1980s and beyond, the Daughters of Sarah, an evangelical feminist group, continued vigorous discussions via a newsletter and at conferences. The Daughters were interested in using female metaphors for God and wrestled with "goddess" language, as they attempted to root their feminist spirituality within biblical tradition. They also struggled with questions of sexuality such as chastity, homosexuality, singleness, and celibacy, as well as issues such as racism, women in the developing world, health care, reproduction, and abortion (about which they still had no consensus in 1987). Given the cultural authority accorded conservative evangelicals with a political inside track, it is startling to discover such a vibrant, open, and radical ongoing conversation among evangelical Christian feminists.

Feminist ideas also continued to evolve in the context of mainstream academic discourses. Over the course of the 1980s, Women's Studies became institutionalized at thousands of colleges and universities, complete with majors, minors, and tenure-track faculty. By the end of the 1980s over two-thirds of all universities, nearly half of all four-year colleges, and about one in four two-year institutions had women's studies courses. Armed with new knowledge, feminist scholars inaugurated a massive effort to transform the entire curriculum in the humanities and social sciences. With initial funds from the Ford Foundation, faculty development seminars at many universities facilitated the revision of courses with the goal of making them more inclusive, not only of women but also of racial and ethnic minorities. Institutes or centers for research on women sprouted on dozens of campuses, winning research grants, developing curricula at the graduate level, and forming a national network through the National Council for Research on Women.[21]

Some disciplines—notably history and English—were altered in fundamental ways. History, for example, shifted away from paradigms of history as public activity, focused on activities of powerful men, to include an enormous range of people (powerful and subordinate) and topics, from housework to popular culture to social movements to legislative activity. Scholarly conference programs once focused primarily on political and military history were, by the 1980s, replete with sessions on women, race, and class. Because feminist approaches built on and supported similar conceptual challenges from scholars interested in studying other previously ignored and subordinated groups, their academic success fueled the political forces aligned against feminism and multiculturalism, resulting by the late 1980s in an increasingly public debate later dubbed the "culture wars."

The National Women's Studies Association (NWSA) followed a path familiar to many other institutional experiments in the 1970s. Noted for large, lively conferences that melded academic discourses with free-spirited expressions of "women's culture," the NWSA could barely subsist from one year to the next. Yet by the mid-1980s, the NWSA gradually began acquiring the accoutrements of a professional association: an academic, peer-reviewed journal, scholarships and book awards, foundation grants, a tiny endowment, and a responsibly managed budget of more than half a million dollars.

Institutionalizing women's studies gave younger generations a new kind of access to feminism. Throughout the 1980s, despite marginalization and stereotypes, on most campuses women's studies classrooms became crucial incubators for a new generation of women by offering a space in which students could debate the meanings of feminism and its implications for life choices. Even as

Paula Kamen interviewed her stereotype-filled cohort, a few voices on the margins gradually became audible in the late 1980s and early 1990s, challenging the fragmentation of the movement.[22]

In the conservative climate of the 1980s, however, feminist-driven changes in the mainstream of higher education provoked growing resistance. Multiculturalism joined feminism and homophobia as touchstones for conservatives emboldened by pronouncements of the National Endowment for the Humanities (NEH) Chair William Bennett and his successor, Lynne V. Cheney.[23] Once again, backlash was a measure of feminist success. Though resources for the humanities were diminishing, feminist scholars were in the vanguard of many disciplines and were beginning to appear in positions of professional prominence. It was their very success, against the grain of official policy, that drove an energetic right-wing assault on liberal education that, by the late 1980s, was gathering considerable momentum.

Even as the "culture wars" gathered steam, however, the feminist spirit of feisty confrontation countered with another round of consciousness-raising activism. In 1985, a group of women artists, writers, performers, and film makers created Guerrilla Girls to protest discrimination against women in the art world.

> Dubbing ourselves the conscience of culture, we declare ourselves feminist counterparts to the mostly male tradition of anonymous do-gooders like Robin Hood, Batman, and the Lone Ranger. We wear gorilla masks to focus on the issues rather than our personalities. We use humor to convey information, provoke discussion, and show that feminists can be funny.[24]

They called attention to the absence of women artists in shows at major galleries such as New York's Metropolitan Museum of Modern Art and the fact that art, like popular culture, had taken a strong turn toward masculine imagery and style. By contrast, female artists, like many feminist thinkers in the 1980s, often focused on women's uniqueness, in particular the maternal values of nurture and cooperation. They curated their own exhibitions to provide women artists with opportunities to exhibit their work, and they showed up in gorilla suits to demonstrate, hand out leaflets, and plaster posters all over town.[25]

The emphasis on maternal values, sometimes referred to as "cultural feminism," led feminist activism in additional new directions in the 1980s focused on the environment and peace. For example, the term "ecofeminism" was coined in 1974 by French feminist Francoise d'Eaubonne, but it did not emerge as a theoretical stream within feminism in the United States until March 1980 at a conference on "Women and Life on Earth" in Amherst, Massachusetts. Ecofeminism grew from important strands in cultural feminism, including writers as diverse as Rosemary Radford Reuther, Mary Daly, Susan Griffin, and Nancy Choderow.[26] What these writers held in common was an analysis that linked patriarchal domination of women with domination of the earth, claiming women had a unique vantage point from which to speak out against both patriarchal domination and ecological devastation. Ynestra King's 1981 manifesto, "The Eco-feminist Imperative," brought the threads together:

> We believe that a culture against nature is a culture against women. We know we must get out from under the feet of men as they go about their projects of violence.... We have to be the voice of the invisible, of nature who cannot speak for herself in the political arenas of our society.[27]

The emphasis on maternal values also contributed to a revival of feminist peace activism in the tradition of Jane Addams' Women's Peace Party during World War I, the Women's International League for Peace and Freedom in the 1920s, and Women Strike for Peace in the 1960s. In the summer of 1983, a Women's Encampment for a Future of Peace and Justice convened for several months in Seneca County, New York. Modeled on the British women's 1981 encampment at Greenham Common, the group framed its opposition to nuclear weapons in the context of "a value system which affirms qualities that have traditionally been considered female: nurturing of life, putting others' well-being before one's own, cooperation, emotional and intuitive sensitivity, attention to detail, the ability to adapt, perseverance." Women provided the backbone of a "nuclear freeze campaign" in 1984, urging a freeze on nuclear weapons.[28]

The internationalism of the women's peace movement highlights the growth of women's activism around the world. Indeed, feminism in the United States and Western Europe had by the 1980s joined forces with insurgent demands from women's organizations in the developing world to produce a massive and multifaceted network of movements and organizations. At the United Nations Decade for Women conference in Nairobi, Kenya, in 1985, 14,000 women from across the globe gathered to debate everything from political participation to family planning to sex trafficking to women's roles in economic development. The International Network for Food and Peace organized a "Peace Tent" with funds provided by an American peace activist and philanthropist. The Peace Tent modeled a new kind of global public space that allowed people to speak and to listen across deep and ancient differences. As a place in which activists on opposite sides of these conflicts could speak directly with each other and engage in a search for common ground, the Peace Tent quickly became the epicenter of ongoing discussions about the Middle East, the Iranian Revolution, apartheid, and raging military conflicts.[29] Rudo Gaidzanwa, a sociologist at the University of Zimbabwe, wrote in retrospect that

> the atmosphere in Nairobi at Forum '85 contained little of the "more feminist than thou" posture of some western women who, in the past, had condemned or decried a Third World woman's desire for family and married life. On the other hand, there was little of the "more political than thou" stance that used to be taken by some Third World women who disapproved of the priorities of western feminists. Generally, these differences in priorities and strategies were taken for granted.[30]

Across the board, the new forms of feminist thought and activism that evolved in 1980s America, for the most part screened from public view by the politically empowered backlash, made it clear that older forms of identity politics were giving way to broad, new coalitions. American women had to rethink their concerns in a global context and acknowledge the enormous range of women's experiences and concerns. Women's issues were no longer separable from issues related to race or class. Similarly the scourge of AIDS in the 1980s brought together feminists and gay rights activists with a broadened community.

Thus, as the 1980s drew to a close, a resurgence of feminist activism was gathering force among young women just coming of age in a world already transformed by their mothers' generation. Paula Kamen wrote her book because she longed for connection with other young feminists, and as she did so others such as Susan Faludi (*Backlash*, 1991), Naomi Wolfe (*The Beauty Myth*, 1992; *Fire with Fire*, 1993), and Rebecca Walker (*To Be Real*, 1995) were incubating their ideas.[31] Women who had been young in the 1980s would view themselves as pioneers, remembering battles over promotion, access, and opportunities, whether or not they ever identified with the label "feminist." Those who were close behind them, in the 1990s, reclaimed feminism by naming themselves the "third wave" and began a conversation about just what female solidarity could mean in a postmodern world.

NOTES

1. Paula Kamen, *Feminist Fatale: Voices from the "Twentysomething" Generation Explore the Future of the Women's Movement* (New York: Donald I. Fine, 1991), quotes on pp. 1, 6, and 2.

2. Nancy Whittier, *Feminist Generations: The Persistence of the Radical Women's Movement* (Philadelphia: Temple University Press, 1995), p. 198; Barbara Ryan, *Feminism and the Women's Movement* (New York: Routledge, 1992), 140–44.

3. See Susan Bolotin, "Voices from the Post-Feminist Generation," *The New York Times Magazine*, October 17, 1982; Eloise Salholz, "Feminism's Identity Crisis," *Newsweek* 107 (March 31, 1986): 58–59.

4. Susan Faludi, *Backlash: The Undeclared War Against American Women* (New York: Crown Publishers, 1991), p. 111.

5. Harry Waters, "Games Singles Play," *Newsweek* 82 (July 16, 1973): 52–58.

6. Quoted in Faludi, *Backlash*, p. 99.

7. See Faludi, *Backlash*.

8. Alex Taylor III, "Why Women Managers Are Bailing Out," *Fortune*, August 18, 1986, 16–23.

9. Felice N. Schwartz, "Management Women and the New Facts of Life," *Harvard Business Review* 67 (January/February 1989): 65–76; Barbara Kantrowitz, "Advocating a 'Mommy Track': An Expert on Career Woman Stirs Up a Controversy," *Newsweek* 113, no. 11 (March 13, 1989): 45(1).

10. Jolie Solomon, "The Invisible Barrier Is Crystal Clear to Many," *Wall Street Journal*, April 20, 1990, p. B: 1.

11. E. J. Dionne, Jr., *Why Americans Hate Politics* (New York: Simon & Schuster, 1991), pp. 105–106.

12. George Gilder, "An Open Letter to Orrin Hatch," *National Review* 40, no. 9 (May 13, 1988): 33–34.

13. Nancy Rubin, "Women vs. Women," *Ladies Home Journal* XCIX, no. 4 (August 1982): 94–96, 100–103.

14. Joan E. McLean, "Emily's List," in Sarah Slavin, ed., *U.S. Women's Interest Groups* (Westport, CT: Greenwood Press, 1995), 175–76.

15. Ethel Klein, *Gender Politics: From Consciousness to Mass Politics* (Cambridge, Mass.: Harvard University Press, 1984), p. 30; R. Darcy, Susan Welch, and Janet Clark, *Women, Elections, & Representation* (Lincoln: University of Nebraska Press, 1994).

16. Susan Cahn, *Coming On Strong: Gender and Sexuality in Twentieth Century Women's Sport* (New York: Free Press, 1994), pp. 258–60.

17. William P. Lawrence, "Clearing the Legal Way for Women In Combat," *The Washington Post*, July 28, 1991, p. C:7; Eric. Schmitt, "War Puts U.S. Service Women Closer Than Ever to Combat," *The New York Times*, January 22, 1991, pp. A:1, 12; Paula Ries and Anne T. Stone, eds., *The American Woman, 1992–93: A Status Report* (New York: W. W. Norton, 1992), pp. 344–45.

18. "More Hymn Changes," *Christian Century* 104 (April 15, 1987): 352; "Avoiding Sexism," *Christian Century* 104 (April 22, 1987): 376.

19. Mary Fainsod Katzenstein, "Feminism within American Institutions: Unobtrusive Mobilization in the 1980s," *Signs: Journal of Women in Culture and Society* 16, no.11 (Autumn 1990): 40.

20. Katzenstein, "Feminism within American Institutions," pp. 42–43.

21. Mariam K. Chamberlain, *Women in Academe: Progress and Prospects* (New York: Russell Sage Foundation, 1988).

22. Barbara Findlen, *Listen Up: Voices from the Next Feminist Generation* (Seattle, WA: Seal Press, 1995); Rebecca Walker, ed., *To Be Real: Telling the Truth and Changing the Face of Feminism* (New York: Anchor Books, 1995).

23. See William J. Bennett, "The Chattered Humanities," *Wall Street Journal*, 31 December 1982, p. 10 and *To Reclaim a Legacy: A Report on the Humanities in Higher Education* (Washington, D.C.: National Endowment for the Humanities, 1984); Lynne V. Cheney, *The Humanities and the American Promise: A Report of the Colloquium on the Humanities and the American People* (Charlottesville, VA: Colloquium on the Humanities and the American People, 1987); *Humanities in America: A Report to the President, the Congress, and the American People* (Washington, D.C.: National Endowment for the Humanities, 1988).

24. Statement on Guerrilla Girls Website: http://www.guerrillagirls.com.

25. See *Confessions of the Guerrilla Girls* (New York: Harperperrennial Library, 1995).

26. See Rosemary Radford Reuther, *New Woman, New Earth: Sexist Ideologies and Human Liberation* (New York: Seabury Press, 1975); Mary Daly, *Gyn/Ecology: The Metaethics of Radical Feminism* (Boston: Beacon Press, 1978); Susan Griffin, *Woman and Nature: The Roaring Inside Her* (New York: Harper & Row, 1978); Nancy Choderow, *The Reproduction of Mothering: Psychoanalysis and the Sociology of Gender* (Berkeley: University of California Press, 1978). For this analysis of the origins and evolution of ecofeminism I am indebted to Catronia Sandilands, *The Good-Natured Feminist: Ecofeminism and the Quest for Democracy* (Minneapolis: University of Minnesota Press, 1999), Chapter 1, "A Genealogy of Ecofeminism," pp. 3–27. See also Carolyn Merchant, *Earthcare: Women and the Environment* (New York: Routledge, 1995).

27. Ynestra King, "The Eco-feminist Imperative (May 1981)," in Leonie Caldecott and Stephanie Leland, eds., *Reclaim the Earth: Women Speak Out for Life on Earth* (London: Women's Press, 1993), quoted in Sandilands, *The Good-Natured Feminist*, p. 15.

28. Louise Krasniewicz, *Nuclear Summer: The Clash of Communities at Seneca Women's Peace Encampment* (New York: Cornell University Press, 1992).

29. Irene Tinker and Jane Jaquette, "UN Decade for Women: Its Impact and Legacy," *World Development* 15 no. 3 (1987): 422–23; Arvonne Fraser, *The UN Decade for Women* (Boulder, CO: Westview Press, 1987).

30. Rudo Gaidzanqa, "Reflections on Forum '85 in Nairobi, Kenya: Voices from the International Women's Studies Community," *Signs: Journal of Women in Culture and Society* 11 no. 3 (1986): 593, 597.

31. Faludi, *Backlash*; Naomi Wolfe, *The Beauty Myth* (New York: Anchor Books, 1992), and *Fire with Fire: The New Female Power and How It Will Change the 21st Century* (New York: Random House, 1993); Walker, *To Be Real*.

Chapter 7

INTELLECTUAL AFFIRMATIVE ACTION: HOW MULTICULTURALISM BECAME MANDATORY AND MAINSTREAM IN HIGHER EDUCATION

Mark Brilliant

On June 28, 1978, a sharply divided United States Supreme Court ruled narrowly in favor of a limited application of affirmative action in higher education admissions. In the landmark case of *University of California Regents v. Bakke*, four justices concurred with enough of Justice Lewis F. Powell, Jr.'s opinion to cobble together a razor thin one-vote majority on behalf of the "consideration of race and ethnic origin" in admissions decisions. Doing so, the Court ruled, contributed to campus "diversity," which in turn met the requisite legal threshold of serving a "substantial interest" on the part of the state.[1]

Buoyed in part by *Bakke*, the proportion of college enrollment in the United States consisting of "American Indian," "Asian," "Black," and "Hispanic" students climbed from 15.9 percent in 1978 to 22.8 percent in 1993.[2] In few places, if any, was this increasing minority matriculation more evident than the university system that gave rise to *Bakke*. Most notably, the University of California, Berkeley campus marked the tenth anniversary of the Supreme Court's historic decision with a demographic watershed in the history of higher education. The beginning of the 1988 school year saw the undergraduate student body become majority minority (51.5 percent)—a first for both "Berkeley, and probably at any academically top-ranked U.S. university," according to the school's Office of Public Information.[3]

Berkeley foreshadowed a broader transformation afoot in the United States to which pundits and publications throughout the 1980s and into the 1990s called attention. Early in 1990, for example, a *Time* magazine cover story on "America's Changing Colors" announced that "Someday soon white Americans will become a minority group."[4]

"Changing demographics," in turn, compelled "an urgent intellectual need to rethink how we deal with diversity," insisted a Berkeley professor, as did a small, but growing, number of other professors and students.[5] The content of the curriculum, they argued, needed to diversify in order to better reflect the composition of the student body. Affirmative action in higher education admissions required a curricular counterpart—or what a handful of Berkeley professors characterized as "intellectual affirmative action."[6] Students must learn "to understand society from a broadly multi-cultural perspective congruent with today's reality," declared Berkeley Chancellor Ira Michael Heyman, and they needed a required course to help them do so.[7]

In choosing the term "multi-cultural," Chancellor Heyman invoked a neologism that was rapidly becoming a mantra, as mandatory multiculturalism courses, such as the one Heyman endorsed at Berkeley, sprung up on campuses across the country in the 1980s.[8] By 1991, according to one study, just over one-third of nearly 200 universities and colleges surveyed had established some sort of "multicultural general education requirement." Some of these requirements, such as "American Cultures" enacted at the University of California, Berkeley in 1989, focused on the United States.[9] Others, such as "Cultures, Ideas, and Values" adopted at Stanford University in 1988, exposed students to non-Western countries and cultures.[10] Most, such as "Race and Ethnicity" implemented at the University of Michigan in 1991, allowed students to satisfy the requirement by taking a course on multiculturalism in either the United States or abroad.[11]

These courses reflected multiculturalism's imperative to "*recognize* the equal value of different cultures," as philosopher Charles Taylor put it in his seminal 1992 essay *Multiculturalism and "The Politics of Recognition."* More specifically, they sought to carve out a "greater place" in the curriculum for "women and . . . people of non-European races and cultures"—in part because "all students may be missing something important through the exclusion of a certain gender or certain races or cultures," and in part to redress the "demeaning picture of themselves" that "women and students from the excluded groups" received from a curriculum that otherwise conveyed the message that "all creativity and worth inhered in males of European provenance." In these ways, multiculturalism sought to combat the harms of "nonrecognition" or "misrecognition."[12]

Like affirmative action in higher education admissions, intellectual affirmative action stoked heated controversy, forming the curricular front of the "culture wars" that ignited across the United States at the very moment that the

Cold War fizzled.[13] As in the Cold War, combatants in the "curricular culture wars" vied for hearts and minds.[14] For them, nothing less than "what it means to be an American"—or "how to understand the American experience and represent it to American students"—was at stake in the myriad campus conflicts over mandating and mainstreaming multiculturalism and the often pugilistic publications about them that rolled off the presses.[15]

The rise of multiculturalism requirements in the 1980s occurred at a time when education—from kindergarten through college—reclaimed a position atop the nation's agenda that it had not occupied since the late 1950s in the aftermath of the Soviet Union's launching of the satellite Sputnik.[16] In 1983, the National Commission on Excellence in Education, which had been convened by President Ronald Reagan's Department of Education in 1981, released its report, *A Nation at Risk*. Focusing on high schools, *A Nation at Risk* warned that America's "once unchallenged preeminence in commerce, industry, science, and technological innovation is being overtaken by competitors throughout the world," likened that threat to "an act of unthinking, unilateral educational disarmament," and recommended that high schools respond, in part, by ratcheting up their graduation requirements.[17] One year later, William Bennett, head of the National Endowment for the Humanities, published *To Reclaim a Legacy*. Unlike *A Nation at Risk*, *To Reclaim a Legacy* concentrated on humanities education at the postsecondary level. However, like *A Nation at Risk*, it called for increased graduation requirements, in particular, "[d]eveloping a common curriculum with the humanities at the core" in order to reverse the "abandoning [of humanities] course requirements" that had occurred since the 1960s, especially in the area of Western Civilization.[18] The drumbeat for more general education (i.e., required courses that all students must take), of which multiculturalism requirements were a contested part, could also be heard in numerous other publications over the course of the 1980s.[19]

The university system forever linked by the Supreme Court to affirmative action in higher education admissions was also home to some of the leading defenders of intellectual affirmative action, which took the form of multiculturalism requirements. Foremost among these was University of California, Berkeley ethnic studies professor Ronald Takaki. For Takaki, the "American mind" needed to be opened to "greater cultural diversity" in order to offset the "multicultural illiteracy" that afflicted it. One means to this end was the "diffusion of ethnic studies throughout the traditional disciplines."[20] In this way, multiculturalism represented the mainstreaming of ethnic studies, the first department of which had been established at Berkeley in 1969.[21]

To promote the dissemination of ethnic studies across the curriculum, Takaki published the first self-proclaimed "multicultural" history of the United States. Entitled *A Different Mirror: A History of Multicultural America*, Takaki's book made the case for multiculturalism as curricular reform in the service of social transformation. The curricular reform involved teaching students to "see events from the viewpoints of different groups," in particular "racial minorities"— African Americans, Asian Americans, Latinos, and Native Americans—who were, as Takaki saw it, "historically set apart" from "European immigrant groups" and relegated to the margins of "a history that has viewed America as European in ancestry." By incorporating the voices and "viewpoints" of these "different groups" into the curriculum, multiculturalism promised to present students with a "more accurate history" than that found in the "established scholarship" and reflected in the existing curriculum, both of which "tended to define America too narrowly."[22]

In the process, multiculturalism served a broader social purpose. By revising the curriculum to reflect "the dramatic change in our nation's ethnic composition," multiculturalism would help ameliorate the "intensifying racial crisis" that accompanied that transformation.[23] On campus, "Racial Tensions—and Violence—Appear on Rise," announced the *New York Times* in 1988.[24] Many other high-profile publications agreed, including a "special report" of the Carnegie Foundation for the Advancement of Teaching, which found that presidents from over two-thirds of research and doctorate granting universities believed that "racial tensions and hostilities" were a " 'moderate' to 'major' problem on their campus."[25] Off campus, the "racial crisis" that motivated Takaki's multiculturalism culminated in the death and destruction that engulfed Los Angeles in 1992 in the aftermath of the acquittal of four police officers who had been videotaped beating black motorist Rodney King following a high-speed car chase. Multiculturalism, as Takaki envisioned it, would provide at least a partial antidote to the conditions that gave rise to what one commentator described in the *Village Voice* as "The First Multicultural Riots."[26] As Takaki asked and answered, "*How* do we work it out in the post-Rodney King era? Certainly one crucial way is for our society's various ethnic groups to develop a greater understanding of each other."[27]

Takaki's colleague, history professor Lawrence Levine, was also a leading defender of multiculturalism. Speaking from one of the most prominent pulpits in the historical profession, Levine used the occasion of his 1993 presidential address to the Organization of American Historians to celebrate the multicultural approach to historical writing and teaching as the culmination of "an increasingly inclusive notion of where the historian's quarry lies." For Levine, like Takaki, exploring "the culture, the thought, the *lives* of people we have previously neglected" possessed both an historical and demographic imperative. Historically, the United States "has always been a multicultural... society." Demographically, university campuses had increasingly grown to reflect the nation's historic multicultural mix. "As the university becomes more open to and representative of the diverse peoples, experiences, traditions, and cultures that compose America," Levine maintained, "it has to enable its students to comprehend the nature of the society to which they belong."[28]

Who could possibly object to this? Quite a few people, as it turns out. Indeed, in Levine's estimation, the effort to infuse multiculturalism into the university curriculum helped explain why "scholarship and the university are being assailed as they have not been since the 1950s."[29]

Among those spearheading this attack were William Bennett, head of the National Endowment of the Humanities from 1981 to 1985 and United States Secretary of Education from 1985 to 1988. Though Bennett shared Takaki's and Levine's belief in knowledge that, as Takaki put it, "an educated and culturally literate person" must possess, the content of the required knowledge that Bennett had in mind diverged significantly from that of the Berkeley professors. In *To Reclaim a Legacy*, Bennett presented the cultural conservative critique of multiculturalism. "We are," Bennett declared, "a product of Western civilization" and therefore "the core of the American college curriculum—its heart and soul—should be the civilization of the West," in particular, the ideas of "Enlightenment England, Renaissance Florence, and Periclean Athens." Americans of all colors and classes, Bennett insisted, "share these beliefs." They were the "glue that binds together our pluralistic nation," which the "virtues of pluralism," Bennett warned in a dig at multiculturalism, "cannot allow us to sacrifice." For this reason, "each college and university should recognize and accept its vital role as conveyor of the accumulated wisdom of our civilization."[30]

University of Chicago philosophy professor Allan Bloom echoed and amplified Bennett's cultural conservative critique of multiculturalism in his best-selling 1987 jeremiad, *The Closing of the American Mind*.[31] For Bloom multiculturalism smacked of cultural relativism. What multiculturalists touted as a virtue—a curriculum of "contested terrains of different points of view," as Takaki put it—cultural conservatives such as Bloom denigrated as a vice—an enervated equality reflected in "the unwillingness and incapacity to make claims of superiority."[32] Bennett, too, subscribed to this view. "Intellectual authority," he lamented, had succumbed to "intellectual relativism as a guiding principle of the curriculum. Because colleges and universities believed they no longer could or should assert the primacy of one fact or one book over another, all knowledge came to be seen as relative in importance."[33] Bloom's colleague and friend, the Nobel Prize winning novelist Saul Bellow, put the matter bluntly. "Who," he asked rhetorically in a *New York Times Magazine* interview, "is the Tolstoy of the Zulus? The Proust of the Papuans?"[34] As Bellow's references to Tolstoy and Proust implied, whereas multiculturalists viewed "culture as a debate," cultural conservatives viewed culture as a canon, a fixed body of "generally recognized classic texts."[35] That the authors of these Great Books so happened to be white men of European descent—Dead White European Males, or DWEMs, as strident opponents of Great Books curricula sometimes derisively referred to them— was beside the point to cultural conservatives. For them, the greatness of the Great Books had nothing whatsoever to do with *who* the authors were, but *what* they had to say, the universal questions they asked, and the timeless answers they gave.[36]

In contrast to cultural conservatives, civic nationalists did not dismiss multiculturalism outright. On the contrary, they embraced a number of basic premises of multiculturalism. As Pulitzer–prize winning historian Arthur M. Schlesinger, Jr. noted in his best-selling manifesto *The Disuniting of America* published in 1992, "Of course, history should be taught from a variety of per-spectives," Schlesinger insisted in a bow to multiculturalism, such as the "arrival of Columbus from the viewpoint of those who met him." Elsewhere Schlesinger maintained, "Let us by all means teach black history, African history, women's history, Hispanic history, Asian history." The different perspectives these dif-ferent histories afforded would help counterbalance a history "long written in the interests of white Anglo-Saxon Protestant males." Moreover, they would help students recognize how "the curse of racism" was "the great failure of the American experiment" and remained "the crippling disease of American life."[37] Along these same lines, New York University historian of education Diane Ravitch praised the long overdue "new [multicultural] history," which she described as "a warts-and-all history" for its "unflinching examination of racism and discrimination in our history."[38]

At this juncture, however, multiculturalists and civic nationalists parted ways. Whereas multiculturalists were content to stop with the "different view-points" that would spark the "intellectual clashes" out of which "students [could] search for truth," as Takaki put it, civic nationalists had their own "truth" about the overarching trajectory of American history that they believed ought to be imparted to students, namely, that over time the "crippling disease" of racism claimed diminishing numbers of victims.[39] As Schlesinger declared, "The steady movement of American life has been from exclusion to inclusion," the creation of an American unum out of an ethnic and racial pluribus.[40] "Warts-and-all,"

Ravitch insisted, the ultimate direction of United States history was neverthe-less one "in which different groups competed, fought, suffered, but ultimately learned to live together in relative peace and even achieved a sense of common nationhood."[41]

This march of progress, civic nationalists maintained, owed to the cura-tive and cohering power of America's civic ideals. Though historically flouted, the "great unifying Western ideas of individual freedom, political democracy, and human rights," which were enshrined in America's Declaration of Inde-pendence and Constitution, contained the self-corrective power that allowed for the ineluctable expansion of America's circle of "We" in the Constitution's "We the people."[42] Simply put, America in democratic practice, civic national-ists believed, increasingly approximated America in democratic theory. To the extent that multiculturalism did not recognize this progressive tendency in American history, civic nationalists found it lacking both "an overall theory" as well as a "vision of what it wants the country to become," as historian John Higham put it.[43]

Unlike civic nationalists who tended to take for granted the categories in which multiculturalism trafficked, cosmopolitans raised concerns about the categories themselves. Whereas civic nationalists took issue with multi-culturalism for accentuating the pluribus over the unum, cosmopolitans took issue with multiculturalism for espousing a rather limited notion of pluribus. K. Anthony Appiah, a professor of Afro-American studies and philosophy at Harvard, levied the cosmopolitan critique in a response to Charles Taylor's 1992 essay *Multiculturalism and "The Politics of Recognition."* Appiah voiced "suspicion" about "multicultural talk," for how it "presupposes conceptions of collective identity that are remarkably unsubtle in their understandings by which identities...develop." In fact, "historical knowledge and philo-sophical reflection" pointed to the existence of "collective identities" that were "radically unlike the identities that now parade before us for recogni-tion." Simply put, multiculturalism's privileged categories—"gender, ethnic-ity, nationality, 'race,' sexuality"—were not only rooted in misconceptions about the formation of collective identity, but they also represented a nar-row range of categories of collective identity. These categories, in turn, came with "scripts," that is, "notions of how a proper person of that kind behaves." Multiculturalism endeavored to flip these scripts. It sought to transform the "negative...life scripts" historically foisted upon, say, African Americans, into "positive life-scripts"—that is, to keep the collective identity but invert its social meaning. Although "sympathetic" with this project, given the negative asso-ciations long ascribed to people inhabiting one or more of multiculturalism's collective identity categories, Appiah worried that even "positive scripts" ran the risk of being, well, "too tightly scripted." He warned, "Demanding respect for people as blacks and as gays [for example] requires that there are some scripts that go with being an African-American or having same-sex desires. There will be proper ways of being black and gay, there will be expectations to be met, demands will be made. It is at this point that someone who takes autonomy seriously will ask whether we have not replaced one kind of tyranny with another."[44]

Ironically, then, in the name of promoting diversity, multiculturalism, according to its cosmopolitan critics, threatened to impede it. As Berkeley history professor David Hollinger explained in his 1995 book, *Postethnic America: Beyond Multiculturalism*, although "the multiculturalism of our time has helped us to recognize and appreciate cultural diversity . . . [it] has too often left the impression that culture follows the lines of shape and color." Multiculturalism, in other words, too easily shaded into multiracialism, with the "multi" that mattered most of all limited to the "ethno-racial pentagon" of black (African American), brown (Latino), red (Native American), white (European American), and yellow (Asian American). Though driven by "enlightened antiracism," multiculturalism's "ethno-racial pentagon" deployed the very same categories as those whose roots ran back to "the most gross and invidious of popular images of what makes human beings different from one another." In doing so, multiculturalism reified race—tightly coupling color with culture—and highlighted "certain differences at the expense of others." This, in turn, obscured the tremendous diversity that existed within any one of the pillars of the "ethno-racial pentagon" (e.g., Chinese American versus Cambodian American), not to mention the myriad other manifestations that culture and collective identities took. Simply put, flipping "scripts," to borrow Appiah's term, was not enough. Instead, "people . . . ought to be more free than they now are from social distinctions visited upon them by others." To this end, the "scripts" themselves—and the categories of collective identity with which they were associated—needed to be subjected to "renewal and critical revision." Multiculturalism, however, militated against this. It took the "ethno-racial pentagon" for granted, as evidenced by mandatory multiculturalism requirements, such as the one enacted at Hollinger's university, which rendered American "cultures" synonymous with "the ethno-racial pentagon."[45]

As Hollinger's reference to Berkeley's American Cultures requirement suggests, a full appreciation for the contours of the curricular culture wars requires looking beyond the ink spilled about them and examining the campus level debates that the passage of multiculturalism requirements sparked. At a time when pundits and publications noted the majority white to majority nonwhite transformation that was overturning the "presumption," as *Time* magazine put it, "that the 'typical' U.S. citizen is someone who traces his or her descent in a direct line to Europe," the University of California, Berkeley was on the cusp of this transformation. Not surprisingly, it was also at the forefront of developing the intellectual affirmative action that multiculturalists believed ought to accompany the demographic changes wrought by affirmative action in higher education admissions—a multiculturalism requirement that Ronald Takaki would describe as "a 'different mirror' in the curriculum."[46]

During the 1985–1986 academic year, a small group of Berkeley student government leaders requested that the faculty's Committee on Educational Policy take steps to establish an undergraduate "Ethnic Studies Graduation Requirement." By this, the students meant a single ethnic studies course, drawn from a list of preapproved ethnic studies department courses, on the "history, values, and experiences of non-White ethnic minorities in California," delineated as "Native American, Chicano, Afro-American, Asian-American, Pacific Islander, and Hispanic." These groups, the students maintained, had deep historical roots in the United States, which included "positive contribution[s]" amid pervasive racial discrimination. They constituted the core of California's "increasingly multi-ethnic society." Yet, they found themselves ghettoized in the university's curriculum, encountered only by the few hundred students each year who elected to enroll in courses taught through the ethnic studies department. A requirement that all students take an ethnic studies course, its student advocates believed, would serve as a necessary response to the state's—and university's—diversifying student body. It would also help foster an "educated citizen[ry]" and combat "racial prejudice."[47]

"United People of Color"—another student group—agreed. A coalition of student groups formed during the 1980s campaign for the University of California to divest from apartheid South Africa, United People of Color linked the fight against apartheid in South Africa with the fight against "curricular apartheid" at the University of California, Berkeley.[48] A "Subject 'E' [for ethnic studies] Requirement," United People of Color contended, would compensate for the "racist interpretations, flagrant distortions, and the exclusion of the issues, culture, and history of People of Color in the United States" across the curriculum.[49] For "White" students, a required ethnic studies course would serve as a "crucial first step in overcoming racism." For "Third World" students, it would "provide an understanding of our true history [and] a sense of identity and pride in our heritage as people of color."[50]

In calling for at least one required course that taught "true history," the Berkeley undergraduates who demanded an ethnic studies graduation require-ment seemed to anticipate the scathing critique of cultural relativism in higher education that Allan Bloom delivered in 1987. In *The Closing of the American Mind*, Bloom lamented the plight of the poor undergraduate faced with a "bewildering variety of departments...a bewildering variety of courses...[and] no official guidance, no university-wide agreement, about what he *should* study."[51] "[U]niversity-wide agreement" for at least one course that all students "*should* study" was precisely what the Berkeley students demanded—only the course they had in mind was a far cry from anything Bloom envisioned.

For Bloom, "the only serious solution" to the "impoverished souls" of undergraduates cast aimlessly adrift in universities that failed to tell them what they "*should* study" was "the good old Great Books approach."[52] For the Berke-ley students lobbying for an ethnic studies requirement, however, the "old Great Books" were precisely the cause of students' "impoverished souls." The course they desired would "counterbalance a curriculum that has traditionally been 'eurocentric.'"[53] It would demonstrate that "the history, culture, and con-cerns of people of color have an equal and necessary place in the education of all students."[54] The editors of the student newspaper agreed: "While an ethnic studies requirement would barely scratch the surface of academia's Euro-centric focus, its implementation would have important symbolic value...and would also provide a refreshing alternative cultural experience to most middle-class kids from suburbia."[55]

Unfortunately for the students seeking an ethnic studies requirement, the Berkeley faculty members who served on the committee that fielded their request proved to be little more disposed to the idea than Bloom would have been had he been a Berkeley professor. For the professors, though, the problem with the proposal was not cultural relativism, but a kind of binary racial reduc-tionism. In particular, the professors recoiled at how the proposed requirement implied an interchangeability in the experiences of "non-White ethnic minori-ties," as if racial discrimination afflicted "non-Whites"—and, by extension, spared "Whites"—in more or less the same way. The proposal, as the professors saw it, posited a racial world divided in half, with the experiences *between* the halves different enough, and the experiences *within* the halves similar enough, to warrant the division down the middle.[56] This logic was implicit in the pro-posal's suggestion that the ethnic studies requirement could be satisfied by a course that focused on a "specific [non-White] ethnic group"—as if the one could serve as a substitute for the rest.[57] It was made explicit the following semester when student representatives of United People of Color shot down an attempt to include "Semites—Arabs and Jews" in the proposed ethnic studies requirement by insisting that "people of color [have] an experience and perspective entirely distinct from all other immigrants."[58]

To this logic the professors on the committee that first addressed the student proposed ethnic studies requirement replied, "We are not sure that there is sufficient commonality among the experiences of, for example, Asians and Native Americans that studying one helps much in understanding the other."[59] This, in turn, raised other concerns. If the experiences of the "non-White ethnic minorities" were not interchangeable, "who would decide which ethnic groups would be included"? Should those eventually encompassed be limited to " 'non-white[s]' " or expanded to encompass all " 'cultural minorities' " some of whom—Jews, for example—were not among the "non-White ethnic minorities" the student advocates for an ethnic studies requirement had in mind?[60]

For these reasons, the professors refused to endorse the students' proposal in both 1986 and 1987, though they did agree to "see what else we can do." In particular, they began to contemplate ways to "transcend the usual categories defined by ethnic studies" by reaching beyond "non-White ethnic minorities."[61] To this end, the faculty Academic Senate created a Special Committee on Education and Ethnicity, with William Simmons, professor of anthropology, as its chair. In February 1988, Simmons' committee discussed a proposal for a "Cultural Pluralism Requirement" drafted by professors L. Ling-chi Wang (Ethnic Studies) and David Lloyd (English) and two graduate students. At the core of the proposed course was a comparative component. "Courses must compare," insisted Wang, by which he meant consideration of "the salient differences and/or similarities between one or more of the core group cultures [identified as African American, Asian American, Chicano/Latino, and Native America] and European ethnic groups as well as the dominant American culture." To meet this criterion, it would not be enough to take a course on, say, Chicanos, but rather a course on "the differences between Chicano and European ethnic groups."[62] This "emphasis" on "comparative or developmental studies" represented a critical difference between the cultural pluralism requirement proposed by the Special Committee on Education and Ethnicity and the ethnic studies requirement initially championed by the students. So, too, did the proposed cultural pluralism requirement's insistence that courses not be limited to those in the ethnic studies department. "The right solution," declared Simmons, "is for an ethnic element to become a part of all departments."[63] Ethnic studies would thus become comparative and mainstream, infusing the entire curriculum.

In these ways, then, members of the Berkeley faculty were beginning to articulate their own vision of what a multicultural education should entail.

Though the Special Committee on Education and Ethnicity's cultural pluralism requirement was, indeed, a requirement, consistent with the original student proposal, its content was more inclusive, more multicultural, and more mainstream. As Simmons put it, the proposed cultural pluralism requirement—which was renamed the "American Cultures" requirement—differed from "what the students originally proposed" inasmuch as it was "not an ethnic studies requirement." Ethnic studies courses, Simmons said, tended to focus on "one or another particular ethnic group." By contrast, the proposed American Cultures requirement represented a "bolder," "comparative" vision.[64] "We want to go beyond Balkanization," Simmons insisted, and examine "the ways in which a diversity of cultures has shaped our society and culture."[65] To this end, the American Cultures requirement that the Simmons's committee submitted to the faculty as a whole for approval in the spring of 1988 called for all Berkeley undergraduates to pass one among a number of courses on "some broad aspect of United States history, society and culture so that the greater part is devoted to the contributions and experiences of racial and cultural minority groups in their relations with white and other ethnic groups, with at least two of the major groups (Afro-American, Asian American, Chicano/Latino, and Native American) represented."[66]

In the report defending the proposed requirement, the Special Committee on Education and Ethnicity stressed the need to equip students with the "tools for understanding cultural pluralism" in light of the "increasing racial and ethnic diversity of our university community." Moreover, the committee maintained, the "exclusion and isolation" of non-European groups over the course of United States history was "qualitatively different" from their European counterparts. Therefore, they should be the focus of American Cultures courses in order to compensate for the historical exclusion of "racial minority groups...from the mainstream curriculum."[67] This repositioning of margin and mainstream represented what Simmons described as "intellectual affirmative action"—a way "to guarantee to our minority students and faculty that [American Cultures] wouldn't turn into a course on Euro-American experience with minorities pushed into the background."[68] One graduate student advocate of the measure called it "affirmative action for...books."[69]

For the undergraduates who wanted a nonwhite ethnic studies requirement taught through the ethnic studies department, the professors' proposed American Cultures alternative was anathema. "They want to distort our vision of ethnic studies," one student charged.[70] More specifically, they rejected what they called the " 'American Cultures' approach," which they understood as advancing the view that "Americans are of many ethnicities—of many cultural identities."

Such a course, they believed, would divert "attention away from the historical oppression" and "perspectives" of "People of Color." Moreover, it would reflect a failure on the part of the university to "demonstrate a...commitment to the advancement of our underrepresented communities."[71]

A majority of the Berkeley faculty proved to be no more enthusiastic about the proposed requirement than these students, though for very different reasons. As the 1987–1988 school year drew to a close, the Academic Senate meeting to vote on the measure devolved into a "shouting match," according to a *Los Angeles Times* account, "the likes of which...had not been seen since the Vietnam protest days" and ultimately left the matter unresolved.[72] Afterward, the student newspaper groaned, "At the rate the Academic Senate is going Earth is going to collide with Jupiter before a decision is made about the American Cultures requirement."[73]

When the Special Committee on Education and Ethnicity reconvened at the beginning of the 1988–1989 school year, Simmons noted, "[We] need to rethink [the] whole orientation."[74] Two weeks later, he observed, "[We] need to expand the 'why' of our proposal. Why mandatory? Why these groups?...Why U.S.?"[75] Sociology professor Bob Blauner was among the first to suggest some answers to these questions. In a memo he sent to Simmons, Blauner recommended revising the proposed American Cultures requirement to allow for courses that compared "white ethnic groups." Such courses, he realized, would "vitiate the present requirement" and likely alienate some "students who will see the broadening I've proposed, the ethnic loophole, as not only a watering down, but a dubious political compromise." Yet, such courses would also help win "support of some fair-minded 'color-blind' liberal faculty." While recommending the creation of a "[white] ethnic loophole," Blauner also called for a better articulation of the "rationale for emphasizing people of color, even though we are no longer limiting the requirement to [them]." Here he made explicit what had been implicit in the case made by proponents of the American Cultures requirement thus far, namely, "that color matters, that race and racism have been among the most fateful elements of American life. And remain so." The vision of a bifurcated racial world, with the experiences between whites (as a whole) and nonwhites (as a whole) different enough to justify the distinction between them in the previous year's American Cultures proposal made eminent sense to Blauner. "I think the argument of race and racism is powerful enough to set off the rationale for the four groups, despite their many differences and variations internally," Blauner wrote.[76] It was, however, an argument that needed to be made rather than a premise to be presumed, with those who did not subscribe to the premise written off as Eurocentrists or worse. As Professor Lloyd of the Special Committee on Education and Ethnicity noted, "We can't just say that the opposition is racist. We have to realize that there are serious concerns."[77]

Blauner's letter presaged many of the reservations that were registered over the course of the 1988–1989 academic year as the proposed American Cultures requirement was revised. Some students did indeed recoil at the prospect of introducing a "[white] ethnic loophole" into the requirement. At an October 1988 meeting of the Special Committee on Education and Ethnicity, a group of 25 students protested any revisions to the existing requirement. "We wanted to let the committee know that...we think [the requirement as spelled out the previous year] is strong enough and we think it is compromised enough," declared student body president Jeff Chang.[78]

Other students, however, expressed an interest in compromise, especially those who felt "that the proposal discredits the contributions and plights of many other ethnic groups," as Valli Israels, a student government leader, explained. "Clearly, there are valid reasons for including other ethnicities in the proposal" and the criteria for inclusion should not be "because [one group] is 'more oppressed' than the next."[79]

Israels' diagnosis of what troubled some of her peers echoed that which members of the Special Committee on Education and Ethnicity deemed to trouble many of their fellow faculty members. "Many liked the idea but didn't like focus on 4 [non-white] ethnic groups," observed one Special Committee on Education and Ethnicity member.[80]

To better gauge where the faculty as a whole stood on the question of the proposed American Cultures requirement from the previous year, and to solicit advice on how to revise it in order to secure majority support in the Academic Senate, the Special Committee on Education and Ethnicity solicited faculty responses to a questionnaire.[81] The majority of the 150 professors who took the time to respond—roughly six out of seven faculty members—opposed the measure. A small number of these opponents expressed their opposition in hostile terms. They derided the measure as the "height of idiocy," "Nazi propaganda," "left-wing ideology," "a device for hiring unqualified persons," and the equivalent of courses on "Marxism-Leninism offered at the universities of Communist societies." In addition, they dismissed the measure's proponents as "destroyers of culture," purveyors of a "freak show," and champions of "reverse racism." If there was a dominant theme running through this small group of staunch opponents, it was that the proposed requirement was a pedagogically bereft bow to politically correct political pressure—"an effort at symbolic appeasement," as one professor put it, which would serve only to legitimate courses "whose message is, to paraphrase Che Guevara, People of Color, Yes. White Man, No."[82]

Hostile responses such as these, however, were dwarfed by those that tended to focus on more substantive reasons. The most common reservation was that the proposed requirement lacked a sufficient rationale for specifying the groups that it did. These opponents described the proposal as "arbitrarily" "includ[ing] some groups and exclud[ing] others." Other respondents questioned the legitimacy of the very categories themselves, suggesting that they had the paradoxical effect of perpetuating the problem they purported to redress. "To maintain these indefensible categories is to perpetuate myths that should be laid to rest," insisted one professor. Similarly, another professor who described himself as a "refugee from earlier schemes of ethnic categorization" expressed reservations over what he took to be "already too much categorization of people by race." What was needed instead was a "more pluralist...approach"—the treatment of "[a]ll ethnic cultures...with complete equality in an American cultures requirement."[83]

Informed by the responses to the questionnaire, members of the Special Committee on Education and Ethnicity devoted the balance of the academic year to revising the proposal. The "Proposal for an American Cultures Breadth Requirement" they eventually arrived at in the second semester of the 1988–1989 school year called for students to pass a one-semester course that would "substantially consider at least three of the five main racial/cultural groups in American society: African American, American Indian, Asian American, Chicano/ Latino, and European American."[84] The principal difference between the new proposal and its predecessor revolved around the place of "European Americans" in the proposed requirement. The 1988 version had called for courses on the "contributions and experiences of racial and cultural minority groups in their relations with white and other ethnic groups, with at least two of the major groups (Afro-American, Asian American, Chicano/Latino, and Native American) represented."[85] In doing so, it drew a line between "whites" on one side and "racial and cultural minority groups" on the other. This binary view of American cultural pluralism, the 1989 proposal maintained, had elicited the "strongest criticism" from the faculty for being, among other things, "too one-sided...a form of reverse racism...white-bashing...and...exclud[ing] or minimiz[ing] European Americans."[86] The 1989 version of the proposed American Cultures requirement did not segregate "European Americans" from the four "major...racial and cultural minority groups." Rather, it located them alongside, as one of the "five main racial/cultural groups" in the United States and from which a course satisfying the proposed American Cultures requirement

On the night of July 3, 1986, the nation celebrated the rededication of the Statue of Liberty after a nearly $300 million renovation of the monument. Many Americans saw the 1980s as a decade of patriotic resurgence. *Courtesy, Ronald Reagan Library.*

Desert sandstorms brought down two American helicopters in Iran on April 26, 1980, causing commandoes to abort a planned rescue of 52 American hostages held by Islamic fundamentalists at the U.S. embassy in Tehran since November 1979. The failed mission symbolized the impotence of America—as well as of President Jimmy Carter. *Courtesy, AP Photo.*

Ronald Reagan and his team helped set the tone of patriotic revivalism during the 1980s. On October 6, 1981, Reagan and key staffers discussed one of many unanticipated crises, the assassination of Egyptian President Anwar Sadat. Pictured from left to right are Michael Deaver, Richard Allen, Vice President George H.W. Bush, James Baker, David Gergen, and Ed Meese. *Courtesy, Ronald Reagan Library.*

Christian Evangelicals were key allies in what became known as the "Reagan Revolution." The Reverend Jerry Falwell led the Moral Majority, which sought to transform the growing religious fervor, especially in the South and West, into a powerful political force. *Courtesy, Liberty University.*

The Speaker of the House, Thomas P. (Tip) O'Neill, was the leader of the political opposition to the Reagan administration. The Massachusetts Democrat defended the
"big government" legacy of Franklin Roosevelt's New Deal and Lyndon Johnson's
Great Society. *Courtesy, Ronald Reagan Library.*

In 1984, Jesse Jackson, shown here with his two main rivals, former Vice President Walter Mondale and Senator Gary Hart, ran for the Democratic nomination for president. During the campaign, Jackson spoke often of a multicultural "Rainbow Coalition" of minorities, the poor, feminists, and organized labor who opposed the policies of the Reagan administration. *Courtesy, Getty.*

In July 1981, Reagan appointed Sandra Day O'Connor as the first woman Justice on the Supreme Court, proving that social changes often transcend ideology. For all the talk of a "backlash" against the civil rights movement, feminism, and environmentalism, many of the innovations of the 1960s became mainstreamed in the 1980s. *Courtesy, Ronald Reagan Library.*

"The Cosby Show" premiered in September 1984. This television sitcom, featuring an upper-middle-class African American family, dominated primetime for the next eight seasons. The show, starring Lisa Bonet, Bill Cosby, Keshia Knight Pulliam, Phylicia Rashad, Sabrina Le Beauf, Tempestt Bledsoe, and Malcolm-Jamal Warner, celebrated both the Huxtables' African American identity as well as their all-American escapades. *Courtesy, Getty.*

The singer Michael Jackson was one of the biggest pop stars of the 1980s. In growing recognition of the power of celebrity, "the King of Pop" joined Ronald and Nancy Reagan at a White House ceremony launching a national campaign against drunk driving on May 14, 1984. *Courtesy, Ronald Reagan Library.*

In 1981, IBM introduced its version of the personal computer (PC). By the end of the decade, the PC became standard in almost every home and changed the way Americans worked and played. The PC revolution was part of a broader technological transformation, much of which was driven by the economic boom of the 1980s. *Courtesy, Erik Klein of Vintage-Computer.com.*

The economic boom of the 1980s also fueled a festival of conspicuous consumption. Television shows such as "Dynasty," which premiered the week Ronald Reagan was inaugurated, helped shape the stereotype of a decade identified by wealth, celebrity, and glitz. *Courtesy, Pictorial Parade/ Getty Images.*

The 1980s was the decade of the "young, urban professional" or "Yuppie" as well as the "Preppie," wherein ambitious lower-class and middle-class youth such as these UCLA students learned to dress like the WASP elite. Both "Yuppies" and "Preppies" exemplified the spread of prosperity, the obsession with style, and the decade's odd mix of class-consciousness and egalitarianism. *Courtesy, Getty Images.*

The AIDS Quilt, spread out on the Ellipse near the White House on October 9, 1989, helped educate the American public about the disease's devastating impact. The AIDS crisis highlighted the decade's constant tug of war between euphoria and despair. *Courtesy, AP Photo/Doug Mills.*

President and Mrs. Reagan honor those Americans killed when Islamic terrorists bombed the American embassy in Beirut, Lebanon, in April 1983. Despite eventual success in the Cold War, Reagan proved less adept in dealing with the complexities of the Middle East, leading to tragedies such as the 1983 embassy bombing, the bombing of the U.S. Marine barracks in Lebanon in October 1983, and the Iran-Contra scandal. *Courtesy, Ronald Reagan Library.*

At the November 20, 1985, Geneva Summit in Switzerland, Ronald Reagan surprised his aides by negotiating with Soviet General Secretary Mikhail Gorbachev alone and emerging with an agreement for future summits. The flexibility of Reagan and the domestic reforms of Gorbachev would soon lead to the end of the Cold War. *Courtesy, Ronald Reagan Library.*

On November 12, 1989, residents of Berlin, Germany, celebrated the dismantling of the hated symbol of Communist control, the Berlin Wall. East Germans could now stream into the free West. The end of the 1980s saw the end of Communist control of Eastern Europe and the beginnings of the disintegration of the Soviet Union. The Cold War was over. *Courtesy, AP Photo/Lionel Cironneau.*

had to "substantially consider" at least three.[87] "Including whites," Professor Simmons believed, had an additional virtue: it "would help the proposal gain support."[88]

Simmons had reason to be optimistic. A little over a month before, he had participated in a public debate over the revised American Cultures requirement during which one of the three professors representing the side opposed to the measure conceded that the "revisions in the American Cultures requirement have...taken some of the starch out of my opposition." Another professor on the opposing side was even more conciliatory. The inclusion of "all American cultures, rather than the four minorities," he said, was a "great improvement over the previous proposals," so much so, in fact, that "I'm not sure I would oppose the proposal any longer."[89] Coming from the same faculty member who, as a member of the Committee on Educational Policy in 1986, had blasted the original student ethnic studies proposal as "a required 'guilt trip' for whites," such sentiments boded well for the passage of the final, faculty shaped American Cultures requirement.[90] They also confirmed another professor's reflections years later that the addition of "European Americans" to the American Cultures requirement was the "big compromise" that broke the "deadlock."[91]

On April 25, 1989, an unusually "large turnout" of over 400 Berkeley professors gathered for a "Special Meeting of the Academic Senate."[92] Over 700 students also flocked to the faculty meeting, which was held just steps away from Sproul Plaza, the campus's center for student protest.[93] By a margin of 227 to 194, the faculty approved the American Cultures requirement.[94] The students greeted the vote for their school's new graduation requirement with a standing ovation. "Today," Ronald Takaki exclaimed, "we articulated the Berkeley vision of an educated person."[95]

It was not, however, the vision that student advocates of the original proposal for an ethnic studies requirement had articulated—and to which some of them still clung. "Unfortunately," lamented the editors of the student newspaper, which had long endorsed an ethnic studies requirement, the professors who crafted the American Cultures requirement "had to make some concessions, such as including 'European American' in the subjects covered." Though regrettable "considering that every other class on campus covers the accomplishments of European Americans extensively and exhaustively," the new requirement was still a "critical step in the right direction."[96] Similarly, the student groups who comprised United People of Color endorsed the American Cultures requirement without acknowledging how their original vision of an ethnic studies requirement had been transformed in the hands of the faculty. Indeed, in their "Student Message to the Faculty on the American Cultures

Requirement," they chose to quote from the part of the Special Committee on Education and Ethnicity's "Proposal for an American Cultures Requirement" that called for courses that would "take substantial account of those racial minority groups such as African Americans, Asian Americans, American Indians, and Chicano/Latinos," while omitting the part of the Special Committee's report that included "European American" alongside the other four groups as the "five main racial/cultural groups" from which American Cultures courses needed to "substantially consider at least three."[97] This "European American" inclusion, after all, was not "the Berkeley vision of an educated person" that these students had in mind, though, in the end, the faculty's "mainstreamed" ethnic studies (i.e., multiculturalism) requirement was the most they would get.[98]

In the decade following the passage of Berkeley's American Cultures requirement, the multicultural "vision of an educated person" that the requirement represented spread to scores of other campuses. As of 2000 a study conducted by the Association of American Colleges and Universities revealed that just under two-thirds of nearly 550 colleges and universities surveyed either had a "diversity requirement" in place or were in the process of implementing one. This proliferation of mandatory multiculturalism received strong public support. According to the Ford Foundation Campus Diversity Initiative, nearly 70 percent of people polled in 1998 registered approval for "requiring students to take at least one cultural or ethnic diversity course in order to graduate."[99] Little wonder, then, that Harvard sociologist Nathan Glazer would claim, in the words of his 1997 book title, *We Are All Multiculturalists Now*. "[M]ulticulturalism in education," Glazer declared, "has...won."[100] No doubt, many of the 110,000 Berkeley students who had enrolled in 1230 American Cultures courses between 1991, when the requirement went into effect, and the end of the 2004 spring semester would have agreed with Glazer—as would the hundreds of thousands of other undergraduates who passed through mandatory multiculturalism courses established at other campuses during the 1980s and 1990s.[101]

But just how secure was the victory that Glazer and others attributed to multiculturalism?

In the same year that *We Are All Multiculturalists Now* appeared, the state of California began implementing Proposition 209, which effectively barred the approach to affirmative action in higher education admissions that the Supreme Court's *Bakke* decision had permitted.[102] As a result, enrollments of African American, American Indian, and Chicano/Latino students plummeted across the University of California system (while Asian American, especially, and white enrollment increased).[103] Ironically, then, even as more Berkeley undergraduates took courses that taught them about African Americans, American Indians, and Chicanos/Latinos, among others, fewer students from these particular groups actually sat in those classrooms. If affirmative action in higher education admissions had contributed to the rise of intellectual affirmative action in the 1980s, would the demise of the former beginning in the late 1990s lead to the demise of the latter and, with it, a return to a more Eurocentric curricular past, albeit perhaps with an Asian twist?

Alternatively, would a new generation of students—led perhaps by those who were the offspring of the ever-increasing number of ethnoracially mixed marriages or those who simply conceived of themselves beyond the collective identity boxes that multiculturalism had bequeathed to them—spearhead a campaign to reconfigure the meaning of multiculturalism? Would they demand a diversification of multiculturalism's particular conceptualization of diversity and thereby point the way toward a more cosmopolitan curricular future?[104]

Simply put, if "[c]hanging demographics" had done so much to trigger the "urgent intellectual need to rethink how we deal with diversity" in the 1980s, then presumably new curricular changes would accompany new demographic changes.[105] If so, multiculturalism's triumph may prove to be fleeting.

NOTES

Special thanks to Victoria Robinson, director of the American Cultures Center at the University of California, Berkeley, for granting me access to the unprocessed files on the passage of the American Cultures requirement. Special thanks, as well, to Candace Khanna for facilitating and indulging my multiple forays into those files while she attended to the business of administering the American Cultures Center. For helpful comments and suggestions, I am grateful to Vincent Cannato, Susan Ferber, David Hollinger, Rob Reich, Jennifer Spear, Justin Suran, and Gil Troy. For directing me to relevant oral historical materials, I am indebted to Lisa Rubens and Nadine Wilmot.

1. *Regents of the University of California v. Bakke*, 438 U.S. 265 (1978), p. 320.

2. "Trends Affecting Affirmative Action," *Chronicle of Higher Education*, 28 April 1995, A22. According to John David Skrentny, though Powell's opinion in *Bakke* did not single out nonwhite groups as the targeted beneficiaries of affirmative action in higher education admissions—and in fact "evinced considerable discomfort" with doing so— "most universities heard him as saying they could prefer the four minorities [i.e., African Americans, Asian Americans, Latinos, and Native Americans] for diversity purposes." John David Skrentny, *The Minority Rights Revolution* (Cambridge: Harvard University Press, 2002), p. 178.

3. Quoted in "Proposal for an American Cultures Breadth Requirement: Report of the Special Committee on Education and Ethnicity," 28 March 1989, University of California, Berkeley, pp. 6–7. As of the fall 1988, 48.5 percent of Berkeley undergraduates were white, 26.5 percent were of Asian descent, 11.1 percent were Latino, 7 percent were African American, and 1.1 percent were Native American. More generally, from 1974 until 1994, the percentage of white undergraduates dropped from 68.6 to 32.4, whereas the percentage of Asian Americans increased from 15.8 to 39.4, Latinos from 3.2 to 13.8, African Americans from 4.4 to 5.5, and Native Americans from 0.5 to 1.1. Lawrence W. Levine, *The Opening of the American Mind* (Boston: Beacon Press, 1996), p. xviii.

4. William A. Henry III, "Beyond the Melting Pot," *Time*, 9 April 1990, p. 28.

5. William Simmons in Minutes of the Special Committee on Education and Ethnicity, 27 October 1988, American Cultures Center (hereinafter AC Center), American Cultures—July 88–Dec 88 file, University of California, Berkeley.

6. William Simmons, letter to David Vogel, 2 May 1988, AC Center, Dept. Responses to 1st Proposal file. See also L. Ling-chi Wang, "Intellectual Affirmative Action: From Ethnic Studies to 'American Cultures,'" circa May 1989, AC Center, Special Committee on Education and Ethnicity file.

7. Ira Michael Heyman, letter to Academic Senate, 17 April 1989, AC Center, Special Committee on Education and Ethnicity file. See also, Heather Jones, "Chancellor supports American cultures," *Daily Californian*, 19 April 1989, p. 1.

8. According to the *Encyclopedia of Multiculturalism*, the term "multiculturalism" with reference to the United States was "coined in the late 1980s"—just a few years before the six-volume *Encyclopedia of Multiculturalism* was published. Susan D. Greenbaum, "Multiculturalism," in *Encyclopedia of Multiculturalism* (New York: Marshall Cavendish, 1994), p. 1178. The United States, however, took a cue from Canada, which was the first country to make "multiculturalism" an official policy in 1971. For more on the meaning of multiculturalism in the Canadian context, see http://www.pch.gc.ca/progs/multi/inclusive_e.cfm.

9. Berkeley's requirement will be discussed at length below.

10. Stanford's requirement emerged in 1988 after 2 years of heated campus deliberations. The new Cultures, Idea, and Values (CIV) requirement retooled the old Western Civ(ilization) requirement for first-year students, supplementing the former course with content drawn from the non-Western (i.e., non-European) world. Lee A. Daniels, "Stanford Alters Western Culture Course," *New York Times*, 2 April 1988, p. 7.

11. For more on Michigan's requirement, see http://141.211.177.75/lsa/detail/0,2034, 4341%255Farticle%255F181,00.html. More generally, see Arthur Levine and Jeanette Cureton, "The Quiet Revolution: Eleven Facts about Multiculturalism," *Change* 24 (January/February 1992): 25–29. As Levine and Cureton categorized the different kinds of "multicultural general education requirement[s]," some of them "focus on domestic diversity (12 percent), more emphasize global multiculturalism (29 percent), and most include both (57 percent). The programs vary in structure, too. An eighth (13 percent) might be called core curricula, meaning all students take the same courses. Another two-thirds (68 percent) could be described as prescribed distributions, in which students are

permitted to choose from a relatively short list of approved courses. And the remainder (19 percent) include every variation of general education known to humankind."

Of course, not all institutions of higher learning adopted multiculturalism requirements. Others, such as Brooklyn College in New York City and St. Joseph's College in Indiana, moved in the opposite direction. See William J. Bennett, *To Reclaim a Legacy: Report on the Humanities in Higher Education* (Washington, D.C.: National Endowment for the Humanities, 1984): pp. 22–24.

12. Charles Taylor, *Multiculturalism and "The Politics of Recognition"* (Princeton: Princeton University Press, 1992), pp. 64, 65, 25.

13. James Davison Hunter, *Culture Wars: The Struggle to Define America* (New York: Basic Books, 1991).

14. I borrow the term "curricular culture wars" from Gil Troy, *Morning in America: How Ronald Reagan Invented the 1980s* (Princeton: Princeton University Press, 2005), p. 268.

15. Arthur M. Schlesinger, Jr., *The Disuniting of America: Reflections on a Multicultural Society* (New York: Norton, 1992), p. 17; "Proposal for an American Cultures Breadth Requirement," p. 2. As evidence of the high stakes and pugilistic nature of the curricular culture wars, consider the titles of this small sampling of books: Todd Gitlin, *The Twilight of Common Dreams: Why America Is Wracked by the Culture Wars* (New York: Metropolitan Books, 1996); Richard Bernstein, *Dictatorship of Virtue: How the Battle Over Multiculturalism Is Reshaping Our Schools, Our Country, and Our Lives* (New York: Knopf, 1994); Russell Jacoby, *Dogmatic Wisdom: How the Culture Wars Divert Education and Distract America* (New York: Free Press, 1994); William J. Bennett, *The De-Valuing of America: The Fight for Our Culture and Our Children* (New York: Summit Books, 1992); Henry Louis Gates, *Loose Canons: Notes on the Culture Wars* (New York: Oxford University Press, 1992); Arthur M. Schlesinger, Jr., *The Disuniting of America: Reflections on a Multicultural Society* (New York: Norton, 1992); Dinesh D'Souza, *Illiberal Education: The Politics of Race and Sex on Campus* (New York: Free Press, 1991); James Davison Hunter, *Culture Wars: The Struggle to Define America* (New York: Basic Books, 1991); Roger Kimball, *Tenured Radicals: How Politics Has Corrupted Our Higher Education* (New York: Harper & Row, 1990); Charles Sykes, *Profscam: Professors and the Demise of Higher Education* (New York: Kampmann, 1988); Allan Bloom, *The Closing of the American Mind: How Higher Education Has Failed Democracy and Impoverished the Souls of Today's Students* (New York: Simon & Schuster, 1987).

16. Jerry G. Gaff, *New Life for the College Curriculum: Assessing Achievements and Furthering Progress in the Reform of General Education* (San Francisco: Jossey-Bass, 1991), p. 5. According to a Gallup Poll, a "large majority" of Americans believed that "education should be at the top of the Nation's agenda." National Commission on Excellence in Education, *A Nation at Risk: The Imperative For Educational Reform* (Washington, D.C.: GPO, 1983), p. 17.

17. *A Nation at Risk*, p. 5.

18. Bennett, *To Reclaim a Legacy*, pp. 7, 20. For more on the demise of Western Civilization, see Gilbert Allardyce, "The Rise and Fall of the Western Civilization Course," *American Historical Review* 87, no. 3 (June 1982): 695–725.

19. See, for example, Ernest L. Boyer and Arthur Levine, *A Quest for Common Learning: The Aims of General Education* (Washington, D.C.: The Carnegie Foundation for the Advancement of Teaching, 1981); *Integrity in the College Curriculum: A Report to the Academic Community* (Washington, D.C.: Association of American Colleges, 1985); Lynne V. Cheney, *50 Hours: A Core Curriculum for College Students* (Washington, D.C.: National Endowment for the Humanities, 1989).

20. Ronald Takaki, "An Educated and Culturally Literate Person Must Study America's Multicultural Reality," *Chronicle of Higher Education*, 8 March 1989, pp. B1–B2.

21. For more on multiculturalism as the mainstreaming of ethnic studies, see Evelyn Hu-DeHart, "Ethnic Studies in U.S. Higher Education: History, Development, Goals," in *Handbook of Research on Multicultural Education* (2nd ed.), James Banks and Cherry A. McGee Banks, eds. (San Francisco: Jossey-Bass, 2004), p. 873: "[T]he variety of educational reforms that are gathered under the rubric of 'multiculturalism' include the integration of ethnic studies into the college and university curriculum. It also means that all students, not just those of color, should be exposed to the histories and cultures of Americans of non-European descent. In other words, ethnic studies is not for minorities only." For more on precursors to multiculturalism besides ethnic studies, see Jonathan Zimmerman, "*Brown*-ing the American Textbook: History, Psychology, and the Origins of Modern Multiculturalism," *History of Education Quarterly* 44, no. 1 (Spring 2004): 44–69 and Nathan Glazer, *We Are All Multiculturalists Now* (Cambridge: Harvard University Press, 1997), pp. 8, 84, 85. According to Glazer, Multiculturalism is "a new word for an old problem: how public education is to respond to and take account of the diversity of backgrounds of public school students, religious, ethnic, racial." Early twentieth century intellectuals—Horace Kallen, Randolph Bourne, and John Dewey—were among the first to make "major arguments in favor of multiculturalism."

22. Ronald Takaki, *A Different Mirror: A History of Multicultural America* (Boston: Little, Brown, and Company, 1993), pp. 4, 10, 6.

23. Takaki, *A Different Mirror*, p. 2. See also, Celeste Sollod, "Takaki Backs Ethnic Studies to Cure Cultural Illiteracy and Racial Tension," *Daily Californian*, 16 March 1988, p. 4.

24. "Campus Racial Tensions—and Violence—Appear on Rise," *New York Times*, 21 February 1988, p. 171. Similarly, the editors of the Berkeley student newspaper observed, "In the past year there has been an alarming increase in racial incidents on America's college campuses," which could be ameliorated in part by changing the curriculum to facilitate "an awareness of and sensitivity for the history, culture and concerns of all racial or linguistic groups that make up the state's population." "Editorial: Diversity Opens Minds," *Daily Californian*, 15 October 1987, p. 4.

25. "Campus Life: In Search of Community" (Princeton: The Carnegie Foundation for the Advancement of Teaching, 1990), p. 27.

26. Peter Kwong, "The First Multicultural Riots," in *Inside the L.A. Riots*, Don Hazen, ed. (New York: Institute for Alternative Journalism, 1992), pp. 88–92.

27. Takaki, *A Different Mirror*, p. 5.

28. Lawrence W. Levine, "Clio, Canons, and Culture," *Journal of American History* 80, no. 3 (December 1993): 850, 864, 862.

29. Levine, "Clio, Canons, and Culture," p. 850.

30. Bennett, *To Reclaim a Legacy*, pp. 30, 29.

31. Allan Bloom, *The Closing of the American Mind: How Higher Education Has Failed Democracy and Impoverished the Souls of Today's Students* (New York: Simon & Schuster, 1988). For a direct rebuttal to Bloom, see Levine, *The Opening of the American Mind*.

32. Ronald Takaki, "Multiculturalism: Battleground or Meeting Ground?," *Annals of the American Academy of Political and Social Science* 530 (November 1993): 116; Bloom, *The Closing of the American Mind*, p. 337.

33. Bennett, *To Reclaim a Legacy*, p. 20.

34. Quoted in James Atlas, "Chicago's Grumpy Guru," *New York Times Magazine*, 3 January 1988, p. 31.

35. Takaki, "Multiculturalism: Battleground or Meeting Ground?," p. 116; Bloom, *The Closing of the American Mind*, p. 344.

36. On this point, see also Dinesh D'Souza, *Illiberal Education: The Politics of Race and Sex on Campus* (New York: Free Press, 1991), p. 85: "It seems unlikely that being white and male are the reasons for anyone's greatness of thought; rather, those are features, historically accidental, that happened to coincide with great minds who were working at particular times in particular environments."

37. Arthur M. Schlesinger, Jr., *The Disuniting of America: Reflections on a Multicultural Society* (New York: Norton, 1992), pp. 15, 99, 53, 14.

38. Diane Ravitch, "Multiculturalism: E Pluribus Plures," *American Scholar* 59, no. 3 (Summer 1990): 340.

39. Takaki, "Multiculturalism: Battleground or Meeting Ground?," p. 116.

40. Schlesinger, Jr., p. 134.

41. Ravitch, p. 340.

42. Schlesinger, Jr., p. 138; I borrow the phrase "circle of 'We'" from David Hollinger, "How Wide the Circle of 'We'? American Intellectuals and the Problem of the Ethnos since World War II," *American Historical Review* 98, no. 2 (April 1993): 317–33.

43. John Higham, "Multiculturalism and Universalism: A History and Critique," *American Quarterly* 45, no. 2 (June 1993): 204, 214.

44. K. Anthony Appiah, "Identity, Authenticity, Survival," in *Multiculturalism: Examining the Politics of Recognition*, Amy Gutman, ed. (Princeton: Princeton University Press, 1994), pp. 156, 162, 163. More recently, Appiah has written that "'multiculturalism'...so often designates the disease it purports to cure." Kwame Anthony Appiah, *Cosmopolitanism: Ethics in a World of Strangers* (New York: Norton, 2006), p. xiii.

45. David Hollinger, *Postethnic America: Beyond Multiculturalism* (New York: Basic Books, 1995), pp. x, 8, 32, 26, 25, 118.

46. Takaki, *A Different Mirror*, p. 429. For a more detailed description of the passage of American Cultures (as well as a kindred requirement at the University of Wisconsin,

Madison), see David Yamane, *Student Movements for Multiculturalism: Challenging the Curricular Color Line in Higher Education* (Baltimore: Johns Hopkins University Press, 2001). As the title suggests, Yamane emphasizes the role of activist students as the driving force behind the attack on "curricular apartheid" (p. 59). By contrast, in what follows I emphasize the role of faculty members at fundamentally reshaping the vision of the requirement that the students initially articulated.

47. ASUC Office of Academic Affairs, "An Ethnic Studies Graduation Requirement," letter to the Committee on Educational Policy of the Berkeley Division of the University of California Academic Senate, 19 March 1986, AC Center, Academic Senate file. The Committee on Educational Policy fielded an earlier student appeal for an "ethnic studies course for graduation" the previous semester. Minutes of the Committee on Educational Policy, 26 November 1985, AC Center, Academic Senate file. See also Debora Vrana, "Ethnic studies may become a requirement at Berkeley," *Daily Californian*, 4 March 1986, p. 1.

48. Yamane, p. 56. See also Pedro Noguera, "Professor of Education, Student Leader during the Anti-Apartheid Campaign," an oral history conducted 1999 by Ann Lage in *The University of California, Office of the President and Its Constituencies, 1983–1985, Volume II: On Campuses: Chancellors, Faculty, Student*, Regional Oral History Office, The Bancroft Library, University of California, Berkeley, 2002. Noguera was president of the Associated Students of the University of California during the years 1985–1986, as well as a leader in the divestment campaign. According to Noguera, "[R]ight after the anti-apartheid issue, then we started dealing with the issue of the American cultures requirement.... [W]e started saying that it's important to be in solidarity with the struggles of South Africa, but we also have issues here to be addressed, and we need, once this is over, to direct some attention on those issues" (p. 126).

49. "Resolution Towards a Subject E Requirement," 15 October 1986, AC Center, Mark Min file #1.

50. United People of Color, "An Ethnic Studies Requirement?," circa fall 1986, AC Center, Mark Min file #1.

51. Bloom, *The Closing of the American Mind*, p. 338.

52. Bloom, *The Closing of the American Mind*, p. 344.

53. "UC Students March for Ethnic Studies," 2 February 1988, AC Center, Mark Min file #2.

54. United People of Color, "An Ethnic Studies Requirement?," circa fall 1986, AC Center, Mark Min file #1.

55. "Editorial: Education Is a Rainbow—Skip the Whitewash," *Daily Californian*, 18 November 1986, p. 4.

56. On this point, see also Michael Omi and Howard Winant, *Racial Formation in the United States: From the 1960s to the 1990s* (New York: Routledge, 1994), who speak of the "qualitative differences between white and non-white groups' encounters with U.S. society" groups such that it makes sense to think of the color line as having been drawn around, rather than within, Europe (pp. 49–50). Along these same lines, Ronald Takaki distinguishes between " 'ethnic' and 'racial' experiences" with the latter being limited to nonwhites. He

writes that "only blacks were enslaved, only Native Americans were removed to reservations, only Chinese were singled out for exclusion, and only Japanese Americans (not Italian Americans or German Americans) were placed in concentration camps." Ronald Takaki, ed., *From Different Shores: Perspectives on Race and Ethnicity in America* (New York: Oxford University Press, 1987), p. 7. Similarly, Evelyn Hu-Dehart distinguishes between those groups "socially constructed as 'minorities'" who are the focus of ethnic studies departments, programs, and courses and "European immigrants and their descendants," with the former having a "shared history of having been racially constructed as distinct" from the latter. Hu-DeHart, "Ethnic Studies in U.S. Higher Education," p. 874. Based on this distinction, Manning Marable suggests using the term "racialized ethnic minorities" to refer to "Asian Americans, American Indians, Latinos, and black Americans," lest they get confused with white ethnic groups. Manning Marable, "The Problematics of Ethnic Studies," *Black Renaissance/Renaissance Noire* 3, no. 1 (Fall 2000): 12.

57. ASUC Office of Academic Affairs, "An Ethnic Studies Graduation Requirement," letter to the Committee on Educational Policy of the Berkeley Division of the University of California Academic Senate, 19 March 1986, AC Center, Academic Senate file.

58. Amy Louise Kazmin, "Tense senate meeting results in delay of bill," *Daily Californian*, 10 October 1986, p. 7; Juliana Chang, Ricky Vincent, United People of Color, "Ethnic Americans," *Daily Californian*, 15 October 1986.

59. Subcommittee on an Ethnic Studies Requirement, Letter to the Committee on Educational Policy, 30 April 1986, AC Center, Mark Min file #1.

60. Minutes of the Committee on Educational Policy, 5 May 1986, AC Center, Academic Senate file.

61. Minutes of the Committee on Educational Policy, 26 February 1987, AC Center, Academic Senate file.

62. Minutes of the Special Committee on Education and Ethnicity, 16 February 1988, AC Center, Special Committee on Education and Ethnicity file.

63. Minutes of the Committee on Educational Policy, 23 March 1988, AC Center, Academic Senate file. Similarly, Professor Wang was on record nearly two years earlier saying it would be a "disaster" to limit any such required course to the ethnic studies department. Melissa Crabbe, "Ethnic studies requirement. Reflection of UC Diversity?," *Daily Californian*, 14 November 1986, pp. 1, 6.

64. William Simmons, Address to Academic Senate, 10 May 1988, AC Center, American Cultures—July 88–Dec. 88 file.

65. William Simmons, letter to David Vogel, 2 May 1988, AC Center, Dept. Responses to 1st Proposal file.

66. "Proposed Amendments to the Regulations of the Berkeley Division," 20 April 1988, AC Center, Mark Min file #1.

67. "Report of the Special Committee on Education and Ethnicity," 11 April 1988, AC Center, Mark Min file #1.

68. William Simmons, letter to David Vogel, 2 May 1988, AC Center, Dept. Responses to 1st Proposal file. See also, L. Ling-chi Wang, "Intellectual Affirmative Action: From

Ethnic Studies to 'American Cultures,'" circa May 1989, AC Center, Special Committee on Education and Ethnicity file. Wang credits David Lloyd, professor of English and member of the Special Committee on Education and Ethnicity, as having coined the term "intellectual affirmative action."

69. Ann Gelder, "Affirmative Action for People *and* Books," *Daily Californian*, 30 January 1989, p. 2.

70. David Ginsborg, "Hundreds of students demonstrate for ethnic studies," *Daily Californian*, 16 March 1988, p. 1.

71. Michael Stoll, Julie Chang, Alfonso Salazar, and Marcella King-Ben, "To: the Committee on Education and Ethnicity," 12 February 1988," AC Center, Special Committee on Education and Ethnicity file.

72. Larry Gordon, "Ethnic and Racial Mix Stirs Dispute Over Berkeley Curriculum Revision," *Los Angeles Times*, 14 November 1988, pp. 3, 24.

73. "Academic Waffling," *Daily Californian*, 20 October 1988, p. 4.

74. Minutes of the Special Committee on Education and Ethnicity, 30 August 1988, AC Center, American Cultures—July 88–Dec. 88 file.

75. Minutes of the Special Committee on Education and Ethnicity, 15 September 1988, AC Center, American Cultures—July 88–Dec. 88 file.

76. Bob Blauner, letter to Bill Simmons, June 1988, AC Center, Mark Min file #1.

77. Quoted in Lynn Kidder, "'Cultures' Proposal Will be Reworked," *Berkeleyan*, 10 January 1989, pp. 1, 8.

78. Amy Louise Kazmin, "Protest against change in Am. Cultures requirement," *Daily Californian*, 11 October 1988, pp. 1, 7.

79. Valli Israels, "Announcement by the ASUC Academic Affairs Vice President," 28 November 1988, AC Center, Academic Senate file.

80. Minutes of the Special Committee on Education and Ethnicity, 22 September 1988, AC Center, American Cultures—July 88–Dec. 88 file.

81. William Simmons, letter and questionnaire to faculty, 9 December 1988, AC Center, American Cultures—Dec. 1988 Questionnaires file.

82. Responses to questionnaire, December 1988, AC Center, American Cultures—Dec 1988 Questionnaires file.

83. Responses to questionnaire, December 1988, AC Center, American Cultures—Dec 1988 Questionnaires file.

84. "Proposal for an American Cultures Breadth Requirement," p. 4.

85. "Proposed Amendments to the Regulations of the Berkeley Division," 20 April 1988, AC Center, Mark Min file #1.

86. "Proposal for an American Cultures Breadth Requirement," p. 18.

87. "Proposal for an American Cultures Breadth Requirement," p. 4.

88. Heather Jones, "American Cultures Proposal Ready for Faculty Vote," *Daily Californian*, 6 April 1989, pp. 1, 3.

89. "Public Debate on the American Cultures Requirement," Sound Recording (Berkeley: University of California, Berkeley Language Laboratory), 28 February 1989.

See also Heather Jones, "American cultures opposition slight," *Daily Californian*, 1 March 1989, p. 1.

90. "First Draft—Ethnic Studies," 11 November 1986, AC Center, Academic Senate file, University of California, Berkeley.

91. Troy Duster, "An Oral History in Progress with Troy Duster," an oral history conducted in 2002 and 2003 by Nadine Wilmot and Richard Candida Smith, Regional Oral History Office, The Bancroft Library. Permission to quote granted by Troy Duster in 2006.

92. Quoted in Heather Jones, "American Cultures Passes," *Daily Californian*, 26 April 1989, pp. 1, 19. Though certainly much larger than a typical Academic Senate meeting, the turnout was still roughly a quarter of the size of the Academic Senate faculty, and less than half the size of the nearly 950 faculty members who voted—824 to 115—in favor of the Free Speech Movement student demands on December 8, 1964. Jo Freeman, *At Berkeley in the Sixties: The Education of an Activist, 1961–1965* (Bloomington: Indiana University Press, 2004), p. 220.

93. Jones, "American Cultures Passes," pp. 1, 19.

94. Minutes of Special Meeting, Berkeley Division, 25 April 1989, AC Center, Minutes of the Subcommittee on the Breadth Requirement in American Cultures file.

95. Quoted in Jones, "American Cultures Passes," pp. 1, 19.

96. "A crucial step," *Daily Californian*, 25 April 1989, 4; "One Battle Won, But What About the War?" *Daily Californian*, 27 April 1989, p. 4.

97. African Studies Association, Asian Students Association, Jeff Chang (ASUC President), MEChA, American Indian Students Association, Agha Saeed (Graduate Assembly Chair), "A Student Message to the Faculty on the American Cultures Requirement," *Daily Californian*, 24 April 1989, p. 9; Proposal for an American Cultures Breadth Requirement," p. 4.

98. On the American Cultures requirement as "mainstreamed" ethnic studies, see Duster, "An Oral History in Progress with Troy Duster": "The original idea was that this will be—the language of the period was something called mainstreamed, like you would break out of the notion that Ethnic Studies owned ethnic studies, that each department would have to deal with the ethnic, racial reconfiguration of America."

99. "National Survey Finds Diversity Requirements Common Around the Country," *Diversity Digest* (Fall 2000), http://www.diversityweb.org/Digest/F00/survey.html.

100. Glazer, *We Are All Multiculturalists Now*, 4. More recently, Richard Thompson Ford echoes Glazer about the triumph of multiculturalism: "Multiculturalism is no longer notable because it is everywhere." Richard Thompson Ford, *Racial Culture: A Critique* (Princeton: Princeton University Press, 2005), p. 42.

101. The data on the number of American Cultures courses and the total student enrollment in them can be found at http://amercult.berkeley.edu/about.html.

102. In 2003, the Supreme Court revisited—and narrowly upheld—*Bakke*, but only for a maximum of twenty-five additional years. "We expect that 25 years from now, the use of racial preferences will no longer be necessary to further the interest approved

today," wrote Justice Sandra Day O'Connor on behalf of the court's five justice majority. *Grutter v. Bollinger* 539 U.S. 306 (2003).

103. Though system wide the number of African American, American Indian, and Chicano/Latino students admitted would eventually return to—and even outstrip, in the case of Chicano/Latino students—what it was prior to Proposition 209; this was not the case at the University of California's Berkeley, Los Angeles, and San Diego campuses as of 2005. For more specific demographic data about applications, admissions, and enrollment at the University of California as a whole, as well as individual campuses within it, see http://www.ucop.edu/news/studstaff.html.

104. For data on interracial marriage rates, see *Table MS-3. Interracial Married Couples: 1980 to 2002*, released by the Census Bureau, 15 September 2004. See also "Yes to Mixing It Up for Mixed-Race," *Daily Californian*, 14 August 2006, http://dailycal.org/sharticle.php?id=21056. According to the editors of the University of California, Berkeley student newspaper, "For years, the UC system has based its compilation of student race data on antiquated U.S. Department of Education standards that deny the existence of mixed-race individuals. The system is flawed and outdated, especially considering that 6.8 million Americans identify themselves as mixed-race, according to 2000 U.S. Census Bureau data. And that is bound to rise—41 percent of those in the mixed-race category are under the age of 18, indicating that mixed-race individuals may mark a new norm for future generations."

105. William Simmons in Minutes of the Special Committee on Education and Ethnicity, 27 October 1988, AC Center, American Cultures—July 88–Dec 88 file. On this point, see also Duster, "An Oral History in Progress with Troy Duster": "[I]f the rationale [for why the American Cultures requirement took the shape that it did] has to do with the nature and character of social and political life in the country and demography, well of course, there will be changes...And those changes perhaps would undermine the argument for the original conception."

Chapter 8

REAGANOMICS: THE REBIRTH OF THE FREE MARKET

Kim Phillips-Fein

Early in 1981, Ronald Reagan proposed a new economic program to Congress, boldly entitled "America's New Beginning."[1] The heart of his vision was tax reduction: across-the-board rate cuts by 30 percent over three years. "In this present crisis, government is not the solution to our problem; government is the problem," he declared in a speech. "It is time to reawaken this industrial giant, to get government back within its means and to lighten our punitive tax burden."[2]

By the end of the year, Congress had passed Reagan's budget. Tax rates were cut (although not by quite as much as Reagan had proposed) and so was funding for many federal programs, ranging from public service jobs to food stamps to child nutrition to mental health expenditures. Celebrating his successful legislative crusade in July, Reagan claimed that it would "mark the beginning of a new renaissance in America."[3] Earlier in the year, he had removed Harry Truman's portrait from its place on the wall of the Cabinet Room and replaced it with one of 1920s president Calvin Coolidge, known for his belief that "the business of America is business." The symbolism was clear: Truman, who had pushed for union rights and public housing, was no longer in vogue—Reagan's inspiration came from the days before the New Deal.[4]

In August of the same year, Reagan took a second major step to transform the American economy when he fired 13,000 air traffic controllers who had voted to go on strike in violation of their contract. Their union, the Professional

Air Traffic Controllers Organization (PATCO), had endorsed Reagan for president, believing that as a former union president, he would be sympathetic to their cause. The strikers thought that they would attract wide public support, since their strike involved issues including long shifts and outdated technology that seemed to impact passenger safety. Instead, Reagan announced that the strikers "are in violation of the law, and if they do not report for work within forty-eight hours, they have forfeited their jobs and will be terminated."[5] Furious at Reagan's threats, the striking workers did not return to their jobs. Ignoring the pleas of Congressional leaders, Reagan kept his word. Not only did he fire all the strikers, but they were also blacklisted—prevented from seeking work in the industry ever again. A few months after the PATCO strike, *Fortune* magazine opined, "Managers are discovering that strikes can be broken, that the cost of breaking them is often lower than the cost of taking them, and that strikebreaking (assuming it to be legal and nonviolent) doesn't have to be a dirty word."[6]

Taken together, the tax initiative of 1981 and the breaking of the PATCO strike symbolized much about Ronald Reagan's economic policy. Throughout his time in office, Reagan sought to reduce the role of the government in economic life by cutting federal spending and lowering tax rates, while also opposing what he perceived as excessive union power. His administration sought to unleash the forces of the free market, limiting the scope of action open to collective institutions such as unions and the state. This faith in the marketplace was not easily separable from Reagan's broader moral and political vision. The same core beliefs shaped both his foreign policy—especially his anticommunist commitments—and his domestic economic agenda. Reagan essentially used economic policy to advance a philosophy of small government and anticommunism. At times, Reagan's absolute belief in the beneficence of the free market caused him to ignore the economic strife that many Americans—especially working-class people—endured during his presidency. But this was not an accident or an oversight; rather, it followed naturally from the depth of his commitment to the ideal of the free market. The word that both supporters and critics used to refer to Reagan's economic agenda, with its emphasis on shrinking the role of the government in the economy by slowing government spending, cutting tax rates, and rolling back regulations, was "Reaganomics."[7]

The Reagan administration inherited a fractured, troubled economy from Jimmy Carter. The strong and steady economic growth that had characterized the entire postwar period seemed to have ground to a halt. Unemployment stood at about 7.5 percent, and inflation was increasing rapidly.[8] What was more, the tried-and-true liberal methods for stimulating economic growth—most importantly, boosting the economy through federal expenditures—no longer seemed to work. The crisis that gripped the United States during the 1970s was not simply economic—it was intellectual and political as well. None of the economic experts who had prided themselves on their "fine-tuning" abilities knew what to do to bring down unemployment and to restore economic health.

By the time Reagan left office, economic growth had been revived. The steep inflation that had characterized the late 1970s disappeared. But the economic growth of the 1980s was distinctly different from what had characterized the country during the period between 1945 and 1973. During the earlier period, the benefits of economic growth had been equally shared, and the nation's wealth grew without accelerating inequality. By contrast, during the 1980s, the gap between rich and poor expanded sharply. When the economy began to grow again after the recessions of the 1970s and early 1980s, the wealthiest people in the country got richer, whereas people in the lower half of the income distribution saw their wages stagnate or even decline.[9] Ronald Reagan's economic policies, focused on cutting taxes and regulations and expanding the role of the free market in the allocation of resources, had profoundly changed the way in which wealth was generated and distributed in the United States.

Equally important, Reagan's approach to the economy had revolutionized the way that people thought about the relationship between government and economic life. Out of all the transformations in American politics, culture, and society that transpired over the course of the 1980s, the changes in economic policy and in economic thought are perhaps the most profound. They did not, of course, begin in the 1980s, nor did they end there. But it was in the 1980s that the idea of the free market's power became the governing philosophy of the United States. As Martin Anderson, a Hoover Institution economist, wrote in his account of the Reagan presidency, "The ultimate irony of the twentieth century may be that lasting, worldwide political revolution was accomplished not by Trotsky and the communists but instead by Reagan and the capitalists."[10]

During his presidency, liberal thinkers often mocked Reagan's Hollywood anti-intellectualism, particularly his free hand with statistics. Reagan did not have a Ph.D. in economics, and to many observers, his ideas seemed hopelessly simplistic and old-fashioned, hearkening back to the faiths of the late nineteenth century and even to a preindustrial America. Many saw Reaganomics as simply the beliefs of an untutored actor. John Kenneth Galbraith, a Harvard economics professor who served in the presidential administration of John F. Kennedy, criticized Reagan's program for being rife with contradictions.[11] Other left-leaning writers saw Reaganomics as no more than an exercise in bad faith, a fig leaf that just barely covered naked class interest. As two journalists wrote in the liberal magazine *The Nation*, Reaganomics "does not really mean getting the government off people's backs; it means repealing the hard-won social gains of the last fifty years and using the government to transfer money to large corporations, high-income earners and military contractors."[12]

These negative assessments fail to give sufficient weight to the significance of the transformations in economic ideology over the 1980s. Reagan was not confused about economics. Nor was he without intellectual models: Nobel Prize winners such as Friedrich Hayek and Milton Friedman (who were also themselves political thinkers and writers) informed his thought. There was, of course, a symbolic element to Reaganomics, but this does not mean that Reagan's economics was merely smoke-and-mirrors hiding his real concerns. Reagan's economic vision expressed a way of looking at the world, a framework for understanding the economy and society and the individual's place within both. It was this market vision that brought working-class voters to Reagan—as least as much as what he himself termed the "so-called social issues—law and order, abortion, busing, quota systems."[13]

To understand the magnitude of the changes that transpired during the Reagan years, it is first necessary to know a little about Keynesian economics. Ever since the Great Depression of the 1930s, economists had believed that the private economy would not always be able to pull out of economic downturns unassisted. They thought that the state, in the hands of capable, responsible economic experts, should play a critical role in managing the economy. John Maynard Keynes (1883–1946), a British economic thinker, argued during the Great Depression that there was no reason to believe that the economy would naturally right itself when it sank into recession. He thought that consumer demand was the key economic variable that determined economic health; if consumers did not possess enough purchasing power, businessmen would never find it profitable to invest. Therefore, in a depression, the state needed to use its economic might to boost demand, and the government also needed to do what it could to support the incomes of workers to make sure that they would have enough purchasing power to drive the economy. The liberal economists who became followers of Keynes believed that labor unions played a central, and necessary, economic role in the economy, as the representative of the workers and the guarantors of the high wages necessary for expanding consumer markets.

The early Keynesians, who formulated their ideas during the Great Depression, were much more deeply sensitive to the political implications of their thought than were the postwar economists.[14] As time went by, the early economists' sense of the role of labor in the economy gave way to a narrower self-assurance regarding the predictive power of the Keynesian models and the infallibility of the new techniques of economic management carried out by the government. Keynesian economists had been supremely confident in their ability to understand the business cycle and forestall economic depressions. In the 1965 report of the Council of Economic Advisors, President Lyndon Johnson proclaimed that he "d[id] not believe recessions [we]re inevitable."[15] Their pride only increased in the early 1960s, with the advent of computers and the development of more sophisticated modeling techniques. Walter Heller, a University of Minnesota economist named by President Kennedy to head the Council of Economic Advisers, enthused, "Our statistical net is now spread wider and brings in its catch faster. Forecasting has the benefit of not only more refined, computer-assisted methods but of improved surveys of consumer and investment intentions."[16] Nobel Prize–winning M.I.T. economist Paul Samuelson, whose elegant synthesis of economic thought was like the Bible for a generation of economics students, wrote in his textbook (*Economics: An Introductory Analysis*) that modern economists "*kn[ew]* how to use monetary and fiscal policy to keep any recessions that br[oke] out from snowballing into *lasting* chronic slumps."[17] They had learned to solve the business cycle, and serious recessions were a thing of the past.

With the economic crises of the 1970s, this certainty evaporated. One of the central tenets of the Keynesian faith had been that there was an inverse relationship between unemployment and inflation. Unemployment indicated underutilized resources; inflation implied insufficient productive capacity. If unemployment rose, then the government could increase spending to lower unemployment. If inflation was rising, the state could cut back to stop the acceleration of prices.

In the late 1960s and early 1970s, both unemployment and inflation began to rise at once. The reasons for the slowdown were many and complex, both cyclical and structural. The government was steadily pumping money into the economy to fund the war in Vietnam, which had the effect of raising prices. The Northeast and Midwest had experienced a slow outflow of manufacturing jobs, as industrial employers closed up to seek cheaper labor in the South and in Mexico. Businessmen were wary about the social and political climate of rising militancy among workers, antiwar youths, and urban populations of African Americans and Hispanics. Large, quasimonopolistic corporations that had been accustomed to raising prices to make up profit shortfalls without facing significant competition were starting to encounter competition from Europe and Japan. Oil shocks in the early 1970s raised the price of energy abruptly.

The causes of the crisis were myriad and murky; however, one thing was clear: the governing faith of the postwar period, the belief that economic cycles could be controlled through increasing or decreasing government spending, no longer seemed to hold true. If the state increased spending, economists feared it would cause runaway inflation. If the state tried to cut back on spending, the ranks of the unemployed would explode. The once-solid faiths of liberal economics suddenly began to feel like a trap. As one Keynesian economist commented, by 1980 it was very difficult to find "an American academic macroeconomist under the age of 40 who professed to be a Keynesian."[18]

Not everyone was surprised by the collapse of Keynes. Throughout the postwar period, economic thinkers such as University of Chicago economist Milton Friedman and the Austrian émigrés Friedrich von Hayek and Ludvig von Mises had been sharply critical of Keynesian economics, seeing it as a precursor to socialism. Keynesianism proclaimed that people could exercise control over the economy. The free-market thinkers argued that this was itself a fallacy—that no human agency could collect the information needed to guide economic life, and that therefore the best the state could do was stick to the most neutral enforcement of rules. In his 1962 classic, *Capitalism and Freedom*, Friedman attacked the concept of countercyclical government spending: "In fiscal policy as in monetary policy, all political considerations aside, we simply do not know enough to be able to use deliberate changes in taxation or expenditures as a sensitive stabilizing mechanism. In the process of trying to do so, we almost surely make matters worse."[19] This simply echoed the idea expressed by Hayek years earlier that the "spontaneous collaboration of free men often creates things which are greater than their individual minds can ever fully comprehend."[20]

When the Keynesians were confronted with a problem for which there was no solution within their framework, their critics' ideas exploded into public view. Milton Friedman argued that economic health would be restored if the Federal Reserve simply adopted a tight monetary policy. Economist Robert Lucas, who invented the school of "rational expectations," insisted that all macroeconomic policies were doomed to failure, since the market would immediately interpret and often circumvent whatever policymakers said they were trying to do. No one entirely agreed as to what should be done, but everyone agreed that the Keynesian solutions had failed, and that the problem had been overestimating the power of government and underestimating the importance of allowing the market to operate without significant restrictions.

Into this intellectual maelstrom came the crisply optimistic vision of supply-side economics. *Wall Street Journal* editorial page writer Jude Wanniski and up-and-coming University of Southern California economics professor Arthur Laffer advanced the argument that there was a declining marginal utility to tax rates: after they rose to a certain level, they would provide such a significant disincentive to earning income that they would actually begin to depress total revenues. The natural correlate was that it might be possible to at once lower taxes and maintain—or, for the true optimists, even increase—the federal government's income. Wanniski celebrated Laffer's theory of taxation in his free-market manifesto, *The Way the World Works*. "The worst mistakes in history," he wrote, "are made by political leaders who, instead of realizing that rates could be lowered as a means of gaining revenues, become alarmed at the fall in revenues as citizens seek to escape high rates by bartering and do-it-yourself work."[21]

Instead of thinking about tax rates and government expenditures in terms of the impact they would have on the flows of income through the economy—from government to consumption to investment—Laffer and Wanniski saw the tax rates primarily in terms of the incentives they would have for producers. The argument was that people who were too heavily taxed would no longer work as hard or as productively as they would if their taxes were lower; therefore, by lowering their taxes, the government would give them an incentive to work harder and produce more overall income.

The economic slowdown of the 1970s made an economic proposal focused on cutting taxes very appealing to many working-class and middle-class voters, who were desperately seeking to maintain their standard of living as prices soared and jobs seemed unstable. Conservatives argued that tax dollars were being taken from hard-working Americans and used to support "welfare queens"—a suggestion that fed off of and exploited the white backlash against the civil rights movement. In some states, such as California and Massachusetts, these antigovernment sentiments led to full-fledged property tax revolts in the late 1970s. These rebellions were motivated not so much by the theory of supply-side economics as by economic anxiety combined with white Americans' distaste for policies that were thought to disproportionately benefit ethnic and racial minorities. But around Reagan, the strongest proponents of cutting taxes articulated their theory in terms of stimulating economic growth. As Congressman Jack Kemp, who proposed tax-cutting legislation in the House in 1978 that would become the prototype for Reagan's tax reduction plan, said in a speech to the Economic Club of New York City that year, "When you tax production, capital, work, savings and entrepreneurial activities, you get less of all of these."[22] Or, to quote Reagan himself, "When I was in the movies, I'd reach a point each year where after the second movie I'd be in the 90 percent bracket. So I just wouldn't make any more movies that year. And it wasn't just me, but Bogart and Gable and the others did the same. We weren't the ones who were hurt. The people who worked the props and the people who worked the yard, they were the ones who were hurt."[23]

Instead of focusing on consumer demand, Reaganomics focused on investors—creating the incentives that would make investors create wealth. Herbert Stein, the Council of Economic Advisers chair under Presidents Nixon and Ford, sneered at the scheme, giving it the derogatory nickname "supply-side economics."[24] But Wanniski loved the phrase, and it stuck.

Supply-side theory optimistically suggested that unemployment and inflation could be solved using the same policies of lowering taxes and cutting regulations. If taxes were cut and incentives adjusted, it should be possible to have real economic growth without inflation. After all, inflation came about only when there were struggles over an existing supply of goods; it reflected a shortage of goods. Once the economy started growing again, after disincentives were decreased, there would be more for everyone. "The most direct thing that we can do to immediately increase the amount of employment, saving and investment is to increase the reward or incentive for the next dollar earned by employment, saving, or investment," Kemp told an audience of union members in 1979. "That means cutting tax rates."[25]

The larger implication of supply-side theory was that the problems the economy faced were not structural—the migration of jobs out of industrial areas, for example—nor did they have to do with the distribution of income, the relationship of the United States to the rest of the world, or the level of aggregate demand. Rather, the problem the American economy faced was essentially that there were too many disincentives to investment. There was, to quote social theorist George Gilder, a "war against the rich."[26] To solve the problem, investors needed to be reassured and catered to, and the barriers that prevented them from investing—such as too-high wages, militant unions, burdensome taxes, and negative cultural attitudes toward businessmen—needed to be removed. Anything that provided a disincentive to invest—in other words, anything that irritated business—would hurt the economy; anything that offered an "incentive" to investment was in the general interest. According to this new logic, unions, high wages, and strikes were bad for the economy, whereas conspicuous displays of personal wealth—the just rewards for wise investments—benefited everyone.

After the punishments for wealth had been eliminated, the economy would grow once again. As Jack Kemp said in 1981, defending Reagan's tax plan, "In the past few years, we have literally been taxed into recession. The way our system is now, the more you work, the more you save, the more you invest—the higher your tax bracket."[27] The answer was to cut taxes, and thus unleash the revolutionary force of self-interest, which would stimulate ever-higher levels of investment, saving, and work. "Under capitalism, when it is working, the rich have the anti-Midas touch, transforming timorous liquidity and unused savings into factories and office towers, farms and laboratories, orchestras and museums," wrote George Gilder in his popular defense of Reaganomics, *Wealth and Poverty*. "That is the function of the rich: fostering opportunities for the classes below them in the continuing drama of the creation of wealth and progress."[28]

Giving money to poor people, or providing state services for them, was, by contrast, perceived as a sink-hole. Programs to help people who were in difficult straits were wrong-headed, because they were rewards for wrong choices. "The only dependable route from poverty is always work, family and faith," as Gilder put it.[29] As followers of Gilder preached, poor people (like everyone else) did not want to work; if the government offered them a less onerous option, such as welfare, they would take it. Welfare payments led to broken families by rendering men obsolete as wage-earners within the home. In this way, welfare only worsened poverty. Both rich and poor people were responding to the incentives established by their government; by changing the incentives, the government would change their actions as well.

Did Reaganomics succeed? It depends on who you ask and on the difficult question of how success is evaluated. Although Reagan's program may have been partly responsible for creating economic conditions in which investors wanted to invest, it helped contribute to a restructuring of the American economy that has meant widening inequalities of income and wealth. Perhaps economic growth could have resumed during the 1980s without these consequences; this is an historical counterfactual, and we don't know the answer. But although people can argue about its impact on the American economy, Reaganomics triumphed in a deep political sense—on some level, the policy vision that Reagan articulated continues to frame the way that many policymakers in both political parties approach economic issues today.

Reagan's policies did not immediately create a new burst of economic growth or a new wave of prosperity for ordinary Americans. In the short term, his economic program seemed to bring about the precise opposite of what it was intended to accomplish. Inflation did flicker away early in the Reagan presidency, but not because of a sudden surge of growth. Rather, in the first two years of the 1980s the country entered a recession fiercer and deeper than any it had known in the 1970s, due in part to the sky-high interest rates pursued by the Federal Reserve. Even though economic growth averaged 4.2 percent between 1982 and 1988, the average rate of growth for the entire 8 years of the Reagan presidency was only 2.8 percent—lower than the 2.9 percent growth averaged during the Carter years—in part because of the sharp downturn of the early 1980s.[30]

Reagan's tax cuts—which decreased the top marginal rates from 70 to 28 percent, and lowered federal taxation as a percentage of GNP from 20 percent in 1981 to 18.6 percent in 1988—did not have the effect that the supply-siders projected on the government budget.[31] "The conjecture that a general reduction in tax rates would increase total tax revenues was clearly refuted," wrote William Niskanen, the head of the libertarian think tank Cato Institute and onetime member of Reagan's Council of Economic Advisors. (Libertarians believe that government is frequently coercive and that individuals should be given maximal freedom in their own lives.)[32] Cutting tax rates while increasing the military budget and maintaining entitlement programs in the 1980s did not unleash growth so rapid that it made up for the loss of revenue; instead, it led to tremendous government deficits. Some of Reagan's aides (such as David Stockman, who headed the Office of Management and Budget) had believed that cutting federal taxes would necessitate cutting government spending. This didn't happen, in part because of Reagan's anticommunist commitments that led to a military buildup throughout the decade. Ballooning government deficits were the result.

Finally, the Reagan "revolution" failed on its own terms in a number of ways, never achieving the broad rollback of the welfare state that had been its ultimate ambition. Aid to Families with Dependent Children, the main welfare program, continued to exist throughout the 1980s. Social Security remained a public program. Despite various cutbacks in funding, Reagan did not abolish any government agencies. Even the much-maligned Departments of Energy and Education exist to the present day.

But at the same time, economic growth did ultimately begin once again, although on terms much less favorable to the American working class and middle class than had been the case earlier in the century. After rising to 10 percent in 1982, unemployment fell to 5.4 percent in 1988 (opponents of the Reagan administration argued that many of these were service-sector jobs that were poorly paid or even part-time).[33] The cutbacks on regulations, the tax cuts, and the overt political support for the market and for business combined with the hostility to organized labor may have played some role in the revival of economic growth, but they certainly helped to guarantee that once growth began again its rewards were far less equally distributed than they had been in the mid-century boom—that working-class wages would stagnate while the incomes of the very rich grew.[34] Reagan was also successful in starting to shrink the welfare state; spending on social spending fell over the 1980s, and Reagan embarked upon a "New Federalism" that sought to shift responsibility for social services to the state level, away from the federal government.[35] In a strange way, the economic restructuring of the Reagan years—which saw the deindustrialization of the Northeast and Midwest, the decline of union power, and dramatic increases in economic inequality—literally made real the free-market faith in the ultimate impotence of collective action, by delivering a series of defeats to the labor movement as well as to broader political movements that sought to use the state to decrease social inequality. The political economy embedded in the free-market program sought to restrict the power of unions and the state, the primary social institutions capable of challenging the power of business, leaving individuals to face their employers and the market alone.

For Ronald Reagan himself, the economic program that he espoused simply expressed the beliefs he had held throughout his life: that the private economy was the source of dynamism and freedom; that capitalism liberated people, whereas liberalism and communism enslaved them; and that only by being part of a market economy could people achieve self-expression, political freedom, and creative power. Perhaps Reagan's most important insight was simply that the economy was not—as the liberals of the mid-twentieth century had it—a realm of technocrats. It was a space of political meaning. As he wrote in the introduction to a book of Congressman Jack Kemp's collected speeches, "Restoring prosperity, rebuilding our national agenda and keeping the peace, recovering the moral foundation of our social order—these goals cannot be isolated one from the other. They cohere. They interrelate. They mutually sustain."[36] Fighting communism, liberating industry, and opposing strikes were all part of a single political program for Reagan. The standard was not "success" or "failure," but simply doing the right thing and advancing the cause of what he understood as freedom.

The longest-lasting impact of Reaganomics is in this intellectual and political realm. For the Reagan Revolution—despite its mixed impact on the economic health of the nation—did decisively transform the way that most policymakers approached the question of the role of the government in economic life. Since Reagan left office, the faith in individual initiative and the free market has largely become the gospel of both political parties. The 1980s also saw a cultural glorification of wealth and material excess, shading at times into commercial indulgence and hedonism reminiscent of a depoliticized counterculture.[37] During the 1990s, the celebration of the free market would reach ever more frantic heights, the national mood rising with each tick of the stock market tape. As the economic expansion swelled and the stock market rose, the national faith in the market that Reagan tried to instill spilled over into politics in a way that it never could during his presidency. Democratic President William Jefferson Clinton transformed the nation's welfare system, ending welfare as an entitlement—something that Reagan was never able to accomplish. The Democratic administration of the late 1990s began a debate over the privatization of Social Security—again, something Reagan was unable to achieve. More recently, the Republican administration of George W. Bush has won additional tax cuts that were clearly inspired by Reagan's.

In short, for years after Reagan's presidency ended, it seemed that both of the major political parties, as well as most mainstream academic and media institutions, had largely accepted the idea that there was little the state could or should do to shape economic growth or patterns of wealth distribution, at least in terms of reducing inequality. Various contemporary challenges such as the accelerating gap between rich and poor, the crisis of New Orleans after the devastation of Hurricane Katrina, environmental degradation, the nation's continued struggles around health care and, most dramatically, the economic meltdown of 2008, revived calls for the government to play a greater role in economic life. But Reagan's economic vision dominated for more than a quarter century after he first entered the White House. Regardless of what one thinks about its impact on the economic health and social fabric of the United States, this political victory is perhaps his greatest success.[38]

NOTES

1. Bruce Schulman, *The Seventies: The Great Shift in American Culture, Society and Politics* (Cambridge: Da Capo Press, 2001), p. 231.

2. Robert Dallek, *Ronald Reagan: The Politics of Symbolism* (Cambridge: Harvard University Press, 1984), p. 64.

3. Lou Cannon, *Reagan* (New York: G.P. Putnam's Sons, 1982), p. 322.

4. Ibid, p. 323.

5. Schulman, *The Seventies*, p. 233.

6. Herbert E. Meyer, "The Decline of Strikes," *Fortune*, November 2, 1981.

7. William A. Niskanen, *Reaganomics: An Insider's Account of the Policies and the People* (New York: Oxford University Press, 1988), gives this basic definition. Niskanen also mentions Reagan's attempts to restrain inflation by controlling the money supply.

8. Dallek, *Ronald Reagan: The Politics of Symbolism*, p. 64.

9. A clear overview of the statistics can be found in Richard Oestreicher, "The Rules of the Game: Class Politics in Twentieth-Century America," in Kevin Boyle, ed., *Organized Labor and American Politics: 1894–1994, The Labor-Liberal Alliance* (Albany: State University of New York at Albany Press, 1998).

10. Martin Anderson, *Revolution: The Reagan Legacy* (Stanford, Calif.: Hoover Institution Press, 1990), p. 37.

11. Cannon, *Reagan*, p. 338.

12. Martin Carnoy and Derek Shearer, "Reaganomics: The Supply Side of the Street," *Nation*, November 7, 1981. Quoted in Schulman, *The Seventies*, p. 235.

13. Cannon, *Reagan*, p. 327.

14. For example, see the work of Leon Keyserling and Chester Bowles.

15. Michael Bernstein, *A Perilous Progress: Economists and the Public Purpose in Twentieth-Century America* (Princeton: Princeton University Press, 2001), p. 118.

16. James Patterson, *Grand Expectations: The United States, 1945–1974* (New York: Oxford University Press, 1994), p. 464.

17. Quoted in Bernstein, *A Perilous Progress*, p. 118.

18. Bernstein, *A Perilous Progress*, p. 159.

19. Milton Friedman, *Capitalism and Freedom* (Chicago: University of Chicago Press, 1962), p. 78.

20. Friedrich Hayek, "Individualism and Social Order," in *Individualism and Economic Order* (Chicago: University of Chicago Press, 1996), p. 6.

21. Jude Wanniski, *The Way the World Works* (Washington, D.C.: Regnery Publishing, 1998), p. 102.

22. Jack Kemp, *American Idea: Ending Limits to Growth* (Washington, D.C.: American Studies Center, 1984), p. 13.

23. Bruce Bartlett, *Reaganomics: Supply-Side Economics in Action* (New York: Quill, 1982), p. 212.

24. Cannon, *Reagan*, p. 322.

25. Ibid, p. 31.

26. George Gilder, *Wealth and Poverty* (San Francisco: Institute for Contemporary Studies, 1993), p. 114.

27. Kemp, *American Idea*, p. 48.

28. Gilder, *Wealth and Poverty*, p. 73.

29. Ibid, p. 79.

30. Nigel Ashford, "The Conservative Agenda and the Reagan Presidency," in Joseph Hogan, ed., *The Reagan Years: The Record in Presidential Leadership* (Manchester and New York: Manchester University Press, 1990), p. 199.

31. Ibid, p. 193.

32. William Niskanen, *Reaganomics: An Insider's Account of the Policies and the People* (New York: Oxford University Press, 1998), p. 333.

33. Ashford, "The Conservative Agenda and the Reagan Presidency," p. 199. Ashford points out that the administration tried to argue that 90 percent of the new jobs were full time jobs and that 85 percent of them paid more than $20,000 a year.

34. Emmanuel Saez and Thomas Piketty, "Income Inequality in the United States, 1913–1998," *Quarterly Journal of Economics*, February 2003 argues that Reagan's tax policies had a significant effect on economic inequality. Economic inequality was likely also exacerbated by the declining role of labor unions and the expansion of jobs in lower-wage areas of the economy.

35. Bruce Schulman, "The Reagan Revolution in International Perspective: Conservative Assaults on the Welfare State Across the Industrialized World in the 1980s," in Richard Conley, ed., *Reassessing the Reagan Presidency* (Lanham, Md.: University Press of America, 2003), p. 101. Schulman argues that the United States embodied a distinctive approach to shrinking the welfare state, something that was happening in many industrialized nations in the 1980s, because the Reagan administration never fully adopted fiscal conservatism, but instead relied on rallying political opposition to the welfare state in a variety of ways over the course of the decade.

36. Kemp, *American Idea* (introduction by Ronald Reagan), p. xiv.

37. See Gil Troy, *Morning in America: How Ronald Reagan Invented the 1980s* (Princeton: Princeton University Press, 2005), pp. 204–35, for a depiction of the culture of wealth in the decade.

38. Many journalists and historians—including Gil Troy, Bruce Schulman, Richard Reeves, Thomas Byrne Edsall, and others—agree that the ideological victories of the Reagan administration in the area of economic policy are in many ways its most significant and enduring legacy. For Reeves, see *President Reagan: The Triumph of Imagination* (New York: Simon & Schuster, 2005). For Thomas Byrne Edsall, see "The Reagan Legacy," in Sidney Blumenthal and Thomas Byrne Edsall, eds., *The Reagan Legacy* (New York: Pantheon Books, 1988). Edsall argues that Reagan's economic policies were able to strengthen the political clout of the affluent, while weakening countervailing forces such as labor unions, and thus that they helped to bring about a political realignment as well.

Chapter 9

DID RONALD REAGAN MAKE THE BERLIN WALL FALL DOWN?

Peter Schweizer

The 1980s witnessed a series of fascinating and important events, but none was as world-changing as the collapse of the Soviet Empire. The demise of the communist edifice in Europe meant close to a billion people found themselves suddenly out from under totalitarian rule. The nuclear sword that had been hanging over the planet seemed to vanish, and the Cold War, which had so dominated American politics for more than a generation, was history. The approach that Ronald Reagan took in challenging the Soviet Union tells us much about why it collapsed, how Reagan viewed the world, and his faith in the revolutionary power of freedom.

Whenever a large empire collapses, historical debate follows. Why did Rome fall? What contributed most to the fading of the British Empire? In the case of the collapse of world communism, the debate seems particularly intense and political. After all, determining what conclusions are reached, and who receives the credit, will undoubtedly influence American foreign policy over the next several generations.

A common explanation for the demise of communism is that it was inevitable; in other words, the system was doomed to failure. This sort of historical determinism, that certain events are inevitable regardless of what actions people take, is problematic. But even granting for a minute that history actually can be seen this way, this explanation is severely limited. The fact is that the Soviet system was flawed from the beginning. Economic trauma, restless nationalities, and a lack of popular support were problems dating back to the 1920s. For 70 years the Soviet economy was in a state of crisis. So why did it collapse when it did?[1]

If credit is given to any one individual, historians will often grant it to Mikhail Gorbachev, the last general secretary of the Soviet Union. Gorbachev is often praised for steering the USSR down the path of radical reform, which invariably caused chaos and then collapse. It was Gorbachev who was the brilliant one, says historian Robert Dallek, who overcame "Reagan's carelessness or shallowness as a foreign policy maker." After all, it was Gorbachev who was *Time* magazine's Man of the Decade; Reagan just showed the good timing of an actor.[2]

Of course, Gorbachev does deserve praise for choosing to allow the peaceful demise of the Soviet empire rather than trying to hold it together with force. But giving Gorbachev most of the credit raises several important questions: Why did the Kremlin feel the need to reform the system so radically in the 1980s? How and why did Gorbachev come to power? Why did the Cold War end on Reagan's terms and not Gorbachev's?

If no one person is considered the author of the Soviet Union's demise, the American policy of containment is often acknowledged as the reason for the end of the Cold War. Containment, the general idea that the United States would limit the Soviet Union and its sphere of influence geographically to prevent its expansion, was developed during Harry Truman's administration and endorsed by every one of his successors. Former President Gerald Ford said the credit did not belong to any one leader but to the American people, as if who happened to be in charge really did not matter. Others, such as former Secretary of State Madeleine Albright, contend that it was the ultimate team effort. "There were the Communists and there were us; the good guys and the bad guys...it was fairly easy to understand." If Reagan did anything, says Dallek, it was simply to stand on the shoulders of every cold war president before him. "By the time of Reagan's presidency," Dallek writes, "the wisdom of containment policy was largely transparent."[3]

Although all of these explanations offer some answers as to why the Soviet Union collapsed, none is sufficient to explain why the Soviet Union collapsed when it did and how the collapse came about. Only by examining the actions and policies of the Reagan administration can the Soviet collapse be fully understood and adequately explained.

Indeed, contrary to the claims of Albright and Dallek, Reagan's strategy was not a simple affirmation of containment. The Reagan approach represented a radical break from that policy. Much as Reagan sought to rewrite American domestic politics, he was determined to transform the superpower relationship. And it was because of these policies that Reagan succeeded in toppling the Soviet Union.

Containment was essentially a defensive strategy that called for the West to meet Soviet challenges and beat back any attempts at expansion. Even anticommunists such as Richard Nixon subscribed to the seductive idea that stability was most important, and that a healthy Soviet Union was important for long-term peace. The 1970s policy of détente was predicated on the idea that a strong Soviet Union would be less aggressive and more cooperative with the West. Even in the pre-détente era, Presidents Dwight Eisenhower, John Kennedy, and Lyndon Johnson espoused their faith in policies that would maintain the status quo between East and West. The Reagan view was quite different. An examination of Reagan's early writings and prepresidential speeches makes it clear that he did not favor coexistence with the Soviet Union as a matter of policy, but instead believed that the United States needed to develop a series of policies designed to eventually defeat it. Once he became president, many of these precepts were formalized into policy.[4]

Reagan's views were particularly bold because they represented a complete break from prevailing wisdom. The rebellion in the 1960s had reinforced the accommodationist strain in American foreign policy. Defeat in Vietnam had shaken the confidence of many who believed that America's best days were behind it. America also witnessed the rise of a new, intensely self-critical "counterestablishment" of well-educated baby boomers often ashamed of America. Doubting both American power and American virtue became a self-fulfilling prophecy. The 1970s became an epoch of national demoralization and of serious foreign policy setbacks. The 1973 Arab Oil Embargo not only generated lengthy gas lines but helped trigger the devastating inflation of the 1970s and a sobering lesson in the limits of American power. The collapse of South Vietnam in 1975 popularized the view of the Vietnam War as a debacle—meaning that Ronald Reagan created quite a controversy when he declared the war was "a noble cause."

Under Jimmy Carter, the transformation of Iran from a valued ally into a hostile Islamic state and the fall of Nicaragua into communist hands made many experts proclaim that the "American century" had ended prematurely. Here, too, Ronald Reagan's faith in the United States and in capitalism placed him in opposition to mainstream media opinion and intellectual conventions. Finally, Jimmy Carter's human rights rhetoric, the SALT treaties he pushed through Congress, and his returning of the Panama Canal to Panamanian sovereignty infuriated Reagan—and millions of other Americans. Reagan ran in

1976, and again in 1980 promising a more assertive and confident foreign policy throughout the world, not just in dealing with the Soviets.

Harvard historian Richard Pipes, who handled Soviet policy on the National Security Council early in the Reagan administration, penned a top secret 1982 study in which he advocated an aggressive policy to seek the "democratization" of the Soviet Union. The study, requested by the president as part of National Security Study Directive (NSSD) 11–82, called for supporting dissident movements, upgrading radio broadcasts from the West, engaging in a battle of ideas with the Kremlin, curtailing technology exports and loans, and building up the military as a means to undermine Soviet power. The goal of American policy, wrote Pipes, should not be coexistence, but rollback.[5]

The text of the document, since declassified, makes it quite clear what Reagan's goals were. "By identifying the promotion of evolutionary change within the Soviet Union itself as an objective of U.S. policy, the United States takes the long-term strategic offensive. This approach therefore contrasts with the essentially reactive and defensive strategy of containment, which concedes the initiative to the Soviet Union and its allies and surrogates," Pipes wrote.

The directive, signed by President Reagan, declared that when it came to economic policy, the goal should be "to avoid subsidizing the Soviet economy or unduly easing the burden of Soviet resource allocation decisions, so as not to dilute pressures for structural change in the Soviet system." On a political level, the document made it U.S. policy to advocate dramatic change in the Soviet system. "U.S. policy toward the Soviet Union must have an ideological thrust which clearly demonstrates the superiority of U.S. and Western values of individual dignity and freedom, a free press, free trade unions, free enterprise, and political democracy over the repressive character of Soviet communism. We should state openly our belief that people in communist countries have the right to democratic systems."

Reagan did indeed make rollback a central component of his policy. In the Top Secret National Security Decision Directive (NSDD)-32, signed on May 20, 1982, Reagan laid out a series of objectives related to his global strategy. These objectives included "to contain and reverse the expansion" of Soviet power; to "weaken the Soviet alliance system by forcing the USSR to bear the brunt of its economic shortcomings, and to encourage long-term liberalizing and nationalist tendencies within the Soviet Union and allied countries." No American administration had ever pledged to go so far in seeking to undermine the Soviet system. If Washington stuck to this policy, Reagan declared in the directive, it "could result in a fundamentally different East-West relationship by the end of the decade."[6] Reagan's secretive directive concerning Soviet policy

(NSDD-75) laid out the same policy goals as did the Pentagon's top secret Five Year Planning Directive.

The Reagan strategy toward the Soviet Union rested on three important components. First, there was the effort to reverse Soviet influence and power around the world. The Soviet Union had established a large collection of client states around the world by 1980, including Ethiopia, Nicaragua, Cuba, Vietnam, and Angola—often by supporting insurgents who seized power. Reagan was determined to reverse this process by using the same approach: backing anticommunist insurgents against communist regimes. By the end of his first term, communist regimes in Central America, Africa, and Asia were under assault. In Afghanistan, where President Jimmy Carter had established an embryonic program to support Afghanistan insurgents in early 1980, Reagan dramatically increased the amount of aid. The goal of American policy also changed. The Carter administration had authorized aid to the Afghan resistance with the goal being the "harassment" of Soviet forces. NSDD-66 made it American policy to seek a complete Soviet retreat from Afghanistan.

This strategy of supporting anticommunist insurgents, dubbed the Reagan Doctrine, was relatively inexpensive for the United States, but it was costly to the Kremlin, a reality that did not go unnoticed in Moscow. "The USA skillfully exploits the fact that in 'low-intensity conflicts' it is much cheaper to support guerrillas than the government," lamented two Soviet officials.[7] The CIA estimated that although the United States was spending $1 billion a year to support anticommunist insurgents, the Kremlin, with a much weaker economy, was spending $8 billion annually on counterinsurgency operations.[8] This successful application of force also produced a ripple effect by making other Soviet clients uneasy. Cuba, anxious about American military maneuvers and contras in Nicaragua, demanded increased military aid. The Kremlin, which had sent $3 billion to Havana between 1974 and 1983, was forced to cough up $7 billion from 1983 to 1987 to calm a nervous ally. No doubt this was a strain for the Kremlin, which had hard currency earnings of approximately $35 billion at the time.[9]

Efforts at curtailing or reducing Soviet power also included less lethal methods. In Eastern Europe, particularly Poland, the Reagan administration developed clever, cost-effective methods to help undermine Soviet power including channeling cash, printing presses, computers, and radio equipment to underground groups. The government-funded National Endowment for Democracy provided support for dissidents in every Eastern European country.

In Poland, Reagan saw a tremendous opportunity to change the status quo ante. The rise of the Solidarity movement in Poland posed a grave threat to

Soviet dominance over Central Europe. The heavy-handed Polish government declared martial law in December 1981 in an attempt to destroy the movement that Reagan was determined to help. "We can't let this revolution against Communism fail without offering a hand," he wrote in his diary shortly after the declaration of martial law in December 1981. "We may never have an opportunity like this in our lifetime." At a meeting of the North Atlantic Congress (NAC), including NATO member countries, the administration successfully lobbied allies to make the loosening of Soviet control a Western objective. "What is at stake in Poland is freedom," declared the official NAC statement. "We in the west have a responsibility not only to preserve our own freedom but to nurture it where it does not exist."[10] To advance that objective, Reagan imposed economic sanctions, upgraded radio broadcasts being beamed behind the Iron Curtain, and provided material assistance covertly to the Polish underground.

Parallel to this geographically based offensive, the Reagan administration embarked on an ideological offensive as Pipes had suggested. Reagan's first term in office saw the greatest programming expansion and radio modernization in the history of international broadcasting. Both Radio Free Europe/Radio Liberty and Voice of America received hundreds of millions of dollars in new resources. In places such as Poland and Czechoslovakia, a high percentage of adults would tune in on a regular basis, and dissidents in Russia such as Anatoly Marchenko and Ludmilla Alexeyeva credit the broadcasts with encouraging resistance to the Soviet regime. Alexeyeva, a veteran Soviet dissident and cofounder of the Moscow Helsinki Watch Committee, saw the radios as spawning a much larger movement inside the Soviet Union. "While our own authorities ignored our calls to dialogue and reform, the West wanted to know all about us.... Without foreign broadcasts, neither the human rights movement nor the religious rebirth in our country would have been possible on anything like the scale which they have attained."[11]

The radio broadcasts had the effect of "broadening the circle" of Polish citizens willing to collaborate with the underground, warned Polish internal security.[12] Colonel Henryk Piecuch, a senior official in the Polish Interior Ministry, saw the transformation in Polish society before his eyes as the radio broadcasts became more pronounced. "Under its influence people simply stopped being afraid, and this is always the beginning of the end of all sorts of tyrannies," he told me in written correspondence. "There wasn't a single coordinating meeting of the special services [secret police] of the Soviet bloc which did not include consideration of matters relating to the radios."[13] KGB agent Oleg Tumanov says that the Kremlin feared these broadcasts "more than any other American weapon."[14]

Reagan personally participated in this ideological offensive with great effect. Past American presidents had condemned Soviet behavior; but Reagan questioned the legitimacy of the Soviet system itself. In a series of speeches early in his administration, Reagan declared that communism had completely failed. "The West will not contain communism, it will transcend communism," he said in one speech at Notre Dame University. "We will not bother to renounce it, we'll dismiss it as a sad, bizarre chapter in human history whose last pages are even now being written." On other occasions he declared it an "evil empire." He also went on Radio Free Europe/Radio Liberty and in an interview declared that it was his hope to "show the captive nations that resisting totalitarianism is possible." No American president had ever uttered such words.[15]

Historians should not underestimate the impact of these powerful words. One of Reagan's good friends, the Associated Press reporter and editor John Koehler, was behind the Iron Curtain when Reagan delivered his speech about communism ending up on the "ash heap" of history. "By coincidence," he wrote the president, "I was in Prague on the day you made your speech at Notre Dame, and within hours, word had gotten around on your statements about communism and there were expressions of glee and I detected some hope over your remarks that it [communism] was a passing phenomenon."[16]

When Reagan delivered his famous "evil empire" speech in 1983, he evoked a similar reaction among political dissidents. Then Soviet political prisoner Natan Sharansky credits the speech with emboldening and encouraging him and his fellow political prisoners to resist the system even further.[17]

Along with rollback and the ideological offensive, Reagan engaged in a fierce economic war against the Kremlin. This was essentially a squeeze play: compel the Kremlin to spend precious assets it did not have by ramping up the arms competition, while at the same time restricting access to western inputs, including technology, currency, and credits. Reagan ramped up the arms race, authorizing the production of 3000 new combat aircraft, 3700 strategic missiles, and 10,000 new tanks during his first term in office. He was well aware that by doing this, he was intensifying an arms competition that the Kremlin could not win. "They cannot vastly increase their military productivity because they've already got their people on a starvation diet," he told one reporter in 1981. With the new American build-up, he said, "they can't keep up."[18]

Reagan's ballistic missile defense program, both mocked and praised by comparison with the blockbuster movie "Star Wars," only added to the pressure. The Strategic Defense Initiative (SDI) was a multibillion dollar research and development program to explore the possibility of creating systems that could intercept ballistic missiles before they hit their target. Although many in the West were skeptical that such a system could work, Kremlin leaders took it very seriously. "For the first weeks that announcement seemed a little bit fantastic," recalled Aleksandr Bessmertnykh, who was working in the foreign ministry when Reagan publicly announced his plans in 1983, and later became Soviet Foreign Minister. "But then it started to come to the minds of the leaders that there might be something very, very dangerous in that."[19] The Soviet intelligence community and military brass shared that concern. General Vladimir Slipchenko, who served on the General Staff of the Soviet Armed Forces, recalled that the SDI put the military "in a state of fear and shock because we understood that this could be realistic due to the economic and financial capabilities of the United States."

Compounding their concerns was their understanding that because of the struggling Soviet economy, the Kremlin "was not ready or prepared to respond adequately," recalls Bessmertnykh.[20] KGB General Sergei Kondrashey remembers that the SDI "influenced the situation in the country to such an extent that it made a necessity of seeking an understanding with the West very acute."[21]

The squeeze play worked: Moscow was determined not to fall behind the West militarily. In late 1981, in response to the Reagan budget, the Politburo approved a 45 percent increase in military expenditures over the next 5 years. It was a massive shift in resources that would weigh heavily on the already weak civilian economy. Two years later, after the SDI announcement, the Politburo would increase military spending another 10 percent. Meanwhile, the production of civilian machinery was frozen at the 1980 level for the next 5 years due to a lack of resources. As a result, consumption by the civilian economy would drop to less than 45 percent of the Gross National Product.

Trying to match the Reagan buildup staggered the Soviet economy. By 1982, according to former Soviet Prime Minister Ryzkhov, civilian consumption stopped rising for the first time since World War II. It was at this point, says Ryzkhov, that the Soviet economic downward slide began.[22]

Reagan and his cabinet were well aware that the military build-up would further strain the Soviet economy, forcing leaders to "confront increasingly difficult economic choices," as one National Intelligence Estimate put it. Slowdowns in the economy would become necessary. "Cutbacks in consumer goods and services could have two unpalatable consequences: a worsening of already poor prospects for improving labor productivity and an increase in worker discontent."[23]

The economic squeeze came from another direction. Western inputs—trade, bank loans, and the theft of western technologies—which had always been so helpful in aiding the poor economy, were also strategically reduced. Early in the Reagan administration, Moscow was expecting a natural gas pipeline running from Soviet production fields to Western Europe to yield a bonanza of perhaps $8 billion a year in hard currency. But pressure from the Reagan administration lead European leaders to dramatically scale the pipeline back. Bank loans were curtailed, and the export of technology items to the Soviet bloc declined substantially. The list of restricted technologies that could not be exported increased dramatically by several hundred items. But perhaps even more importantly, neutral countries such as Austria and Sweden, which had for decades served as transshipment points for technologies going to the Soviet bloc, agreed to limit high-tech exports. The Kremlin became so frustrated that it even went so far as to register a formal complaint against the Reagan administration with the General Agreement on Tariffs and Trade (GATT). If Reagan's efforts continued, the Soviets complained, the wheel would soon be a restricted export. All of this amounted to an additional burden on an economy with hard currency earnings of just $32 billion a year.[24]

By the mid-1980s the aging Soviet leadership faced a critical decision: How would they confront the Reagan challenge? The great debate came to a head in early 1985 when General Secretary Konstantin Chernenko died. Hard-liners and reformers quickly formed up sides to decide on a new leader. In the end it was the leaders of the institutions most concerned about the Reagan challenge, the foreign ministry, the KGB, and the military—who swung the balance of support behind Mikhail Gorbachev, a young and reform-minded party leader. "International circumstances" was cited by these institutions as a major reason for their choice of a reformist path. Gorbachev, in a very real sense, owed his ascendance as General Secretary to the pressures Reagan was exerting on the Soviet system. Georgy Shaknazarov, one of Gorbachev's foreign policy advisers, said that Gorbachev's selection was a result of "internal domestic pressures and Reagan's rigid position and that of his administration." The simple fact was that the Soviet Union was "falling behind" the United States and reform offered the only opportunity to catch up.[25]

Prior to the Reagan presidency, especially since the Nixon presidency, the United States had generally sought accommodation with Moscow. Détente and cooperation had in a very direct way strengthened the hand of Soviet hard-liners. Economic reforms, making difficult choices about military spending, and fundamental structural changes to Soviet society simply did not need to be considered because Moscow could remain competitive with the West. Hence, during the era of détente, Soviet hard-liners were on the ascent. But the Reagan challenge, which called into question their military status and demonstrated in glaring terms Soviet economic deficiencies, forced the Kremlin to consider radical structural change.

Typically, for the times, Reagan's success in pressuring Moscow did not necessarily translate into popularity at home or abroad. Reagan endured intense criticism in the media, among academics, and from liberals and Democrats for being too hard on the Soviet Union. His SDI "Star Wars" program was mocked and his "Evil Empire" speech was condemned for being too aggressive and endangering world peace.

Liberals whipped themselves into a panic, convinced that Reagan's anti-communism would trigger a nuclear war. A vocal No-Nukes movement fed off this fear, resulting in a rally against nuclear proliferation that drew as many as 750,000 people to New York's Central Park in 1982. A year later, the made for TV movie "The Day After" captivated Americans' attention in its graphic depiction of what would happen if nuclear missiles fell on the American heartland.

Reagan's credibility with these critics was so low that even when he introduced sweeping disarmament proposals at the Reykjavik summit in 1986, many left-leaning experts dismissed him. These academics and diplomats were so comfortable with the idea of MAD, mutually assured destruction, that Reagan's outrage at such a potentially destructive standoff terrified them. Many mocked Reagan as stupid for not understanding their sophisticated balance of power, when, in fact, Reagan on principle felt this kind of standoff was itself immoral and unstable.

Whereas in the United States, the rejuvenated conservatives somewhat balanced out these harsh critics from the left, in Europe, the denunciations were far more ubiquitous and vociferous. Even though many Europeans had dismissed Jimmy Carter as too willing to appease the Soviets, Europeans denounced Reagan as a warmonger and a dangerous cowboy. This constant attack on Reagan's political smarts and peaceful intentions made the eventual fall of the Soviets, and Reagan's triumph, all the more surprising for so many.

Unfortunately, the further away from anticommunism and the Soviet orbit Reagan wandered, the weaker his foreign policy was. One of his great successes—again despite harsh condemnation—was his consistent support for the "Contra" anticommunist insurgency in Nicaragua and the anticommunist government in El Salvador. In both Central American countries, the results in the long term were two relatively stable democracies and a defeat for Soviet-supported Marxist-Leninists. In South Africa, however, Reagan's anticommunism blinded him to the abuses of the racist Apartheid regime and, in the rest of Africa, the lack of a serious communist threat in most countries meant that Reagan was mostly disinterested.

Reagan experienced his greatest failures in the Middle East. His decision to deploy marines in Lebanon after the Israeli-Lebanon war of 1982 ended disastrously. In October 1983, Hezbollah-backed terrorists triggered a truck bomb that nearly leveled the barracks in which marines were sleeping, murdering 241 American soldiers. Despite Reagan's blustery rhetoric, he soon ordered the marines to retreat from Beirut and the deaths went unavenged.

Reagan's lack of clarity about the Middle East combined with his boldness in fighting communism also produced the great debacle known as the Iran-Contra scandal of 1986 and 1987. Reagan tried freeing American hostages held in Beirut by using a back channel to Iranians who were supposedly moderate. The arms sales these Iranians demanded did not free the hostages but did generate secret profits that were then funneled to Nicaraguan Contras, to contravene congressional restrictions on American funding for the contras. When word of this scheme was leaked—from the Middle East, of course—Reagan appeared to contradict his asserted policies by negotiating with terrorists. He seemed weak for failing to free the hostages or woo Iran and he seemed dishonest for funding the Contras surreptitiously. The resulting rounds of investigations and revelations derailed Reagan's second term. Moreover, the broader demonstration of American impotence in the Middle East throughout the 1980s emboldened the Islamic terrorists in targeting Americans and, ultimately, America itself. Considering all these troubles, the progress with Gorbachev and the Soviets actually helped redeem Reagan's second term—and his historical legacy.

No one factor can be singled out as the cause of the Soviet demise. The communist system was inefficient, unpopular, and bankrupt. However, those factors were always present in the Soviet Union; they do not fully explain why the Soviet edifice collapsed when it did. Mikhail Gorbachev chose in the end not to use violence to hold the empire in place. But Reagan's radical (and highly controversial) policies played a central role in the Soviet collapse. Like a heavy pile of snow weighing heavily on an old and shaky structure, Reagan provided the weight necessary to cause the collapse.

Much as Reagan put his faith in the free market and free trade to strengthen the American economy, Reagan saw freedom as a powerful tool and ally in international affairs. But Reagan was no pure idealist in its application. He distinguished between totalitarian regimes that restricted almost all freedoms from authoritarian regimes that simply restricted political freedoms. So while Nicaragua would receive criticism for its repressive actions, an ally such as the dictator Ferdinand Marcos in the Philippines could expect no similar treatment. In foreign affairs Reagan was a realist who believed he needed to act in the fundamental interests of the United States. But he was also an idealist who believed in the power of ideas and individuals. As in domestic affairs, Reagan, the conservative, was in the true sense of the term quite a revolutionary.

NOTES

1. For more on the perpetual crisis of the Soviet economy, see Gordon M. Hahn, "An Autopsy of the Soviet Economy: Soviet Documents Now in the Hoover Archives Reveal Seventy Years of Economic Bungling," *Hoover Digest* no. 4, 1998: 174–77.

2. Robert Dallek, *Ronald Reagan: The Politics of Symbolism* (Cambridge, Mass.: Harvard University Press, 1999), p. x.

3. Quoted in Lawrence Kaplan, "We're All Cold Warriors Now," *Wall Street Journal*, January 18, 2000, and Dallek, *Ronald Reagan: The Politics of Symbolism*, p. xviii.

4. I explore this in depth in Peter Schweizer, *Reagan's War: The Epic Story of His Forty Year Struggle and Final Triumph Over Communism* (Doubleday, 2002). See also Kiron K. Skinner, Annelise Anderson, and Martin Anderson, eds., *Reagan In His Own Hand: The Writings of Ronald Reagan That Reveal His Revolutionary Vision for America* (Free Press, 2001), and his early speeches reprinted in Davis Houck, ed., *Actor, Ideologue, Politician: The Public Speeches of Ronald Reagan* (Greenwood Press, 1993), and Ronald Reagan, *The Creative Society: Some Comments on Problems Facing America* (Devin-Adair, 1968).

5. "Response to NSSD 11–82: U.S. Relations with the USSR," National Security Council, December 6, 1982, pp. 1–43.

6. "U.S. National Security Strategy," National Security Decision Directive 32, May 20, 1982.

7. Alexei Izyumov and Andrei Kortunov, "The Soviet Union in a Changing world," *International Affairs (Moscow)* no. 8 (August 1988): 52.

8. William J. Casey, "Collapse of the Marxist Model: America's New Calling." Speech to the Union League Club, New York, January 9, 1985.

9. "Costs of Soviet Support to Cuba," State Department Briefing Paper, p. 1.

10. Quoted in Schweizer, *Reagan's War*, pp. 166, 169.

11. Ludmilla Alexeyeva and Paul Goldberg, *The Thaw Generation: Coming of Age in the Post-Stalin Era* (Boston: Little, Brown, and Co., 1990), pp. 181–82.

12. Quoted in Schweizer, *Reagan's War*, p. 198.

13. Colonel Henryk Piecuch, correspondence with the author.

14. Oleg Tumanov, *Confessions of a KGB Agent* (Chicago: Edition Q, 1993), pp. 66–95.

15. "Reagan Lashes Communism," *Washington Post*, June 15, 1985.

16. Koehler's letter of June 1, 1981 to Reagan. Obtained from Mr. Koehler.

17. Natan Sharansky, "Afraid of the Truth," *Washington Post*, October 12, 2000.

18. "Interview with the President," October 16, 1981. Presidential Documents, vol. 17 (October 26, 1981), pp. 1160–61.

19. Comments in William Wohlforth, ed., *Witnesses to the End of the Cold War* (Baltimore: Johns Hopkins University Press, 1986), p. 33.

20. Comments are from "Understanding the End of the Cold War, 1980–1987: An Oral History Conference," Brown University, May 7–10, 1998.

21. "Messengers from Moscow," A Barraclough Casey Production in association with Thirteen/WNET and PACEM Productions, Inc. for the British Broadcasting Corporation. Post-Production Script, 1994, pp. 34–35.

22. Ryzkhov's statement is from Izvestiya, June 8, 1989. For Soviet military budget increases see Army General V.N. Lobov, "Voennaya reforma: istoricheskie predposylki I osno-vonye napravleniya," *Voenno-Istorischeskii Zhurna*, no. 11 (1991): 3; Marshal Ogarkov's comment in Izvestiya, May 9, 1983 and the General Staff statement in *Pravda*, March 9, 1985.

23. "Soviet Potential to Respond to US Strategic Force Improvements, and Foreign Reactions," SNIE 11–4/2–81.

24. Foreign Broadcast International Service (USSR International Affairs, United States and Canada), December 26, 1985, p. A4.

25. Georgy Shakhazarov, comments in "Understanding the End of the Cold War," p. 27.

Chapter 10

WHERE IS GRACELAND? 1980S POP CULTURE THROUGH MUSIC

Steve Greenberg

In the fall of 1979 the disco boom, which had dominated the pop music landscape over the previous three years, ended abruptly. That summer, in Chicago, a radio Disco Jockey named Steve Dahl led an antidisco rally at Comiskey Park between games of a White Sox double-header. A box overflowing with fan's disco records was detonated in the outfield as the overwhelmingly white male crowd shouted "Disco sucks." Racial and homophobic epithets were thrown into the mix, reflecting disdain for disco's roots in the black and gay communities. The ensuing riot forced the White Sox to forfeit the second game of the double-header.[1]

Coming the same month as President Carter's "malaise" speech, in which the Chief Executive mostly blamed the nation's economic woes on the public's bad attitude, the rally further indicated that there was a deep dissatisfaction in the land. For what really occurred at Comiskey Park was a public lynching, a backlash against the perceived dominance of black and gay culture in white America. White men were demanding a return to cultural preeminence. That yearned-for resurgence of white rock hegemony would arrive, but like all movements based on a return to the past, it would not last.

The backlash would, however, help shape the decade to come. With the demise of disco, the story of eighties music would begin. As in the rest of America, it would be a story of patriotic resurgence and occasional racial progress, of growing prosperity and greater addiction to technology, of continuing rebellion and bursts of anxiety about modern America's morality and destiny.

For disco, the end came quickly thereafter, as the cry of the "Disco sucks" forces reverberated. The same week as the rally, "Good Times" by Chic debuted in the Top 10. No one knew it at the time, but it would be the last hit of the disco era. And a fitting close it was. Against icy percussion and an unforgettable bass line, Chic's female vocalists sang "These are the good times," in an emotionally drained fashion that let listeners know those heady, hedonistic days actually were ending. "Time marches on/It's getting late/You silly fools/ You can't change your fate," they prophesized. Journalist Dave Marsh has noted that "Good Times" captured "the heady disintegrating atmosphere of...the late 70's, as both local and national government abandoned any hope of social equity and opened the door for the ruthless laissez-faire heyday of upper and lower-class criminality that characterized the 80's."[2]

When "Good Times" entered the Top 10 on July 21, 1979, the top six records in the country were all disco records. By the time it fell out of the Top 10 on September 22, there were none.[3] Disco was declared dead; white kids, the media reported in relieved, even celebratory tones, were dancing to rock and roll again. A new wave rock record called "My Sharona" by the Knack replaced "Good Times" at number one and stayed there until October. "Good Times" fell out of the Top 40 later that same month, coinciding with the release of the very first rap record, "Rappers' Delight," by the Sugarhill Gang, which used Chic's bass line as its instrumental underpinning. The glossy fantasy world of disco was being replaced by a harsher street cousin.

Within a month, two events signaled that the seventies party was over in the world at large as well. November saw both the abduction of American hostages in Iran and Ronald Reagan announcing his candidacy for the presidency. The eighties had been jump-started a bit early; the civil rights movement had run out of steam, and powerlessness, retrenchment, and xenophobia were in the air.

Whether by sheer coincidence or communal instinct, that same month witnessed the chart debut of "Coward of the County," a country song by Kenny Rogers, which audiences immediately heard as a parable for America's perceived paralysis and the country's need to reassert itself in order to regain the world's respect. The song tells of young Tommy, whose father taught him to avoid trouble. But when the "Gatling Boys" rape his darling Becky, Tommy takes his revenge, releasing twenty years of bottled up anger. "Papa, I sure hope you understand," the song ends. "Sometimes you gotta fight when you're a man." Simultaneously, back-pedaling Top 40 programmers began shying away from all records by black artists, trying to stay as far from the disco tag as possible.

Adding to this mix, a seismic technological shift occurred on the pop radio dial: The immediate postdisco era saw a rise in "specialized formats" on the FM dial, which in 1979 supplanted mass-audience AM Top 40 radio as the prime source of radio music. At the end of the seventies, 50.1 percent of radio listeners were tuned to FM, ending AM's historical dominance and hastening the demise of the mass-audience Top 40 stations that had dominated the radio ratings since the 1950s. By 1982, FM commanded 70 percent of the audience—and among the twelve- to twenty-four-year-old demographic group, it was 84 percent.

Consequently, a mass pop music audience that crossed demographic lines could not be sustained. Instead of listening to stations that offered "the best of everything" as they had on AM, the abundance of choice on FM afforded listeners the luxury of hearing only the musical subgenre they liked, without having to wade through everything else. The result of this shift was that each audience segment had only limited exposure to the music played on the formats targeted to other audience groups. Billboard columnist Mike Harrison noted in 1981 that "No longer is there an exclusive Top 40 anything, but rather an ever-changing multitude of Top 40's, depending upon the genre one wants to research or focus on." He added: "Those who enjoy a-little-bit-of-this-and-a-little-bit-of-that...constitute a minority."[4]

Precision targeting of audiences meant that radio stations needed to avoid playing anything that fell outside their listeners' most narrowly defined tastes. Failure to do this would lead to listener "tune-out," the fatal turning of the dial. In the AM Top 40 days, listeners sat through records they may not have liked, suffering through "Hello Dolly," say, to get to the Beatles, because there was nowhere else to turn on the dial. On FM, greater choice meant greater choosiness. The fear of tune-out led many stations to turn to newly sophisticated forms of "passive research" to set their playlists. This telephone-based research determined which songs would make listeners least likely to turn to another station. It led to radio stations programming records that the least number of people actively disliked, rather than those that generated the most excitement. This ethos encouraged a certain bland quality on radio stations, as the new and exciting lost out to the tried-and-true.

With the last of the baby boomers coming into adulthood, radio stations had less incentive to cater to the rapidly shrinking demographic slice made up of teens—the group that usually drive innovation in the music marketplace. All together, these developments led to a period of doldrums and the rise of the so-called faceless bands of 1981, whose "musical wallpaper" symbolized the era. Styx, Journey, REO Speedwagon, and Foreigner were the most popular of these bands. They possessed little personality, projected almost no image, and offered bland adult rock with a similar sound—making them ideal for stations directed by passive telephone research.

Likewise, the period was marked by a continued rise of adult-oriented country music on pop radio, peaking with the "Urban Cowboy" fad of 1980–1981. This was yet another grown-up boomer rejection of the disco era. The film "Urban Cowboy" starred John Travolta, who just three years earlier had been the poster boy for white America's love affair with disco music as the star of "Saturday Night Fever." His perceived "conversion" seemed to represent the ultimate triumph of the antidisco ethos. Actually, the baby boomer move toward country signified that this generation was aging and would no longer be at the cutting edge of musical taste. Disco would prove to be the last mass musical revolution the baby boom audience triggered.

This overall situation led *Newsweek*, in April 1982, to state: "the Big Beat is sounding more and more like the muzak of 1984."[5] Increased fragmentation had drained much of the excitement from the pop scene, as there was no longer much cross-fertilization between musical styles. Especially hard hit was black music, which had been banished from most white-oriented radio stations after the fall of disco and the demise of Top 40 radio. Ghettoized on urban contemporary radio, black artists began to disappear from mainstream pop culture in the early years of the decade: in 1979, nearly half of the weekly Billboard Hot 100 pop chart could also be found on the urban contemporary chart. By 1982, that number was down almost 80 percent. By the fall of that year, the height of early-eighties musical fragmentation, not a single record by a black person could be found in the Top 20 on the albums chart or singles chart for three consecutive weeks—a phenomenon unseen since before the creation of Top 40 radio in the mid-1950s.[6]

In this environment, number one urban contemporary hits, such as Roger Troutman's "Heard It Through the Grapevine" or "Burn Rubber" by the Gap Band, failed to even crack the pop Top 40. Prince's "1999," which would later emerge as a pop culture anthem, flopped at Top 40 radio even as it soared up the urban chart. A black superstar like Rick James could sell over 4 million albums while remaining unknown to most listeners of white-oriented radio.

A seemingly impenetrable wall had been erected between the black listening audience and its white counterpart; for the most part, neither black kids nor white kids had any idea what the other was listening to. Consequently, the nascent rap movement, which by decade's end would reinvigorate American musical culture, was developing exclusively in front of a black audience, with most white American music fans barely aware of its existence.

The *Newsweek* article on rock's "doldrums" ended with nostalgia. In the "good old days," Elvis Presley and the Beatles created excitement by providing an identifiable center to the pop music world, recording music that the various segments of the pop music audience could all share. According to *Newsweek*, Elvis and the Beatles were "Phenomena produced by a nation responding in unison to the sounds on every Top 40 radio station." The magazine went on to predict that "In today's fragmented music marketplace, no rock star can hope to have that kind of impact."[7]

Within a year, *Newsweek*'s prediction would prove spectacularly wrong, as a star appeared on the scene with unprecedented impact on the various fragments making up the marketplace. What enabled Michael Jackson to become such a dominant figure, and what eroded the lines of demarcation, reuniting the various segments of the pop audience, was the emergence of the decade's most important pop culture innovation: MTV.

The growing popularity of cable television in the early 1980s was the technological development that made MTV possible. With dozens of underdeveloped channels on the cable dial, Warner-Amex Satellite Entertainment, an adjunct to one of the nation's largest cable providers, decided to create a twenty-four-hour channel for young people that would play music videos in rotation, much as radio stations played a rotation of hit records. MTV was launched in August 1981; at its inception it reached only 8 million homes, mostly in small towns and suburbs. But its impact was immediate and dramatic: In markets in which MTV was available, music industry insiders were astonished that records featured on their playlist began to pick up sales without any radio airplay.[8]

Why did MTV choose to play videos of songs that were not on the radio, rather than concentrating on the biggest pop hits? Quite simply, music videos for most of the American hit records of the day did not exist. Desperate to fill a round-the-clock schedule with videos, MTV's initial playlists were full of clips by British New Wave acts unfamiliar to American radio audiences. British videos were easy to come by since they had been a staple of UK pop music TV programs such as "Top of the Pops" since the mid-seventies. And so, seemingly out of nowhere, British groups such as Soft Cell and the Human League were "moving units" in places such as Tulsa and Columbus, and fans were calling their local radio stations to request their records.[9]

Famously, the very first clip played by MTV was a British hit called "Video Killed the Radio Star" by the Buggles. Although this choice accurately foretold the decline of radio's dominance as pop's gate-keeper—to be replaced by MTV itself—it also suggested an important generational shift that MTV was about to impose on the pop music world. The record itself was a synth-pop ditty of the sort that was quite popular among British teens and preteens; in fact, it had climbed all the way to number one on the British charts. But it had been shut out of American radio, which was still chasing the aging boomers with a classic rock sound.

Synth-pop, as its name suggests, was music made almost entirely using synthesizers, which had only recently become affordable to aspiring musicians. The music sounded intentionally artificial—the synthesizers were not used to imitate acoustic instruments—and the rhythms had a mechanized feel. It was music perfectly attuned to the emerging tastes of a generation that was spending an increasing percentage of its leisure time playing electronic video arcade games, such as Asteroids and Pac-Man.

Measured against MTV's playlist, the fare being offered on American "pop" radio stations—Christopher Cross, Eddie Rabbit—began to seem very tired, indeed. Britain was still experiencing the aesthetic fallout of the punk/new wave revolution, which had never gained traction in the American mainstream. Now it was serving up artists who were younger, flashier, and more innovative than their "faceless" U.S. counterparts. MTV's embrace of this aesthetic was an implicit announcement that the baby boomers' demographic reign was nearing its end, at least as far as music was concerned.[10]

The first real breakout celebrities to emerge from MTV belonged to the English band Duran Duran. Their video for the song "Girls on Film" was produced the same month that MTV made its U.S. debut, but it was made with the British market in mind—no one in the band imagined that there would be an outlet for it stateside. The video, which featured topless women mud wrestling, was banned by the BBC. In Britain, this was a time-honored means of creating a sensation. MTV, however, simply edited out the most offensive scenes and played "Girls on Film" in heavy rotation. It became the first "must-see" music video. That fall, the band toured America to sell-out crowds. But U.S. radio would not come to the party. When asked why his station was not playing the song, the music director of Washington, D.C.'s top-rated pop station (which favored the music of Jackson Browne, Linda Ronstadt, and other over-thirty rockers) responded, "Are you kidding? I hear one of them has green hair!" Bob Dylan's famous 1960s line, "Something's happening and you don't know what it is, do you, Mr. Jones?" was being played out once again, but this time with the boomers themselves in the role of the clueless Mr. Jones.

MTV's true impact was not fully felt until the channel made its debut in the New York and Los Angeles areas in September 1982. Suddenly, what was a whispered rumor wafting in from the heartland became a resounding thunder-clap rousing the cultural agenda setters in the nation's twin media capitals. A plethora of print and television news articles appeared, declaring the dawn of the video era. British new wave acts crashed their way onto the national charts in a seemingly endless succession—Adam and the Ants, Culture Club, Flock of Seagulls, Haircut 100, Duran Duran, etc. American pop radio, which had resisted this assault for a year, finally gave up in response to listener demand. And American record labels scrambled to find younger, hipper acts of their own that would look good in videos.

MTV's early embrace of British new wave was matched by its unstated closed-door policy toward black music. Launched at the height of radio playlist segregation, the channel at first could not fathom its largely white audience wanting to hear black records, with which they were unfamiliar. The previously mentioned nadir of a black presence on the pop sales charts in fact coincides precisely with the launch of MTV in New York and Los Angeles—a moment that saw black music entirely shut out on both pop radio *and* the nation's only important music video channel.

Enter Michael Jackson. By the time his album "Thriller" was released in 1982, Michael Jackson had been a top recording star for over a dozen years. But his most recent album, the mega-hit "Off the Wall," had been released in 1979, before the wall separating black and white music on the radio arose. Executives at CBS records, Jackson's label, knew there were no black records in the pop Top 20 the week they sent the debut single from "Thriller" to radio in October 1982. Faced with the very real possibility that Jackson's record would fail to become exposed to a crossover radio audience, the record company took no chances. That first single, "The Girl Is Mine," was a gentle duet with the ex-Beatle Paul McCartney, who was still a pop radio mainstay in the early eighties. McCartney's presence ensured the song's acceptance at white radio. And, noticing that MTV did not play videos by black artists, CBS simply did not make one for Jackson's single.

On the strength of the number two pop chart peak of "The Girl Is Mine," Jackson's "Thriller" LP became a certified retail hit that Christmas. As 1983 began, the label prepared its campaign for the album's second single, the more "urban" sounding "Billie Jean." The strategy of opening with the McCartney duet paid off, as pop radio started to play this follow-up song as well. But with MTV the rage of the music world that winter, there was no way Jackson could occupy the central spot in a multiformat pop culture without its support.

CBS gambled and filmed expensive videos for both "Billie Jean" and the next single, "Beat It"—videos that were a joy to behold. Jackson was a natural video star, his era's premiere song and dance man. The two videos introduced a standard of choreography previously unseen in music videos, arguably surpassing even James Brown's 1960s live work, until then the gold standard against whom all rhythm and blues dancers were judged.

As a visual art form, music video is naturally suited to choreography. Yet with the exception of middle-aged Toni Basil's "Mickey" clip from the previous fall, there really had not been any accomplished dancing featured on MTV. This was largely due to the fact that the music business had not in recent years nurtured artists who could dance—even the stars of disco music were not consummate dancers themselves. All that would soon change, with Madonna, Michael's sister Janet Jackson, and Paula Abdul, among others. But in the meantime, Michael Jackson had the MTV dance floor to himself.

Despite the obvious quality of the Jackson videos, MTV initially resisted playing them. Wielding its muscle, CBS threatened to withhold all its artists' videos unless the channel featured Jackson. As it turned out, MTV's capitulation to this threat was the thing that put both Michael Jackson and MTV itself over the top. Featuring Jackson's videos widened the video-clip channel's appeal as much as airplay on MTV widened the appeal of Michael Jackson. "Billie Jean" spent seven weeks at number one, followed by three weeks at the summit for "Beat It." The album went on to become the best selling record of all time, moving more than 40 million units over the course of two years. It spent thirty-seven weeks at number one, spawned seven hit singles, and won eight Grammys. The thirteen-minute video of the title track became the best selling music videocassette of all time.[11] And lest there be any doubt that this album truly did unify all corners of the pop audience, it won the hipper-than-thou *Village Voice* critics' poll for album of the year in addition to all the relevant Grammy awards.

For MTV's part, breaking Michael Jackson's "Thriller" on such a grand scale offered proof of the channel's new status as the most powerful single force in pop music as well as in all of youth culture. By 1984 MTV was reaching 1.2 percent of the daily total television audience and more than a quarter of daily teen viewers. Children of the eighties would henceforth be known as "the MTV Generation."

As the channel opened itself up to more videos by other black artists, it single-handedly forced pop radio to reintroduce black music into its mix: after all, MTV viewers, now accustomed to seeing black artists and white artists on the same video channel, came to expect the same mix of music on pop radio. It was impossible to keep the various fragments of the audience isolated from one another. Top 40 radio itself made a big comeback due to this seismic shift. Beginning in January 1983 in Philadelphia, and rapidly spreading through the country, one or more FM stations in every city switched to Top 40 and many rose to the top of the ratings playing the mix of music made popular by MTV—young rock and urban hits.

In this environment, black music made a resounding comeback on the pop charts. If 1982 was the genre's low point in terms of pop success, by 1985 more than one-third of all the hits on the Billboard Hot 100 were of urban radio origin. Even Prince's "1999" single, shut out of pop radio upon its initial release in 1982, was relaunched in mid-1983 and off the back of its MTV exposure became a huge pop radio success the second time around. Thus, in a way few historians appreciate, MTV proved itself a remarkably progressive force, helping to reintegrate a fragmented popular culture at the dawn of the Reagan era.

Conversely, the rise of MTV spelled doom for country music's fortunes in the pop world. Prior to MTV, country music had, since the early seventies, become increasingly strong at pop radio, with its popularity culminating in the summer of 1981, during the "Urban Cowboy" craze, just as MTV was being launched. That summer, there were an average of 11 country records on the Billboard Hot 100 in any given week—an all-time high, reflecting the shifting tastes of the now adult boomers.[12] But MTV decided from day one that country music would not be part of its programming—the look of country videos was deemed incompatible with the rest of the channel's youthful fare. Country's performance on pop radio steadily nosedived from that point onward. As MTV solidified its status as arbiter of "what's in," country music found itself standing outside the mainstream. Since the dawn of Top 40 radio, there had always been a country presence on the pop playlist. After MTV emerged, that ceased to be the case, and soon country records were completely shut out of the Hot 100. The old adage "out of sight out of mind" proved true, and it took country music a decade to once again find a mainstream audience—as the baby boomers reached middle age.

MTV had, for the time being, cured rock's doldrums. According to Rick Sklar, the legendary AM Top 40 programming wizard of the 1960s and 1970s, "Video is helping to make music once again a vital part of the culture."[13] Robert Chistgau, the dean of rock critics, proclaimed in the *Village Voice* that 1984 was the greatest year for pop singles since the height of Beatlemania, crediting MTV and the resultant revival of Top 40 radio for this development.[14] The profile of pop music had been raised higher than it had ever been due to its presence on television. Record company profits rose to new heights; the press and advertisers showed vastly increased interest in the music; even Hollywood came calling, with everyone trying to grab a piece of what MTV had created.

Pop performers immediately grasped the reality that they now had to appear in videos to be considered part of the mainstream. Bruce Springsteen, who had staunchly vowed he would not make videos, finally succumbed in 1984. Springsteen realized that spurning videos would relegate him to the fringes of the pop world. What he got as a result was the phenomenal success of "Born in the USA," which catapulted him from the status of mere rock superstar to the top of the pop culture pantheon. This level of popularity had its price; inevitably, the nuances of Springsteen's politically charged lyrics were lost when adopted by such a large mass audience. "Born in the USA's" scathing criticism of America was taken as a celebration of patriotism, annoying the artist so much he took Republican political candidates to task for coopting his song in their Reagan-era campaigns. Still, Bruce Springsteen, after more than a decade of record making, saw his popularity sent into the stratosphere by MTV, just like Michael Jackson.

With pop stars now doubling as TV stars, it was time for some serious muscle flexing. In November 1984, a group of top British pop stars joined together to record "Do They Know It's Christmas," a charity single to aid African famine victims. The video for this record, featuring members of U2, Wham, Culture Club, the Police, Duran Duran, and many other leading British performers all singing in unison, was an unprecedented collaboration—and it was compelling viewing. It became the biggest selling single ever in England and a major hit in the United States.

In response, Michael Jackson and Lionel Richie brought together an even more impressive grouping of American artists to record their African charity single "We Are the World." This video made its debut in March 1985 on network television, but it required multiple viewings on MTV to identify all the superstars in the room: in addition to Jackson and Richie, the video included performances by Springsteen, Ray Charles, Bob Dylan, Willie Nelson, Billy Joel, Paul Simon, Tina Turner, Stevie Wonder, and almost all of the other top stars of the day. Pop, rock, urban—even country music was represented, uniting the music world on record and underlining the shared experience of the music audience in the MTV era.

The stars of "We Are the World" and those who joined together at the July 1985 Live Aid charity concerts held simultaneously in London and Philadelphia were the most familiar faces on the cultural scene. They derived their drawing power from the unprecedented combination of exposure on both MTV and radio and the collateral interest this exposure afforded them in the press. The concerts, broadcast live on television (MTV and broadcast TV) and radio, were seen by over one billion people worldwide. They became a giant coming out party for the MTV generation. It is doubtful whether a similar effort by the "faceless" pop stars of four years earlier could have aroused the support of all corners of American society the way Live Aid's stars did. Due to television's magnifying power, pop stardom had simply become a bigger proposition—and it could strike an artist with unprecedented velocity. Members of the Irish rock band U2, merely cult favorites in the United States until that time, seized the Live Aid spotlight with their televised London performance to become "overnight" U.S. superstars, soon thereafter being dubbed "the band of the 80's" by *Rolling Stone* magazine.

Of the first generation of new stars to emerge as a result of the MTV/radio nexus, none shone brighter than Madonna. Using the visual element of music video in a remarkably sophisticated way, she projected multiple images, changing her look and music to remain provocative and fresh. Never hailed as a great vocalist, she was a top-flight dancer, the first woman to use dance as effectively as Michael Jackson had. Her sense of style—manipulating sexual imagery, melding it to the cultural zeitgeist—was unfailing. Madonna's entire career would have been unfathomable without the visual medium. Soon, a generation of teenage girls known as "Madonna Wannabees" arose, adopting her sartorial affect and taking to heart her message of female empowerment. For this, Madonna was condemned by church groups, accused of fostering a generation of "sluts." Once MTV solidified her standing as a star on the small screen, it was not long before she began to star in movies, making her omnipresent. She consistently used the visual medium to fuel controversy; her 1989 "Like a Prayer" video featured stigmata and burning crosses and was condemned as blasphemous by the Vatican.

Prince traveled much the same career trajectory as Madonna throughout the eighties: provocative music, arresting visual image, hit records, hit videos, films, controversy, and condemnation. In 1984, his "Purple Rain" was the number one film, single, and album in the country simultaneously, ultimately winning Grammys and an Oscar for "Best Song Score." But Prince's erotic lyrics eventually brought intense scrutiny from parents and illustrated the risks inherent in pop's newfound popularity. The lyrics of "Darling Nikki" triggered a political backlash: "I knew a girl named Nikki/I guess you could say she was a sex fiend/I met her in a hotel lobby/Masturbating with a magazine." Upon hearing her eight-year-old daughter listening to that song, Tipper Gore, the wife of then-Senator Al Gore, was moved to put together the Parents Music Resource Center, in tandem with Susan Baker, the wife of then-Treasury Secretary James A. Baker, III.

This alliance between Mrs. Gore, a Democrat, and Mrs. Baker, a Republican, proved potent. Along with the wives of fourteen other legislators, Mrs. Gore and Mrs. Baker sent a letter on May 31, 1985 to the head of the Recording Industry Association of America (RIAA) that demanded a record industry ratings code for music that "portrays explicit sex and violence and glorifies the use of drugs and alcohol." The record industry, anxious to maintain congressional support for a separate bill that would have levied a tax on blank recording tape, quickly agreed to put warning stickers on potentially offensive releases. But this was not enough for the Parents Music Resource Center (PMRC). The women demanded a standardized ratings system, with specific symbols to be used to identify profanity, violence, suicide, or sexually explicit lyrics, including "fornication, sado-masochism, incest, homosexuality, beastiality and necrophilia." Further ratings would identify albums that glorified drug and alcohol abuse or that featured lyrics about the occult. Record retailers responded to the call for ratings by voicing concern that such ratings would force them to stop selling questionable material, lest they lose their mall leases. The PMRC also asked that the RIAA "encourage record companies to reassess contracting artists who engage in violence, substance abuse and/or explicit sexual behavior in concerts where minors are admitted." Civil libertarians immediately accused the PMRC of calling for a blacklist. The PMRC crusade ignited a media firestorm, culminating in the Senate Commerce Committee.[15]

With five members of the committee married to women who had signed the PMRC letter, it should come as no surprise that the hearings came under attack for bias. Critics accused the senators of asking "sharp and nasty" questions of the witnesses from the music industry, who included the avant garde rocker Frank Zappa and Twisted Sister's Dee Snider, while being "unfailingly polite" to Mrs. Gore and "placing her group in the most favorable light."[16] Accusations that the hearings were a "show trial" had some basis in truth. In the final analysis, Zappa stole the show by facing down Senator Gore's questions with humor and conviction. "Taken as a whole," Zappa argued before the committee, "the complete list of PMRC demands reads like an instruction manual for some sinister kind of 'toilet training program' to housebreak all composers and performers because of the lyrics of a few. Ladies, how dare you?" He concluded his statement by cautioning the committee that "There's an awful lot of smoke pouring out of the legislative machinery used by the PMRC to inflate this issue. Try not to inhale it."[17]

The ratings system was never imposed legally, nor was it adopted by the industry voluntarily. However, the PMRC letter marked the beginning of an extended period during which the music industry understood itself to be under intense scrutiny, with calls for self-censorship coming regularly from parent and church groups. And those calls were often heeded: At first, heavy metal rock bands bore the brunt of the scrutiny. When religious groups complained about the cover artwork for Guns and Roses' album "Appetite for Destruction" (featuring a dagger-toothed monster and a robot rapist) some retailers refused to sell the album. The cover was changed to something less objectionable. Similarly, the rock group Bon Jovi's plans to feature women's breasts on the cover of their album "Slippery When Wet" were scuttled by their record company after the PMRC preemptively objected.

More importantly, the women of the PMRC were the spiritual foremothers to those forces that took a heightened interest in rap lyrics once hip hop music finally began to gain a white suburban audience—largely due to the debut of the television program "Yo! MTV Raps"—as the decade neared its end. The 1989 release of the rap group N.W.A.'s "Straight Outta Compton" album led to N.W.A.'s record label receiving a letter from the FBI criticizing their song "Fuck tha Police." When N.W.A. went on tour, they were dogged by a police fax campaign urging local police departments to make efforts to get their shows canceled.[18] As the 1990s dawned, some on the cultural right condemned all rap as "antisocial noise" and the calls for self-censorship rose to such a pitch that Time Warner divested itself of Interscope Records, distributor of the Death Row label that released much of the most popular "gangster rap" of the day.

But the calls to condemn rap could not slow the genre's rise to preeminence as the eighties closed. A decade of gestating in the underground, away from the pop spotlight, fighting off regular accusations that it was nothing more than a passing fad, had caused hip-hop to take hold in a lasting and organic way, and the nineties would in large part belong to rap. After mostly ignoring rap since its inception, MTV would ride the hip-hop bandwagon into the new millennium and beyond.

Rap's only competition in the next decade's early years came from another genre that spent the eighties fermenting in the underground: alternative rock—and its subgenre grunge rock. Unified by their collective debt to the unglamorous style and do-it-yourself ethos of seventies punk, alternative rock acolytes spent the eighties working to make their music take hold at a grassroots level on college radio, in fanzines, and in live venues. At the outset the genre offered fans a welcome relief from the image-driven "corporate rock" that came to be identified with MTV as the channel became more and more omnipotent. What had once seemed fresh now felt oppressive to those who wanted their pop culture raw, less Hollywood-beautiful, and messier.

In 1989, the tiny Sub-Pop label released the Seattle-based grunge rock band Nirvana's first album. Nirvana was a decidedly post–baby boom band; the leader, Kurt Cobain, was fourteen years old when MTV made its debut. By the release of the band's next album "Nevermind" in 1991, the band was poised to become the Next Big Thing, and the early nineties would in major part be dominated by Nirvana—christened by the media as "the flagship band of Generation X"—and its musical offspring. MTV embraced the band's dark, angst-ridden breakthrough single "Smells Like Teen Spirit" and its equally disorienting video. After all, Cobain, in spite of his own best efforts to the contrary, looked like a star and wrote terrific pop songs.

MTV was not only an invention of the 1980s—it helped define the decade. MTV helped shape the eighties sound, refine the eighties look, and trigger some quintessential eighties controversies. Due to MTV, American culture was glitzier, more visually oriented, more racially integrated, more technologically savvy, and more in synch with Reaganite prosperity, indulgence, and selfishness.

In the wake of rap and Nirvana, MTV simply discarded one pop aesthetic—the glitter of dance and metal, the laboratory sterility of synth-pop—and embraced another—the unvarnished "street" look, harsh lyrical perspective, and unpretty sonic landscapes that were the hallmarks of grunge and rap. It was this aesthetic that would mark the subsequent decade. By that point, MTV had become an institution unto itself: protean, ready to claim whatever came next as its own. In this fashion, it had figured out how to own the nineties as well.

NOTES

1. Bill Brewster and Frank Broughton, *Last Night a DJ Saved My Life: The History of the Disc Jockey* (New York: Grove Press, 1999), p. 269.

2. Dave Marsh, *The Heart of Rock and Soul: The 1001 Greatest Singles Ever Made* (New York: Plume, 1989), p. 52.

3. Joel Whitburn, *Billboard Top 10 Pop Singles, 1955–1988* (Menomonee Falls, WI: Record Research, 1988), pp. 386–89.

4. Mike Harrison, "In Search of the Disappearing Mass," *Billboard*, August 8, 1981, p. 25.

5. Jim Miller et al., "Is Rock On the Rocks?," *Newsweek*, April 19, 1982, pp. 104–7.

6. Steve Greenberg, "Broadcast Media and the Pop Music Audience," unpublished Masters thesis (Palo Alto: Stanford University Department of Communication, 1985).

7. Miller et al., p. 25.

8. John Sippel and Laura Foti, "Survey Finds MTV Strongly Affecting Record Sales," *Billboard*, September 11, 1982, p. 3.

9. Simon Reynolds, *Rip It Up and Start Again: Postpunk 1878–1984* (New York: Penguin Books, 2006), p. 338.

10. Jim Curtis, *Rock Eras: Interpretations of Music and Society 1954–1984* (Bowling Green, OH: Bowling Green State University Popular Press, 1987), p. 326.

11. Ian Ralfini, "The Care and Feeding of Video Music," *Billboard*, November 10, 1984, p. 10.

12. Greenberg.

13. Rick Sklar, personal interview, May 1, 1985.

14. Robert Christgau, "Village Voice Pazz and Jop Poll," *Village Voice*, February 12, 1985.

15. Danny Goldberg, *Dispatches from the Culture Wars: How the Left Lost Teen Spirit* (New York: Miramax Books, 2003), Chapter 5.

16. Dave Marsh, "Sympathy for the Devil," *Village Voice*, October 8, 1985, pp. 13–15.

17. Frank Zappa, "Statement to Congress, 19 September, 1985," in *The De Capo Book of Rock & Roll Writing*, Clinton Heylin, ed. (New York: De Capo, 2000), pp. 501–9.

18. Nelson George, "Buppies, B-Boys, Baps and Bohos," *Village Voice*, March 17, 1992, p. 40.

Chapter 11

THE PRIVATIZATION OF EVERYDAY LIFE: PUBLIC POLICY, PUBLIC SERVICES, AND PUBLIC SPACE IN THE 1980S

Bruce J. Schulman

In October 1981, President Ronald Reagan appeared before the National Assembly of Business at the Sheraton Washington Hotel. In his typically folksy style, Reagan saluted those better days before Big Government corrupted American life. He recalled a bygone era of volunteerism, when neighbor helped neighbor and neither besuited bureaucrats nor soul-sapping social workers intruded into the wholesome worlds of church, town, and family.

"What exactly is volunteerism?" Reagan asked. Predictably, he found the answer in Hollywood's golden age, citing Gary Cooper's classic role in "Mr. Deeds Goes to Town." "Americans have always extended their hands in gestures of assistance," Reagan explained. "They helped build a neighbor's barn when it burned down, and then formed a volunteer fire department so it wouldn't burn down again.... They took for granted that neighbor would care for neighbor."[1]

Reagan's homily by way of Frank Capra was no hollow, feel-good speech. He was not merely lauding the volunteer social work that his successor, George Bush, would dub the Thousand Points of Light. Reagan's nostalgic appeals blurred voluntarism and for-profit business. Invoking the nation's tradition of civic participation, he celebrated a realm of religious, fraternal, and associational connection superior to the state. But many of the voluntary associations in American history had been organized precisely to secure government assistance.[2] Reagan also ignored voluntarism's historic role as America's antidote to capitalist excess, with not-for-profit churches, clubs, and charities often arrayed against corporate power.

The president did not really want to restore the small town world America had lost. Reagan proposed to free business from government regulation, with business taking over the traditional functions of public life. The private sector, Reagan maintained, worked better than government, offering "creative, less expensive and more efficient alternatives to solving our social problems."[3] Private organizations such as the Boy Scouts could provide public services far more effectively than hated government agencies. As "an efficient, nongovernmental activity, scouting costs a total of only 187 million dollars a year," Reagan announced in 1982. But if it were government run, it would cost 30 times as much, more than five and a half billion dollars.[4]

The president's suggestive analogy possessed no meaningful policy implications. What did he mean by "if scouting were government run"? Where did he come up with the hypothetical costs for a mythical program? Still, on this matter and many others like it, only a few largely unheeded critics carped about the president's reasoning and data. The story's basic thrust confirmed a broader conviction that private institutions functioned better than public ones and that the private sphere was more responsive and more effective, fairer, and cheaper.

Reagan did not always practice what he preached. Still, his sermons helped build the case for privatization on the state and local level. With acts of omission as well as commission, his presidency influenced American attitudes about public and private life, eventually altering Americans' everyday lives.

To be precise, Reagan did not so much change the nation's mind as validate an ongoing trend in American life. During the 1980s, Americans increasingly deserted parks for private health clubs, abandoned town squares for shopping malls, enrolled their children in private schools, and moved into gated communities governed by neighborhood associations and policed by private security patrols. Ronald Reagan's speeches answered a nostalgic longing for the small town America of Frank Capra's movies, where neighbors gathered on the village green and boy met girl at the soda fountain on Main Street and where you trusted the corner storekeeper and suspected the Big Company trying to replace his shop with an impersonal department store. But Americans instead found themselves entering a brave new world in which the soda fountain had closed, gunfire echoed through the town square, and the big business wore the white hat.

"Do we really need to waste money on luxuries like parks, schools, and libraries?" one antitax activist in California demanded.[5] In the two decades after Ronald Reagan's inauguration, many Americans answered no. Corporations and private organizations gradually assumed control over many basic services, the spaces in which citizens congregated, and even the nation's hallowed instruments of self-rule.

THE EROSION OF PUBLIC SERVICES

The rich had always avoided the hurly burly of public life, sending their children to prep schools, lunching at their own clubs, and excluding "undesirables" from their golf courses and tennis courts. After 1980, this familiar secession of the rich spread downward. Aggrieved by the decay of public amenities, more and more Americans began buying their own—relying on corporations to supply the services, the gathering places, and the institutions that their towns, counties, and Washington had previously provided. Without a stake in public facilities, taxpayers increasingly resented government expenditures from which they perceived so little benefit.

Some withdrew from public parks and recreational facilities to repudiate racial desegregation. In Sumter County, Georgia, President Jimmy Carter's birthplace, white residents undermined the civil rights movement's long-delayed victories by largely abandoning town and county facilities. Whites "effectively ced[ed] pools, parks, and schools to the local African-American community,"[6] one Georgia historian concluded.

Parks and recreation facilities, the great jewels of American public life, decayed. By the 1980s, the long, slow decline of the nation's center cities had turned many of the nation's landmark urban parks into dens of crime, drugs, and violence. Meanwhile, the tax revolt and Reagan-era budget cutbacks strangled state park systems around the country. Gymnasiums and workshops closed. Shards of broken glass covered playgrounds. Pools remained closed because municipalities could not hire lifeguards. Communities reduced hours of operation at gyms, theaters, and senior centers.

Instead of patronizing public facilities, those with the means opted for private health clubs. To be sure, the fitness boom reflected broader concerns with wellness in 1980s America, but the almost complete privatization of recreational activity reflected the Reagan era's political imperatives. In the mid-1970s, just 2000 health clubs served the entire United States. By the end of the 1980s, 12,000 spas in suburban shopping centers and tony urban neighborhoods generated more than six billion dollars in annual revenues. As spa membership became a way of life for millions, this aerobics generation had little use for parks and playgrounds.[7]

Libraries also felt the wrath of tax rebels and the indifference of former patrons. Library lions had long guarded the American dream for thousands of poor citizens, especially immigrant children. During the 1980s, libraries suffered from the fiscal crises and budgetary cutbacks, closing branches and cutting hours.

Eventually, businesses stepped into the breech. A new breed of bookstore appeared in the late 1980s. These giant "superstores" carried nearly 100,000 titles, more than most community libraries. They allowed customers to browse the stacks, or to sit and read in comfortable chairs. Barnes and Noble Superstores and Border's Books filled many of the needs public libraries had previously served with organized readings, children's story hours, and book discussion groups. Still, the stores served suburban shopping centers and affluent urban neighborhoods; immigrant children in the 1980s rarely found their way inside a superstore.[8]

Few public amenities escaped the cycle of cutback, privatization, exclusion, and decay during the 1980s. After Proposition 2½ cut state property taxes, many Massachusetts communities required citizens to pay for their own snow removal and garbage collection. Wealthier neighborhoods generally acquired improved services for their outlays, whereas poorer communities cut other services to keep streets clean. Five Bay State communities simply turned off their streetlights,[9] while across the continent, San Francisco pioneered bum-proof benches for bus shelters—revolving slats just wide enough for a rider to sit on, but impossible to recline across. Most cities closed public restrooms, making certain areas less attractive to "undesirables" and assuming businesses would take up the slack.[10]

Visceral concerns about public safety underlay these decisions and accelerated middle-class flight from public facilities in general. One 1982 survey reported that 50 percent of all Americans feared leaving their homes at night. Parks, playgrounds, public rest rooms, and even libraries bristled with danger. The suburban crime rate also exploded in the 1970s and 1980s, jumping by nearly 300 percent.[11]

Not surprisingly, businesses, and those affluent neighborhoods that could, took policing into their own hands, fueling the burgeoning private security industry. These security forces aggrandized police power without public control or democratic accountability.[12] The privatization of policing became particularly apparent in the world of commerce. As businesses moved from main streets to shopping malls, the store security guard or mall patrol replaced the cop on the beat.

Privatizing basic services such as sanitation and policing eroded the very institutions of democratic self-government. Hard-pressed local governments cut budgets by "load shedding," contracting out basic services to private companies. Americans developed new instruments of self-rule: private governments controlling either suburban communities or special districts of major cities—private associations with all the power of duly elected governments, but fewer restraints and less democratic accountability.[13]

These private "shadow governments" emerged in "packaged communities," the gated utopias that arose on the fringes of metropolitan areas and often as retirement communities during the 1970s and 1980s. Private communities became the fastest growing residential neighborhoods in the United States. Millions of middle-class families, of nonretirement age, even in largely white, racially homogeneous areas of the country, opted for private government, schools, and police.[14]

"There is a new park, every blade of grass in shape—but for members only," the *New York Times* reported from Bear Creek, Washington, one of these "serene fortresses." Private guards manned the entrances around the clock, electronic monitors ensured that dogs never strayed onto a neighbor's lawn, and by-laws dictated house colors and shrubbery heights. The streets were private. The sewers were private. The subdivision arranged for itself "everything that local government used to do."[15]

The most common and most powerful governmental form such communities assumed was the residential community association—homeowners' organizations that residents joined automatically when they purchased a property. In 1970, 4000 community associations were scattered sparsely across the United States. By the mid-1990s, the Community Associations Institute counted more than 66,000 associations governing about 28 million Americans. These associations collected mandatory dues and promulgated rules for all homeowners in the community.[16]

Like regular governments, these associations possessed the power to tax, legislate, and coerce obedience (by repossessing the homes of scofflaws). But these quasi-governments were not simply the efficient, privatized identical twins of the towns and counties they superseded. Association managers rarely found themselves accountable to their "constituents" in a general election. Even those neighborhood organizations that voted regularly often apportioned ballots according to the value of the investment (one dollar, one vote) rather than the principle of one person, one vote. Constitutional limitations on governmental authority did not apply in these private bodies nor did many constitutional protections for individual residents. Homeowners Associations could regulate the color of members' houses, the plants in their gardens, and the furnishings in their living rooms.[17]

Shadow governments also appeared within the borders of the nation's cities. Emulating the burgeoning homeowners associations, merchants and bankers guilds created so-called business industrial districts (BIDs) and urban special service districts to wrest political and economic power away from city governments. Between 1975 and 1995 business groups established more than 1000 BIDs across the country. BIDs rebuilt sidewalks and rekindled broken streetlights; they also hired guards to move vagrants away from storefronts and ATM machines. These self-taxing private entities cleaned, policed, and refurbished their neighborhoods—supplanting municipal government in the process.[18] In Virginia, for example, the creation of a special business district around Dulles International Airport fast-tracked approval for new construction and stripped local citizens and their duly elected governments of the power to control development.[19]

NEW PLACES, NEW SPACES

The privatization of services contributed to the transformation of public spaces in which people could meet. As Americans left the streets behind and strolled instead through the overhead skyway or the upscale Galleria, actual physical contact between different types of people diminished—between people of different ethnic and racial backgrounds, different lifestyles, different tastes and values, and different economic status. Certainly, some citizens had never received warm welcomes in public places. But for more than half a century, Americans had shared a wide-open world of public amusements, a "magical corner of the city" in which solidarity reigned and "social distinctions faded." Diverse strangers had regularly rubbed shoulders in neighborhood ballparks, movie palaces, arcades, department stores, fair grounds, and amusement parks. Without that regular contact, critics feared, Americans' sense of togetherness, of shared national identity, would atrophy.[20]

To be sure, genuine problems animated the retreat from public places; racial tensions, crime, and urban decay all reduced the opportunities for casual mingling. But the disappearance of democratic public space never erased the national hunger for meeting places. Americans created, in the words of one architectural historian, "substitutes for streets, which are now so pervasively associated with danger and dirt." Yet these "nodes of concentration in a sprawl" could not recreate real public spaces. The nation's new semipublic gathering places accentuated the stratification and balkanization of American life.[21]

A stampede of commerce and culture out of American downtowns further drained the cities' nearly empty coffers. Movie theaters were boarded up or converted into porno grind houses. Corporate headquarters followed their workers and executives to the suburbs, sweeping the amenities of urban life out with them. Restaurants darkened, stores closed before nightfall, and pedestrians deserted once lively streets. In Milwaukee, one downtown merchant noted with amazement that even the taverns closed at dusk.[22]

Pundits began touting the suburban mall as the nation's new civic center, its new town squares; the mall seemed to be "replacing the old corner drugstore, the city park and Main Street as the core of community 'belonging' in America." Patrons told reporters that they looked increasingly to malls for noncommercial services, such as libraries, teen centers, and even churches. Many of the enclosed shopping centers responded, sponsoring beauty contests, fly-casting demonstrations, flower shows, and high school proms.[23]

Enclosed malls had flourished in the United States, slowly sprouting across the country in the three decades after the Midwestern developer Victor Gruen opened Southdale in Edina, Minnesota in 1956. By 1987, there were more malls in the United States than cities, four-year colleges, or secondary schools. These ubiquitous commercial and social centers dominated the American landscape, real and imagined. Films such as *Fast Times at Ridgemont High* (1982) depicted tony shopping palaces as the center of their characters' worlds—the site for love, loss, birth, death, triumph, and betrayal. In 1982, Southern California's mall culture spawned an entire new language when Moon Unit Zappa "totally" focused the nation's attention on the "Valley Girl, fer shure, fer shure."[24]

The mall industry reached its economic peak around 1980 when annual average sales approached $200 per square foot. In the 1980s developers responded to the more ferocious competitive environment by constructing megamalls, transforming shopping centers into "destinations, an idealized community fun." Shopping mall design had originally reflected the political and aesthetic values of suburban homes. Set amid mazes of parking lots in the middle of nowhere, malls withdrew from nearby streets just as suburban homeowners had traded the front stoops of the city for the private backyard.

During the 1980s, however, malls began to recreate the urban environments their patrons had left behind. They became entertainment centers with movie theaters, restaurants, video arcades, and skating rinks. Dentists moved their offices to malls. Senior citizens arrived early in the morning for organized mall walking groups. Car companies displayed new models. Museums and art galleries hung exhibitions.[25]

Americans, it seemed, had recreated the lost, decaying town squares and city plazas under the fluorescent lights of suburban malls. To be sure, these shopping centers had taken on many of the social tasks that streets, parks, and plazas fulfilled. But private, controlled malls could not be a substitute for genuine public spaces. Malls regulated not only the climate, but also the nature, appearance, and business practices of their tenants. Owners dictated the lettering on stores' signs, their hours of operation, and even the way they displayed their merchandise. No downtown shopping district maintained such rigorous control over the appearance, products, and procedures of its businesses.

Mall operators regulated common spaces even more strictly, fixing seating and traffic patterns and manipulating music and climate controls to encourage consumption and influence patrons' behavior. Private security forces removed vagrants, quieted boisterous teens, and harassed loiterers. In the early 1980s, the Centers Company, one of the largest managers of suburban malls, began arming their security guards.[26]

Malls thrived on exclusion. They offered not just physical safety, but cultural and social security, gathering places free of people from other racial and ethnic backgrounds. Most suburban malls served all-white clienteles; in areas in which a substantial black middle class emerged, such as suburban Prince Georges County outside of Washington, D.C., nearly all-black shopping centers such as the Landover Mall appeared.[27]

Malls also segregated by income and lifestyle. Unlike downtowns or city plazas, enclosed emporia guaranteed that their favored clientele would mix only with the right type of people. Even the megamalls, which served a wide variety of people, began carefully monitoring patronage and locating stores so as to segment areas of the mall by demographic groups.

Private ownership allowed rigid control of mall spaces and raised the issue of citizens' rights within the new agora. Not surprisingly, disputes about the status of shopping malls soon reached the courts. Were shopping centers public spaces or private property? Did the First Amendment apply? In 1980, the Supreme Court effectively turned the issue over to the state courts. In *PruneYard Shopping Center v. Robins*, the court decided that although the Constitution did not guarantee free speech in privately owned shopping centers, no matter how much they mimicked and supplanted the old downtowns, federal law did not prohibit individual states from protecting free speech in private places under their own constitutions.[28]

The *PruneYard* decision stimulated a round of state-level lawsuits across the nation throughout the decade. Connecticut upheld mall owners' property rights, authorizing them to ban pickets and leafleteers. New York, North Carolina, Michigan, Florida, and Maryland all followed suit. Pennsylvania, California, and New Jersey took the other side.[29] Malls failed as town centers; their owners feared that democratic debate was bad for business.[30]

At the end of the decade, a University of Connecticut sociologist published a study of shopping mall culture. "I expected to find the center for some kind of new community, particularly for suburbia, and a unique gathering place for people who live in the city" she told the *New York Times*. "But I found that the mall was not a community at all.... The issues that are part of our everyday community are not discussed there so it doesn't function as a community." Built along standardized models, malls stamped out local idiosyncrasies and regional diversity. People came together around the fountains and food courts, but interaction among them was truncated, rigidly demarcated, and regulated.[31]

THE ARCHITECTURE OF AVOIDANCE

Privatized public spaces burgeoned not only in suburbia. They spread across the country, coming to dominate even the life of the great cities. By the early 1980s, urban marketplaces such as Boston's Quincy Market and St. Louis's Union Station even rivaled the suburban mall as the nation's premier gathering place. Overbuilding, the exhaustion of prime locations, and the Reagan recession crippled suburban retailers during the early 1980s. At the same time, the 1979 oil crisis fueled a burst of new construction in the cities, as Americans wearied of long, expensive drives to fume-choked suburban parking lots. Vertical malls proliferated across the country. "City Sidewalks Move Indoors," the *New York Times* reported in 1983.[32]

But these vertical boulevards barely resembled the horizontal ones they supplanted. In some communities developers went so far as to create analogous cities, privatized avenues above or below the real streets. Minneapolis pioneered the skyway concept, a template followed in other cities, including Atlanta, Detroit, San Francisco, Charlotte, and Miami. As skyways lifted middle-class office workers and shoppers above the city, street conditions toughened. Even in Minneapolis, a racially homogeneous and politically liberal city, the skyways became a refuge from the street, an escape from its problems, and a curtain that hid unpleasant realties below.

In other places the shadow city produced an even starker form of segregation. Developments such as Charlotte's Overstreet Mall attracted middle-class whites within its elevated tubes, dramatically separating them from the mainly minority populations on the ground that several urban analysts decried the new downtown as a kind of spatial apartheid.

The privatization of everyday life depleted America's stock of responsive, democratic, meaningful public space, but never entirely erased the nation's desire to rediscover and resuscitate these.[33] The renewed popularity of farmer's markets and coffee houses, the attempts to design "pedestrian pockets" in suburbs and small towns, the efforts of advocacy groups such as New York's Project for Public Spaces to revive streets and public parks—all these attested to a continuing desire for public places to walk, talk, eat, drink, garden, exercise, and discover oneself or other people. But restoring public space required concerted government action and Reagan's America showed little stomach for such a venture. The nation lacked not only the fiscal and political will to rebuild its parks, streets, hospitals, and downtowns, but also the ideological conviction to attempt the job. The late 1970s and 1980s witnessed a renaissance of free market ideas, a shared sense that the private sphere worked better than the public sphere, that markets operated more fairly and efficiently than government, that the excesses of capitalism were to be applauded or chuckled about rather than checked, and that business deserved praise and encouragement rather than stern and wary monitoring.[34]

By the end of Reagan's presidency, serious criticism of business and skepticism about the beneficence of markets had all but vanished from the American political mainstream. In 1978, Milton Friedman had complained that "the market has no press agents who will trumpet its successes and gloss over its failures; the bureaucracy does." A decade later the private sphere could find dedicated publicists among progressive entrepreneurs and conservative ideologues, mall walkers, local governments, and health club members. The president decorated Milton Friedman with the nation's highest civilian honor; no one championed public servants now routinely regarded as feckless, detestable bureaucrats. The greatness of America, Ronald Reagan repeatedly asserted throughout his presidency, lay in its private and voluntary associations—its businesses, its churches, its clubs, and its families.[35]

The privatization of services and spaces, then, formed one component of a broader, more thoroughgoing shift in American public life. The contemporary United States did not echo Central Europe or eighteenth-century France: contrary to the arguments of President Reagan and numerous conservative intellectuals, the retreat of government did not open cultural space for voluntary civic participation.[36] In fact, recently minted voluntary organizations have been almost exclusively staff-led, professional lobbying outfits such as the American Association of Retired Persons. They have no local chapters and little grassroots participation; membership is simply a matter of paying dues, receiving a newsletter, and supporting the lobbying and organizing efforts of the professional staff.[37]

During the 1980s, President Reagan and his administration would preach privatization more than it practiced it, at least so far as the federal government was concerned. But the gospel of "a buck for business" to serve the nation's social needs spread far and wide, shaping the policies of towns and cities, the behavior of businesses and developers, and the expectations of ordinary citizens. Over the succeeding twenty-five years, privatization would transform American politics. As communities relied more and more on private firms to provide basic services and public amenities, Reagan's successors would advance privatization beyond the president's wildest dreams. In the twenty-first century, President George W. Bush would attempt to privatize Social Security, that most popular of New Deal era public programs that politicians in the 1980s thought the virtually untouchable "third rail of American politics." Reagan's once-controversial arguments about the superiority of the private sphere and the futility of public action had become an almost unchallenged assumption of American life.

NOTES

1. Ronald W. Reagan, "Remarks at the Annual Meeting of the National Alliance of Business," *Public Papers of the Presidents of the United States: Ronald Reagan*, October 5, 1981, p. 883.

2. Theda Skocpol, "The Tocqueville Problem." Presidential Address before the Annual Meeting of the Social Science History Association, New Orleans, LA, 12 Oct 1996.

3. Ibid., p. 882.

4. Ronald Reagan, "Remarks on Private Sector Initiatives," *Public Papers*, April 27, 1982, p. 522.

5. Quoted in David Koistenen, "Resentment Against Government and Taxes and the Rightward Shift in American Politics: The California Tax Revolt," unpublished ms. Koistenen, a Ph.D. candidate at Yale University has interviewed numerous grassroots antitax activists, collected the newsletters and correspondence of local tax revolt organizations, and scoured the records of politicians such as California Governor Edmund Brown, Jr. for constituent letters on the tax issue.

6. Pamela Tyler, "My Roots Are Showing: Southern Politics as Local History." Paper presented at the First Biennial Southern National Bank Conference on the History of the South, Rice University, Houston, Texas, February 27, 2005, p. 32.

7. U.S. Census Bureau, *Statistical Abstract of the United States, 1991*, p. 240. "The Not-So-Healthy Health-Spa Industry," *U.S. News & World Report*, November 7, 1983, pp. 60–62. Consella A. Lee, "Healthy Profits: Gym Chains Don't Sweat Recession as Working Out Becomes a Way of Life," *Los Angeles Times*, 16 October 1992, pp. D1, D4.

8. Lawrence Susskind, *Proposition 2 1/2* (Cambridge: Oegelschlager, Gunn & Hain, 1983), p. 406.

9. Susskind, *Proposition 2 1/2*, pp. 435–50.

10. Mike Davis, "Fortress Los Angeles," in Michael Sorkin, ed., *Variations on a Theme Park* (New York: Hill and Wang, 1992), pp. 161–63. See also Mike Davis, *City of Quartz* (New York: Verso, 1990).

11. For a vivid account of popular fears of park crime, see "Fear of Crime Is Changing How People Use Two Parks," *New York Times*, May 24, 1982. See also Dolores Hayden, *Redesigning the American Dream* (New York: W.W. Norton and Co, 1984), p. 215. William Severini Kowinski, *The Malling of America* (New York: William Morrow, 1985), p. 363.

12. Joel Garreau, *Edge City* (New York: Anchor Books, 1991), pp. 50–51.

13. William J. Mallett, "Private Government Formation in the DC Metropolitan Area," *Growth and Change* 24 (Summer 1993): 385–415. "Many Seek Security in Private Communities," *New York Times*, 3 September 1995, pp. 1, 22.

14. Many Seek Security in Private Communities," *New York Times*, 3 September 1995, p. 1.

15. Ibid.

16. Ibid., pp. 1, 22. U.S. Advisory Commission on Intergovernmental Relations, *Residential Community Associations: Private Governments in the Intergovernmental System* (Washington, D.C.: Advisory Commission on Intergovernmental Relations, 1989). Garreau, *Edge City*, p. 187. Mallett, "Private Government Formation." About 12 percent of the nation's households in 1989 fit into such categories. In booming suburban areas, such as Fairfax County Virginia around Washington's Dulles Airport, southern Florida, or Maricopa County, Arizona—the Greater Phoenix area, practically every home is part of such an association.

17. Ibid. Garreau, *Edge City*, pp. 184–87. Frug quoted on p. 185.

18. Thomas J. Lueck, "Business Districts Grow at Price of Accountability," *New York Times*, November 20, 1994, pp. 1, 46. Mallett, "Private Government Formation." Michael Sorkin, "Introduction," in Sorkin, ed., *Variations*, p. xiv.

19. Ibid. In Fairfax County, an antigrowth candidate won election as Chairman of the Board of Supervisors and attempted to downzone property along the Route 28 corridor near Dulles Airport and slow development. But the developers received relief in the law establishing the special district that freed them from such regulation.

20. On the shared world of public amusements in early twentieth-century America, see David Nasaw, *Going Out* (New York: Basic Books, 1993). The quotation is from p. 2.

21. Neil Harris, "Spaced-Out at the Shopping Center," *The New Republic*, December 13, 1975, pp. 23–26. See also Trevor Boddy, "Underground and Overhead: Building the Analogous City," in Sorkin, ed., *Variations*, p. 151.

22. Ibid. See also Andrew Malcolm, "Look at All These People, Milwaukee Says of $70 Million Downtown Mall," *New York Times*, October 1, 1982, p. 12.

23. *New York Times*, December 6, 1970. "How Shopping Malls Are Changing Life in US," *U.S. News & World Report*, June 18, 1973, pp. 43–46. Gary Breckenfield, " 'Downtown' Has Fled to the Suburbs," *Fortune*, October 1972, pp. 80–87, 156–62. For other commentaries on the mall as civic center in the early 1970s, see *Business Week*, November 10, 1973 and *New York Times*, February 7, 1971.

24. Frank Zappa and Moon Unit Zappa, "Valley Girl," Barking Pumpkin Records, 1982. Mary Corey and Victoria Westermark, *Fer Shurr! How to Be a Valley Girl—Totally!* (New York: Bantam, 1982). On Victor Gruen, see M. Jeffrey Hardwick, *Mall Maker* (Philadelphia: University of Pennsylvania Press, 2003).

25. Stoffel, Where America Goes." Karlen, "Mall That Ate Minnesota." Crawford, "World in a Mall," pp. 15–22. On dentists, see Dylan Landis, "Dentists Leave 'Elm Street' for Malls," *New York Times*, April 21, 1982, p. D4. On mall walkers, consult Olga Wickerhauser, "In Sweat Suits and Jogging Shoes, Walkers Are Taking to the Malls," *New York Times*, February 12, 1989, Sec. 12, p. 1. Jack Curry, "Mall Walkers Leave Shopping and the Weather Behind," *New York Times*, May 28, 1989, Sec. 22, p. 35. Joseph P. Kahn, "Going After the New Bottom Line," *Boston Globe*, November 15, 1994, pp. 69, 72. On auto shows, art, church, and travel, respectively, see "Detroit Hits the Road With New Shopping Mall Shows," *Business Week*, April 23, 1984, p. 47. Michael Cunningham, "Shopping-Mall Art," *Esquire*, November 1983, p. 222. Eric Hubler, "Four Million Square Feet of Mall, *New York Times*, October 25, 1992, p. 33. Lois Anne Naylor, "Mega Malls: Beyond Shopping," *Better Homes and Gardens*, November 1992, pp. 213–20.

26. Harris, "Spaced-Out at the Shopping Center," p. 26. Kowinski, *Malling*, pp. 55–56, 251–53.

27. Kowinski, *Malling*, pp. 158–60, 251–53.

28. Linda Greenhouse, "Petitioning Upheld at Shopping Malls," *New York Times*, June 10, 1980, pp. 1, B14. Margolick, "Mall Owners' Rights," *New York Times*, January 19, 1984, p. B2. Kowinski, *Malling*, pp. 355–56. Crawford, "The World in a Shopping Mall," pp. 22–23.

29. Robert Lindsey, "A Patchwork of Rulings on Free Speech at Malls," *New York Times*, February 10, 1986, p. A12.

30. Sam Roberts, "Now, Public Rights in Private Domains," *New York Times*, December 25, 1994, p. E3. On various decisions concerning free speech in malls, see *New York Times*, December 24, 1985, p. 16. David Margolick, "Albany High Court Lets Malls Restrict Leafletting," *New York Times*, December 20, 1985, p. 1. Laura Herbst, "Albany Ponders Free Speech in Malls," *New York Times*, June 19, 1988, pp. LL1, LL9.

31. Jacqueline Weaver, "Shopping Malls No Bargain, Study Finds," *New York Times*, April 22, 1990, Sec. 12 (Connecticut edition), p. 3.

32. Sam Roberts, "Vertical Malls: City Sidewalks Move Indoors," *New York Times*, June 8, 1983, Sec. 2, p. 1. On the effects of the gas shortage and economic recession on malls, see Pamela G. Hollie, "Mall Merchants Lose Sales to Local Streets," *New York Times*, July 6, 1979. "Melancholy Mall," *Time*, October 20, 1980. "Suburban Malls Go Downtown," *Business Week*, November 10, 1973, pp. 90–94. Howard Rudnitsky, "A Battle No Longer One-Sided," *Forbes*, September 17, 1979, pp. 129–35.

33. Carr et al., *Public Space*, pp. 7, 19–20, 130–31. Sandy Coleman, "Wanted: Ideas for City Hall Plaza," *Boston Globe*, September 25, 1994. Witold Rybczynski, "This old House," *The New Republic*, May 8, 1995, pp. 14–16. James H. Kunstler, *The Geography of Nowhere* (New York: Touchstone Books, 1993), pp. 260–61. Martin Gottlied, "One Who Would Like to See Most Architects Hit the Road," *New York Times*, March 28, 1993, p. E7.

34. Daniel Rodgers, "Vanishing Acts: Power and Society in American Social Thought in the 1980s." Paper presented before the Miller Center Program in American Political Development, Miller Center for public Affairs, University of Virginia, Charlottesville, Virginia, October 2004.

35. Milton Friedman, "Preface," in William Simon, *A Time for Truth*, p. xii. For a prominent example of this rhetoric, see Reagan's Address to the National Association of Evangelicals, Orlando, Florida, March 8, 1983.

36. Robert D. Putnam, "Bowling Alone: America's Declining Social Capital," *Journal of Democracy* 6 (January 1995): 65–78. Gerald Gamm and Robert D. Putnam, "Association-Building in America, 1850–1920." The November 1996 version of a paper originally presented at the 1996 Annual Meeting of the Social Science History Association, 10–13 Oct 1996, New Orleans, Louisiana (available through Ms. Louise Kennedy, J.F.K. School of Government, Harvard University). Skocpol, "The Tocqueville Problem."

37. Since World War II, six new voluntary associations have formed that have claimed national memberships equal to about 1 percent of the nation's population (a level of support that older organizations such as the Boy Scouts and Girl Scouts, the Teamsters, Steelworkers and UAW, the VFW, the WCTU, and Farmers Alliance have enjoyed). They are the American Baptist Women Ministries (1951), the American Association of Retired Persons (1958), the National Right to Life Committee (1973), Citizen Action (1979), Mothers Against Drunk Driving (1980), and (if its membership claims are credible) the Christian Coalition (1989). Nearly all of these groups have no local chapters or membership activities per se; membership is simply a matter of paying dues, receiving a newsletter, and supporting the lobbying/organizing efforts of a professional staff.

Chapter 12

REAGANIZING RELIGION: CHANGING POLITICAL AND CULTURAL NORMS AMONG EVANGELICALS IN RONALD REAGAN'S AMERICA

Lauren F. Winner

The 1980s saw the rise of the Religious Right—a movement within American Christianity that yoked together conservative theology with conservative politics, and that encouraged evangelical Christians to organize on behalf of a conservative social and political agenda. Evangelical Christians, who had for the fifty years largely eschewed involvement in politics, emerged by the early 1980s as a political force to be reckoned with. Their support for Ronald Reagan helped reshape American politics and culture—and their encounter with Reagan's America also reshaped, if more subtly, the culture and priorities of the evangelical church.

Who are evangelicals? Scholars of religion have sometimes found a three-part definition useful: an evangelical Christian is someone who identifies the Bible as the highest authority in life, and who may perhaps take the Bible seriously to the point of a literal interpretation; who practices a type of piety that privileges an intimate, "personal" relationship with Jesus; and who describes his or her religious autobiography in terms of a datable conversion experience, a particular moment at which she committed her life to Jesus and was "saved" or "born-again." (The term "born-again" comes from the Gospel of John, in which Jesus says, "I tell you the truth, no one can see the kingdom of God unless he is born again.")

In the nineteenth century, most Americans were Christians, and most Christians in America were, by default, evangelicals. Evangelicals participated in a host of social reform activities, embracing a varied slate of causes that don't fit neatly into today's categories of "left" or "right": prohibition, the campaign against dueling, and antiprostitution. Harriet Beecher Stowe, the abolitionist novelist whom President Lincoln would credit with starting the Civil War, was an evangelical Christian—as were the leading pro-slavery theorists of the antebellum South. William Jennings Bryan, one of America's most outspoken progressive politicians, took his marching orders from Scripture.

Throughout the 1800s, evangelicals felt at ease in American culture. But around the turn of the century, things began to change. Higher criticism of the Bible—a scholarly approach to reading Scripture, developed in Germany, that did not assume divine authorship—was gaining currency in the United States. A wave of immigration that began in the late nineteenth century brought to America's shores many immigrants with different religious commitments. American evangelicals were growing uncomfortable.

That discomfort crystallized in 1925, in a courtroom in tiny Dayton, Tennessee, where biology teacher John Scopes was tried for violating a recently passed state law that prohibited public school teachers from teaching Darwinism. Clarence Darrow, the provocative lawyer whose roster of clients included American Railway Union president Eugene V. Debs and the youthfully nihilistic murderers Nathan Leopold and Richard Loeb, came to Dayton to defend Scopes, and none other than an aging William Jennings Bryan took the case for the state. Though Scopes was found guilty in court (a decision ultimately overturned on a technicality), he won in the court of public opinion: the many journalists who flocked to Dayton to cover the trial derided the rural evangelical Christians who were so wedded to their literalistic account of Creation. H. L. Mencken, writing in the *Baltimore Sun*, mercilessly mocked the Christians he met in Dayton: "It may seem fabulous, but it is a sober fact that a sound Episcopalian or even a Northern Methodist would be regarded as virtually an atheist in Dayton.... To call a man a doubter in these parts is equal to accusing him of cannibalism.... people are simply unable to imagine a man who rejects the literal authority of the Bible. The most they can conjure up, straining until they are red in the face, is a man who is in error about the meaning of this or that text. Thus one accused of heresy among them is like one accused of boiling his grandmother to make soap in Maryland."[1] Two years later, Sinclair Lewis's novel *Elmer Gantry*, with its scathing portrait of the titular revivalist, echoed the theme: fundamentalists "saw that a proper school should teach nothing but bookkeeping, agriculture, geometry, dead languages made deader by leaving out all the amusing literature, and the Hebrew Bible as interpreted by men superbly trained to ignore contradictions."[2] Times had changed: American culture had grown more critical and intellectual, and evangelical Protestants had grown more entrenched, no longer interested in fighting battles for social reform, but instead devoting their energies to battles over biblical authority. Evangelicals no longer felt at home in American culture.

And so, in the 1920s, evangelicals withdrew from the larger currents of American society and created an elaborate subculture. Fearing that they would be tainted by participation in cultural institutions that were hostile to their version of Christianity, evangelicals constructed their own schools and colleges, summer camps, and publishing houses.[3] Even the architecture of the buildings evangelicals built in these years is revealing. Bob Jones University, for example, which moved from its Tennessee campus to a campus in Greenville, South Carolina, in the 1940s, looks like nothing so much as a fortress, with high walls and a coppice of even taller trees ringing the quad, keeping out the surrounding city.

If we can date evangelicals going underground to the 1925 Scopes trial, we can date their tentative reacquaintance with American culture to 1957, when Billy Graham, the young and beloved evangelist, preached a revival in New York City. Graham had his evangelical bona fides firmly in place: he was an ordained Southern Baptist preacher; he was a graduate of Wheaton College, evangelicalism's premier liberal arts college; he was married to the daughter of missionaries; and he believed unshakably in Scripture's authority. For Graham, New York City was more Gemorrah than Gotham, and he was going there to help save sinners from a life of temptation and decay, and an eternity in hell. And yet when Graham went to New York, he did not confine his meetings to evangelicals. Eager to ensure that the men and women converted at his revival would have churches to go to after the revivalists left town, Graham met with Christian ministers of all different stripes, including liberal Protestants, mainliners, and Catholics. Those ecumenical overtures may seem harmless today, but in 1957, after thirty years in which evangelicals kept to themselves and even derided other Christians as false prophets, Graham's partnering with nonevangelical Christians was scandalous: the likes of Bob Jones (of the eponymous aforementioned university) and John R. Rice (author of the 1941 screed *Bobbed Hair, Bossy Wives, and Women Preachers*) denounced Graham, who stood his ground, insisting that the "fighting, feuding and controversies among God's people...is a very poor example" and that "God has people in all his churches."[4] The fracas over Graham's New York revival exposed differences that had been threatening to fracture the evangelical movement for some time. Indeed, the stand-off between Jones and Graham is one way into the sometimes seemingly elusive distinction between evangelicals and fundamentalists. The latter, with

Jones, were somewhat more hostile to the surrounding culture, and remain in a modified version of the defensive retreat initiated after the Scopes trial. Today, fundamentalists tend to be more suspicious of interfaith conversations, more suspicious of movie theaters, and more suspicious of public schools. Evangelicals, on the other hand, followed Graham's lead in 1957, and began a sort of reentry into the surrounding culture, shedding some of their defenses and beginning to reintegrate into mainstream American society.

But there was a large gap between Graham's ecumenism and the 1950s politicking of the Religious Right. An enormous change occurred in the minds of conservative evangelicals between 1960 and 1980 about the propriety of political engagement. Consider Jerry Falwell. In the mid-1960s, Falwell denounced clergy and other religious figures who became involved in the Civil Rights movement: "Preachers are not called to be politicians, but soul-winners," he said.[5] Fifteen years later, Falwell founded the Moral Majority, an umbrella organization for conservative Christian political action committees, whose purpose, Falwell later explained, was "to give a voice to the millions of decent, law abiding, God-fearing Americans who want to do something about the moral decline of our country." It aimed to educate voters "regarding moral issues that affect our traditional family values" and "to influence Congress" to pass bills that coincided with those values and "to defeat any legislation that would further erode our constitutionally guaranteed freedoms."[6] In particular, the Moral Majority sought to organize voters around opposition to the Equal Rights Amendment (ERA) and gay rights, and "prolife, protraditional family, promoral...and pro-American, which means strong national defense and [backing] the State of Israel."[7] From denouncing all political engagement to sophisticated political organizing—what changed?

Several events in the 1970s helped politicize American evangelicalism.[8] Some were motivated by concern about public education. For example, in 1970, Alice Moore, a pastor's wife in Kanawha County, West Virginia, ran for a seat on her local school board because she was concerned about sex education. Four years later, Moore led a paralyzing public school boycott, aimed at keeping a "godless and un-American" language arts curriculum, which included *The Catcher in the Rye* and *Soul on Ice*, out of the classrooms.[9] Another radicalizing event was the 1977 "Save Our Children" crusade. This crusade, led by Anita Bryant, a Southern Baptist singer well known for her orange juice commercials, protested a local gay rights' ordinance in Dade County, Florida. Throughout the decade, evangelicals also made common cause with Catholics to protest *Roe v. Wade*, the 1973 Supreme Court decision guaranteeing women's right to abortion, and to defeat the proposed ERA. All of these issues had common themes: concerns about sexuality, about children, about gender roles, and about the family. Those themes would thread throughout the political and cultural concerns of the Religious Right throughout the 1980s and beyond. And in working to defeat the ERA and halt gay rights legislation, evangelicals used strategies that would be featured in their political strategies in the 1980s: direct mailing, fund-raising, and lobbying legislators.[10]

Another mark of the growing politicization of evangelicals was the 1976 election of a self-proclaimed born-again Christian to the White House. Many evangelicals embraced Jimmy Carter, the farmer from Plains, Georgia, who had had a dramatic conversion experience in 1966 and enjoyed teaching Sunday School at his Southern Baptist church. He was one of their own, and evangelical leaders urged their flocks to "get involved politically" and support Carter. Evangelical Christians who had for years "shun[ned] involvement in politics in an effort to remain 'pure'" were now taken to task for "handing over by default an important realm of life" to non-Christians. Carter seemed like an earnest and honest candidate, two qualities in short supply after Watergate.

Christian voters thought his "family life...exemplary," even noting that he seemed to have a closer relationship with his brother than had Ford and Nixon. Even before Ronald Reagan lost the Republican primary, Carter had the evangelical vote sewn up: "If Reagan wins the Republican nomination, he will siphon off conservative votes in the evangelical community that would otherwise go to Carter," predicted *Christianity Today*, American evangelicalism's flagship magazine, in June of 1976, but "Even so, the largest chunk of the evangelical vote should remain intact for Carter," who was evangelicals' preferred candidate because "Evangelicals and Carter speak the same born-again, Christ-is-my-Savior language."[11]

When Carter won a narrow victory over Gerald Ford, not all evangelicals were thrilled. As early as the summer of 1976, some were voicing the concerns that would culminate in evangelicals voting for Reagan in 1980. If Carter's religious idiom resonated, his political views did not. A Southern Baptist minister was concerned that Carter expressed "ambiguity on the issues."[12] Jerry Falwell, then known as host of the televised "Old-Time Gospel Hour Program," and W. A. Criswell, pastor of Dallas's First Baptist church (then the largest Southern Baptist Church in the nation, numbering 19,000 members) and an (ostensibly erstwhile) arch-segregationist, both criticized Carter for his much ballyhooed interview in *Playboy*. A Christian leader ought not to be airing his views in smutty magazines, Falwell and Criswell said.[13] Other Christians wondered why "so few of Carter's family or his closest aides share the vigor of his faith," and asked pointedly "Has he ever witnessed to them?"[14] (That is, has Carter ever sat his staff down, narrated his own conversion, and encouraged his staff to make a commitment to Jesus?) Notably, by 1978, the editors of *Christianity Today* were giving their features on Carter titles such as "Does Carter's Christianity Count?" The answer was maybe not.

When the time came to run for reelection, Carter was in trouble with evangelical voters.[15] In February 1980, Carter met for a grits and eggs breakfast with a dozen members of the National Religious Broadcasters—Jim Bakker was present, as were Tim LaHaye and Charles Stanley. They discussed the president's views on prayer in school and gender roles, and asked why Carter hadn't appointed more evangelicals to prominent positions in the government. Bakker and company were not satisfied with the president's answers. True to his Southern Baptist heritage—though the Southern Baptist Convention's current efforts belie their heritage, the Baptist faith has long-standing commitments to the separation of church and state—Carter was opposed to prayer in school. Nor did he support an antiabortion amendment to the Constitution. He "rejected the notion that the Equal Rights Amendment might harm the family."[16]

It is important to emphasize that American evangelicals were not in the 1980s—nor are they now—politically monolithic. If late twentieth century evangelicals were by definition theologically conservative, they were not all politically conservative. In 1973, at a conference at the evangelical school Calvin College, about forty evangelical leaders wrote and signed the Chicago Declaration of Evangelical Social Concern, which committed evangelicals to a program of antiracism and antisexism. Out of that 1973 meeting came the group Evangelicals for Social Action. In 1979, around the time that Jerry Falwell was founding the Moral Majority, leftist evangelicals such as Jim Wallis were organizing against the spread of nuclear weapons. But in the late 1970s, the politically conservative evangelicals had more money and a more wide-reaching presence on the airwaves than the progressives, and were ultimately able to organize more votes.

Enter Ronald Reagan, who became the favored candidate of those politically conservative evangelicals who felt dissatisfied with—even betrayed by— Carter. Reagan wasn't the first choice of the activists who would soon become known as the "religious right." They would have preferred former governor John Connally of Texas or Representative Philip Crane of Illinois. But as it became clear that neither Connally nor Crane were serious candidates, evangelicals latched onto Reagan. Falwell said the Moral Majority would do all in their power to get Reagan elected "even if he has the devil running with him."[17] Reagan didn't quite echo the "born-again, Christ-is-my-Savior language" that came so naturally to Carter. Indeed, the Great Communicator seemed to be intentionally avoiding commonplace evangelical formulations. In an interview with talk show host George Otis, Reagan's efforts to speak about his personal faith sounded somewhat mealy-mouthed: "I certainly know what the meaning of 'born again' is today among those who believe in that. I can't remember a time in my life when I didn't call upon God....In my own experience there came a time when there developed a new relationship with God and it grew out of need. So, yes, I have had an experience that could be described as 'born again.'" But the gifted orator did not falter when describing a socially conservative agenda that was music to the ears of politically conservative evangelicals: he wanted to lead a revolution against the "humanism and hedonism in the land," to "return to a belief in moral absolutes," and to challenge an interpretation of church–state separation that had led to God's being "expelled" from the schools.[18]

By 1980, Christians were no longer "divided over whether they should or should not be involved in political campaigns to begin with."[19] Now, politically conservative evangelicals were clear: they were to "refuse to opt out of the human race" by getting involved in the presidential race. They were to get "God's Kingdom into politics."[20] They were to "Work vigorously to expose amoral candidates and incumbents" and "Consider running for public office."[21] (Indeed, Protestant ministers ran for local office in record numbers.) Registering Christians to vote was now understood to be a "clear Christian duty."[22] During campaign season, evangelicals held a "Washington for Jesus" rally; 200,000 evangelicals came to the mall to pray against abortion, homosexuality, and other sins afflicting the Untied States. An evangelical group called the National Christian Action Coalition—a lobbying group founded originally to keep track of legislation pertaining to private Christian schools—compiled an index that assessed members of Congress's voting records on "family issues." The same organization produced a film that taught previously apolitical Christians how to vote and organize, and the National Christian Action Coalition's (NCAC's) head, Robert Billings, wrote a guide to organizing called *The Christian's Political Action Manual.*[23] Evangelicals in the 1980s did not shy away from the larger society—they wanted to transform it. (It is revealing that when Joel Belz founded his evangelical magazine in 1986, he chose a word that an earlier generation of evangelicals would have considered an epithet: *World.*)

Reagan tapped into evangelicals' new sense of their political power, asking evangelical audiences, "If *you* do not speak your mind and cast your ballots, then who will speak for the ideals we cherish?"[24] That question galvanized politically conservative evangelicals—some of them first-time voters—to support not only Reagan, but also to vote disproportionately for conservative Republican candidates for the Senate and House. Key issues for these newly politicized evangelicals were opposition to abortion, support of prayer in schools, and a general sense that government was too powerful. Sociologists Arthur H. Miller and Martin P. Wattenberg found that politically conservative evangelical activists were most successfully able to organize voters who espoused "social traditionalism, militant anticommunism, and economic libertarianism."[25]

The newly baptized Religious Right was initially thrilled with Reagan's victory. Some even spoke of his presidency in terms of divine appointment. Jerry Falwell, using language that recalls the biblical story of the men on the road to Emmaus who see the resurrected Jesus, left a 1980 meeting with Reagan "with a fire burning in my heart. In answer to prayer and hard work, God had given us a great leader."[26] On his television show, "The 700 Club," Pat Robertson spoke with Harald Bredesen, a member of the board of directors of Christian Broadcasting Network, about an encounter Bredesen had with Reagan during his campaign for governor of California in 1970.

> *ROBERTSON*: I understand after the discussion of Bible things [you] began to pray. Did you join hands, you and Pat Boone, George Otis and Ronald Reagan?
>
> *BREDESEN*: Yeah, that's right.... George had his left hand, I had his right hand and we prayed, and George led out in prayer and suddenly his prayer changed into prophecy. I'm sure you've seen this happen. And in it God was saying that if he would walk in His ways, He said, "I will put you in 1700 Pennsylvania Avenue," which is the address of the White House.
>
> *ROBERTSON*: Whoa! Wait! That's 1970 and George Otis, speaking in prophesy as unto the Lord said, "I will put you in 1700?" Whew! That's electrifying.
>
> *BREDESEN*: Well, I'll tell you—was *Reagan* electrified! I had his right hand and, Pat, it was wobbling like this. Honestly, I've never seen an arm so wave under the anointing of God!
>
> *ROBERTSON*: It's incredible!.... Somebody just said by the way...it's *1600* Pennsylvania Avenue. That was my fault. It's 1600...[27]

But this electoral victory was no time for evangelicals to rest on their laurels. The election proved to evangelicals that they not only had an opportunity but also a "responsibility" to shape the "destiny of [the] nation." "One grand splurge on a presidential race every four years is useless," intoned the editors of *Christianity Today* in a postelection op-ed. "Evangelicals must set themselves to a rigorous agenda for the next ten years."[28]

Those next ten years turned out not to be the decade the Religious Right had hoped—their actual political impact is difficult to assess. Political scientists concluded that the Religious Right actually had a fairly negligible impact on the 1980 presidential election. Their impact on Congress may have been more significant—George McGovern, Birch Bayh, and other Democratic senators that Christian right groups had targeted lost their seats. And four years later? Religious Right activism was successful in getting out Christian votes for Reagan, but some political scientists hypothesized that in the 1984 presidential election, the Christian right's politicizing helped the Democrats, because it inspired anti-Christian right voters to cast votes for Democratic candidate Walter Mondale. Again, the Religious Right had a clearer impact on state-wide races. In particular, they helped Jesse Helms, the ultraconservative senator from North Carolina, get reelected.[29]

In terms of actually getting their policies implemented, the Religious Right was not especially successful during the 1980s.[30] Religious conservatives were disappointed that the Reagan years did not result in a complete roll-back on abortion. Reagan did not defer to the Religious Right regarding Cabinet and judicial appointments. The Religious Right viewed the Supreme Court appointment of Sandra Day O'Connor, whom they deemed soft on abortion and whose support for the ERA they disdained, as something of a betrayal. Conservative activist Connie Marshner captured the feelings of many in the Religious Right: "With this nomination, the Administration effectively said, 'Good-bye, we don't need you.'" They were pleased with Reagan's selecting C. Everett Koop for surgeon general; Robert Billings, of the NCAC, served as undersecretary of education, but many had hoped he would land a more important post.[31]

Reagan knew he needed to keep the favor of the Religious Right and he sometimes threw them a rhetorical bone—announcing in his 1983 State of the Union address, for example, that he supported a constitutional amendment to protect prayer in schools. All in all, the Religious Right succeeded in getting some of their key social issues onto the Congressional agenda—abortion, school prayer, pornography—but they did not get much legislation that met their socially conservative agenda through Congress. Overall, the evangelical entry into politics had a clearer impact on the state and local level. Conservative Christians, for example, successfully lobbied for the passage of a home-schooling bill in Oregon in 1986; the Oregon House Education Committee chair said he had never been lobbied with such fervor on any issue before.[32] State supreme courts to whom socially conservative evangelicals had been appointed were more likely than other courts to hand down conservative rulings on pornography and gender discrimination cases.[33] Perhaps the most even-handed assessment of the actual impact of the Religious Right is that of political scientist Matthew C. Moen: the Religious Right was "effective in shaping the public and legislative agendas, and in checking some of the cultural trends of the previous decades; they were generally unsuccessful in enacting desired public policies." Even when it did not result in legislation, the lobbying of the Religious Right got otherwise dormant issues, such as tax credits to parents who sent their children to private schools, onto the congressional agenda. And the Religious Right, by garnering extensive coverage in newspapers and news magazines, brought these issues to the breakfast table of millions of American families. Thus, the Religious Right significantly reshaped public discourse during the 1980s.[34]

Assessing the political impact of the Religious Right is one way of thinking about the relationship between evangelicalism and American culture—but when trying to understand evangelicalism in the 1980s, another question presents itself, too: not how did the politically conservative activist evangelicals of the Religious Right shape American culture and politics during the 1980s, but how did larger cultural shifts during the same decade reshape, however subtly, evangelicalism? Yes, evangelicals—at least those on the Religious Right—wanted to remake America in their own image. But at the same time, pockets of evangelicalism were being subtly remade in the image of Ronald Reagan's America.

That evangelicalism changed in response to shifting cultural norms is no surprise, since evangelicalism has always adapted itself to the American landscape. Indeed, evangelicalism's long career in the American religious landscape was due in part to the fact that evangelicalism is tensile, always ready to bend and morph to fit new circumstances. In the Second Great Awakening of the early nineteenth century, for example, evangelicalism was transformed by its move from New England to the American South. Theretofore, northern evangelicals had denounced slavery—but evangelicalism's attitudes toward slavery changed when it began to gain converts south of the Mason-Dixon line, and within a few years a decidedly proslavery Gospel was heard on the tongues of southern evangelists.[35] In the early twentieth century, evangelicalism proved its adaptability through its ready embrace of technology—radio, television, whatever would help spread the word. So, even as evangelical politicking was motivated in part by a resistance to certain changes that were afoot in 1980s America—feminism, changing sexual mores, and the perceived liberalizing of public school curricula, to name just three—evangelicalism also absorbed some of the cultural traits of 1980s America.

For example, pockets of evangelicalism in the 1980s readily adapted to the larger culture's pursuit of wealth. Reagan's America was famously a culture in love with money and materialism—it was, in the words of Gil Troy, "the new Gilded Age, the Greed Decade," when Americans' "celebration of free enterprise" presided over a "mad rush toward materialism."[36] Evangelicals were not immune to this cultural shift. In the 1980s, preaching and teaching encouraged American evangelicals to think about their pocketbooks and bank accounts in providential terms. In October 1981, a Pentecostal pastor from Forth Worth, Texas, named Jerry Savelle, awoke early one morning to devote himself to a few hours of prayer before leading the East Coast Believers' Conference in Charlotte, North Carolina. "The Lord supernaturally appeared unto me in my motel room" Savelle explained later. "He had some vital things to share with me—vital, that is, for the whole body of Christ." God's message for Savelle was that "My people are in financial famine, and I'm giving you the assignment to go tell them how to get out." And so, taking as his key biblical text Proverbs 10:22—"The blessing of the Lord brings wealth, and he adds no trouble to it"— Savelle began to proclaim that "God's will is your prosperity."[37]

Savelle was just one of many preachers who, in the 1980s, began preaching the so-called Prosperity Gospel, or prosperity theology. This had its roots in nineteenth-century New Thought discourses about prosperity[38] and in early-twentieth-century Pentecostal revivals, which emphasized God's power to heal the halt and the lame. In Reagan's America, the message that God wanted to reward faithful people with monetary success gained new traction among a broader swath of evangelicals. *How God Taught Me About Prosperity* captures prosperity theology in its cover art: sitting atop an open Bible is a roomy suburban house, a swanky car, a stack of greenbacks and three stacks of coins, and, as a nod to more obviously biblical imagery, some fruit and sheaves of wheat. This is not a book about taking up one's Cross. It is a book that reconciled "the Greed Decade" with Scripture.[39] Pat Robertson gave voice to this in a 1983 interview with *Charisma* magazine. Explaining the fundraising strategies of his Christian Broadcasting Network, Robertson said: "We're putting into practice the Law of Reciprocity, which says if you give it will be given to you."[40] Jim Bakker famously urged his TV audience not to settle for Chevys—if they really wanted Cadillacs, they should pray for Cadillacs.[41] Perhaps the most influential prosperity gospeller was Kenneth Hagin, whose *How God Taught Me About Prosperity* was first originally published in 1985. After telling readers for 20 pages to simply "claim...what [you] need," the booklet ends with a decidedly Reagan-esque indictment: "[R]emember, it is not God withholding your needs and wants." This was Christian spirituality spiced with a diffuse cultural Reaganomics—if a person didn't have what he wanted, he had no one to blame but himself. Neither God, nor social structures, were to blame for your lack of wealth.

Another way in which 1980s evangelicalism bore the marks of the larger culture concerns divorce. If Reagan symbolized a desire for wealth, he also, personally and politically, suggested changing American standards and habits about divorce, changes to which evangelicalism accommodated itself during the 1980s. Evangelicals who had cooed over Carter's cozy relationship with his brother were hard pressed to find many warm and fuzzy things to say about the familial arrangements of Carter's successor. Reagan and his first wife, Jane Wyman, had divorced in 1948. In 1952, he remarried. Not too many years before Reagan rode into the White House, divorce and remarriage was enough to derail a candidacy, as Nelson Rockefeller could attest: Rockefeller's 1963 divorce squashed his hopes for the 1964 Republican nomination, for which he had once been thought a shoe-in.[42]

Reagan also helped usher in sweeping policy change about divorce. He signed California's no-fault divorce law on September 4, 1969, during his first term as governor. Leave it to the children to point out the sins of their father: none other than Reagan's son Michael wondered "And why did Ronald Reagan, the pro-family conservative, sign such a law? I believe that some of his reasons were personal. Notice that Dad signed the no-fault divorce law some twenty years after going through his own divorce. His wife, Jane Wyman, had divorced him on grounds of 'mental cruelty.' Even though listing grounds for divorce was largely a formality, those words were probably a bitter pill for him to swallow. He wanted to do something to make the divorce process less acrimonious, less contentious, and less expensive."[43]

Over thirty years later, socially conservative evangelicals would look back ruefully on this decision, with a tone of "forgive him father, he knows not what he does," and would in fact use Reagan's signing the no-fault divorce law in a campaign against gay marriage. Glenn T. Stanton, Director of Social Research and Cultural Affairs and Senior Analyst for Marriage and Sexuality at Focus on the Family (a Christian organization, founded by James Dobson, that aims to support "traditional" family life) made the connection when he explained that "The Gipper unwittingly tinkered with a fundamental part of marriage, launching a family revolution. This brings us to same-sex marriage. If the essential 'as long as we both shall live' quality of marriage becomes optional, why not the 'husband and wife' part? Tinkering with the fundamentals of marriage begets more tinkering with fundamentals."[44]

Reagan's divorce and remarriage posed something of a problem for his evangelical supporters. Through the 1970s, evangelicals pointed to divorce as one of America's most urgent problems. Combating divorce and rescuing the American family from collapse was part of the reason evangelicals were now supposed to roll up their sleeves and get involved in American politics. Evangelicals, after all, had always been clear about how to interpret the Bible's word on divorce: divorce is forbidden, except in cases of adultery. Evangelicals had historically read the New Testament as also prohibiting remarriage after divorce. And yet, the hero of the Moral Majority, the president who was going to restore America's "profamily" commitments, was a divorced, remarried man.

So it is perhaps no surprise that evangelical discourse on the questions of divorce and remarriage became more liberal during the Reagan years. Larry Richards's *A Healing Gift from God*, which aimed to read the Bible's verses about divorce and remarriage through the "theological concepts of sin, grace, and creation of man as a sexual being with companionship needs," was published in 1981. When one brought those concerns to bear on the question of divorce and remarriage, Richards argues, one landed in a somewhat more "compassionate" place: a recognition that while God has "commanded permanence" in marriage, "God, in his grace meets the [divorced] couple, forgives their sin, and permits them to try again through remarriage."[45] This marks, in essence, a shift in strategies for interpreting the Bible—rather than take Jesus' words in a narrow, literalistic sense, Richards was urging they be read against a broader biblical narrative of sin and redemption. By 2001, evangelical publishing houses could calmly publish books with titles such as *Saving Your Second Marriage Before It Starts*, a self-help book that urged readers to consider their motives for remarriage, cautioning them not to do so if their main motivation was warding off loneliness or shoring up their bank accounts. That *Saving Your Second Marriage Before It Starts* has nary a word to say about the New Testament's views on remarriage is striking; that the epigram with which chapter one opens is from Harry Emerson Fosdick, the liberal Presbyterian preacher who, for most of the twentieth century, was evangelicalism's favorite whipping boy, is astounding.[46]

Evangelicalism's accommodation to the shifts in American divorce law was, of course, subtle. There was not a wholesale rethinking of divorce and remarriage in all corners of evangelicalism, and certainly America's theologically conservative Protestant churches did not enthusiastically embrace divorce; many of those churches continue to criticize what they see as a larger cultural ethic that values self-actualization over commitment. But by the end of the Reagan years, combating divorce no longer occupied as central a role in evangelical politics and cultural engagement as it once had. Historian Randall Balmer has calibrated evangelicalism's waning interest in divorce by looking at *Christianity Today*, America's flagship evangelical magazine. Balmer found that in the 1970s, at least eight articles denouncing divorce ran in *Christianity Today*—but in the 1980s, they dropped off.

What replaced divorce as politically conservative evangelicals' key issue? Abortion. In the years just before and after the *Roe v. Wade* decision, evangelical sentiment about abortion was inconsistent (or, more charitably, nuanced). In 1971, the Southern Baptist Convention (SBC) passed a resolution calling for the SBC to "work for legislation that will allow the possibility of abortion under such conditions as rape, incest, clear evidence of severe fetal deformity, and carefully ascertained evidence of the likelihood of damage to the emotional, mental, and physical health of the mother." After the *Roe* decision, W. A. Criswell—the same Criswell who would later denounce Carter for talking to *Playboy*—said "I have always felt that it was only after a child was born and had a life separate from its mother that it became an individual person...and it has always, therefore, seemed to me that what is best for the mother and for the future should be allowed." During the late 1970s and 1980s, abortion gelled as a central plank of evangelical political life.[47]

When evangelicals did turn their attention to abortion, they took their cues from a seemingly unlikely source. In what is perhaps the consummate example of evangelicals' adapting to the idiom and strategy of their larger, surrounding culture, evangelical antiabortion activists learned how to do political action from the nonviolent protestors of the 1960s. As historian Grace Hale has shown, antiabortion activists borrowed the tactics of nonviolent resistance that had been articulated by Gandhi and Thoreau (and of course, before that, Jesus) and adapted to the cause of Civil Rights by Martin Luther King, Jr. Though many political progressives would vehemently disagree, Christian antiabortion activists saw themselves as the heirs of the Civil Rights movement. From the earliest days of the antiabortion movement, they self-consciously modeled their strategy on the Civil Rights activists. In the 1970s, antiabortion activist Charles Fager wrote a book about the march at Selma, urging antiabortion activists to learn from the movement, and in 1975, Catholic activist Burke Balch spent a day at the Library of Congress, reading up on Quaker nonviolent resistance. There he discovered *A Manual for Direct Action*, by peace and civil rights activists Martin Oppenheimer and George Lakey. The guide, which once influenced SNCC leaders, soon became the tactical Bible of Christian antiabortion activists. In 1988, Operation Rescue's founder Randall Terry, while sitting in an Atlanta jail, wrote a political treatise expressly modeled on King's "Letter from Birmingham Jail."[48]

Ever protean, evangelicalism had once again adapted itself to the mainstream American culture that it sought to transform.

NOTES

1. H. L. Mencken, "Mencken Likens Trial to a Religious Orgy, with Defendant a Beelzebub," *The Baltimore Evening Sun*, July 11, 1925.

2. Quoted in George Marsden, *Fundamentalism and American Culture*, 2nd ed. (New York: Oxford University Press, 2006), pp. 188–89.

3. Randal Balmer, *Mine Eyes Have Seen the Glory: A Journey into the Evangelical Subculture of America*, 4th ed. (New York: Oxford University Press, 2006), p. 132, passim. My periodization of twentieth-century American evangelical history relies on Balmer. See also Randall Balmer and Lauren F. Winner, *Protestantism in America* (New York: Columbia University Press, 2002), pp. 37–68.

4. William Martin, *A Prophet With Honor: The Billy Graham Story* (New York: William Morrow and Company, 1991), pp. 220–22.

5. Falwell quoted in Napp Nazworth, "Institutionalization of the Christian Right," Ph.D. dissertation, University of Florida, 2006, p. 53.

6. William R. Goodman, Jr., and James J. H. Price, *Jerry Falwell: An Unauthorized Profile* (Lynchburg, VA: Paris and Associates, 1981), p. 25. Moral Majority Report, May 1985, p. 23.

7. Susan Friend Harding, *The Book of Jerry Falwell: Fundamentalist Language and Politics* (Princeton: Princeton University Press, 2000), pp. 128–29. Joseph B. Tamney and Stephen D. Johnson, "The Moral Majority in Middletown," *Journal for the Scientific Study of Religion* 2, no. 2 (June 1983): 145.

8. Robert Wuthnow, "The Political Rebirth of American Evangelicals," in *The New Christian Right*, Robert C. Liebman and Robert Wuthnow, eds. (Hawthorne, NY: Aldine, 1983), pp. 168–87.

9. Ted Hartzell, Charleston, West Virginia, The Associated Press, March 22, 1979.

10. Another feature of the 1970s activism would reappear in the 1980s and beyond: the leadership of women (leadership that, in a context such as defeating the ERA, seems at first blush quite ironic). Although beyond the scope of this essay, it is worth noting that this strategy had roots in the nineteenth century, when many women turned their status as mothers into the justification for political activism on issues of special concern to women and children. Thus, it is neither surprising nor, in fact, ironic that politically and religiously conservative women would adopt similar strategies in the 1970s and 1980s.

11. Edward E. Plowman, "An Election Year to Remember," *Christianity Today* [hereafter cited as *CT*], May 7, 1976, p. 37. Wesley G. Pippert, "Viewing the Family from the Oval Office," *CT*, September 9, 1977, p. 60. Albert J. Menendez, "Will Evangelicals Swing the Election?," *CT*, June 18, 1976, pp. 32–33.

12. Edward W. Plowman, "Southern Baptists: Platform for Presidents," *CT*, July 16, 1976, p. 48.

13. "Crusade for the White House: Skirmishes in a 'Holy War,'" *CT*, November 19, 1976, pp. 48–49.

14. "Does Carter's Christianity Count," *CT*, November 3, 1978, p. 19.

15. See, e.g., Richard Viguerie, *The New Right: We're Ready to Lead* (Falls Church, Va.: The Viguerie Company, 1980), p. 156, passim.

16. Edward E. Plowman, "Carter's Presence Confirms Clout of Evangelical Broadcasters," *CT*, February 22, 1980, 48. Goodman and Price, *Jerry Falwell: An Unauthorized Profile, p.* 25. Moral Majority Report, May 1985, p. 23.

17. A. James Reichley, "Religion and the Future of American Politics," *Political Science Quarterly* 101, no. 1 (1986): 26.

18. "Reagan on God and Morality," *CT*, July 2, 1976, p. 39.

19. "Should Christians Vote for Christians?," *CT*, June 18, 1976, p. 20.

20. "Getting God's Kingdom into Politics," *CT*, September 19, 1980, pp. 10–11.

21. James Davison Hunter, *American Evangelicalism: Conservative Religion and the Quandary of Modernity* (New Brunswick, NJ: Rutgers University Press, 1983), p. 116.

22. "Just Because Reagan Has Won..." *CT*, December 12, 1980, p. 14.

23. Matthew C. Moen, *The Christian Right and Congress* (Tuscaloosa: The University of Alabama Press, 1989), pp. 79, 191, fn 29.

24. Reichley, p. 26.

25. In both the 1980 and 1984 elections, Reagan appealed to well-educated Christian voters, often younger voters who had not spent as many years in the isolating evangelical subculture. Arthur H. Miller and Martin P. Wattenberg, "Politics from the Pulpit: Religiosity and the 1980 Elections," *Public Opinion Quarterly* 48 (Spring 1984): 301–17.

26. Jerry Falwell, "Ronald Reagan, my Political Hero." Posted: August 17, 2002, 1:00 A.M. Eastern, *www.WorldNetDaily.com*.

27. Flo Conway and Jim Siegelman, *Holy Terror: The Fundamentalist War on America's Freedoms in Religion, Politics, and Our Private Lives* (New York: Doubleday, 1982), p. 293.

28. "Just Because Reagan Has Won..." *CT*, December 12, 1980, p. 15.

29. John C. Green and James L. Guth, "The Christian Right in the Republican Party: The Case of Pat Robertson's Supporters," *The Journal of Politics* 50, no. 1 (February 1988), pp. 150–65. Daniel Kenneth Williams, "From the Pews to the Polls: The Formation of a Southern Christian Right," Ph.D. dissertation (Brown University, 2005), pp. 377–87.

30. The goals of the Religious right were not just domestic. They also had foreign policy aims. In the mid-1980s, Christian right leaders came out strongly against a nuclear freeze. The Christian Broadcasting Network, for example, "contributed between $3 million and $7 million to U.S.-backed, anticommunist Contras in Nicaragua and Honduras." Arguably, the Religious Right had more success having their foreign policy aims implemented. The melding of right-wing Christianity and Reagan's economic agenda may be seen in documents such as the Santa Fe document, adopted by the Reagan administration, which noted "US foreign policy must begin to counter...liberation theology as it is utilized in

Latin America by the liberation clergy. The role of the church in Latin America is vital to the concept of political freedom....private property and productive capitalism." Jeffrey Marishane, "Prayer, Profit and Power: US Religious Right and Foreign Policy," *Review of African Political Economy no.* 52 (November 1991): 76, 81. William Martin, "The Christian Right and American Foreign Policy," *Foreign Policy no.* 114 (Spring, 1999): 66–80.

31. Matthew C. Moen, "The Evolving Politics of the Christian Right," *PS: Political Science and Politics* 29 (1996): 461–64. Stephen Johnson and Joseph Tamney, "The Christian Right and the 1980 Presidential Election," *Journal for the Scientific Study of Religion* 21 (1982): 123–31. Idem., "The Christian Right and the 1984 Presidential Election, *Review of Religious Research* 27 (1985): 124–33. William Martin, *With God on Our Side: The Rise of the Religious Right in America* (New York: Broadway, 1996), pp. 226–30, 238–43, passim.

32. Vernon L. Bates, "Lobbying for the Lord: The New Christian Right Home-Schooling Movement and Grassroots Lobbying," *Review of Religious Research* 33 (1991): 3–17.

33. Donald R. Songer and Susan J. Tabrizi, "The Religious Right in Court: The Decision Making of Christian Evangelicals in State Supreme Courts," *The Journal of Politics* 61 (1999): 521.

34. At the level of discourse, the Religious Right's influence extended to the Democratic Party. As Roy Jones, legislative director of the Moral Majority, noted after hearing Mario Cuomo's address to the 1984 Democratic national convention: "At the Democratic Convention last night, you had a keynote speaker talking about issues of the New right like the importance of the family. It was astounding to those of us associated with the Christian right that at a Democratic Convention, the topic of discussion was essentially...[our] issues." Moen, *Congress, pp.* 142–47.

35. Christine Leigh Heryman, *Southern Cross: The Beginnings of the Bible Belt* (Chapel Hill: University of North Carolina Press, 1998), pp. 64–98, passim.

36. Gil Troy, *Morning in America: How Ronald Reagan Invented the 1980's* (Princeton: Princeton University Press, 2005), pp. 204–06.

37. Mark Vermaire, "Living With Wealth: One Way to an Answer," *The Banner,* December 11, 1989, p. 6.

38. See, for example, Ralph Waldo Trine's 1897 best-seller *In Tune with the Infinite*: "Suggest prosperity to yourself. See yourself in a prosperous condition. Affirm that you will before long be in a prosperous condition. Affirm it calmly and quietly, but strongly and confidently....Expect it—keep it continually watered with expectation. You thus make yourself a magnet to attract the things that you desire."

39. Kenneth E. Hagin, *How God Taught Me About Prosperity* (Tulsa: Kenneth Hagin Ministries, 1991 [3rd printing]), pp. 22, 29, passim.

40. "Interview with Pat Robertson," *Charisma*, April 1983, p. 26.

41. Philip Yancey, "Jim Bakker Made Me Do It," *CT*, October 16, 1987, p. 64.

42. See Rick Perlstein, *Before the Storm: Barry Goldwater and the Unmaking of the American Consensus* (New York: FSG, 2001), p. 162. As Perlstein dryly notes: "There had been a divorced presidential candidate before. That candidate was Adlai Stevenson."

43. Michael Reagan, with Jim Denney, *Twice Adopted* (Nashville, Tenn.: Broadman and Holman Publishers, 2004), p. 44.

44. Glenn T. Stanton, "What No-Fault Divorce Can Teach Us About Same-Sex Marriage," June 17, 2004, http://www.family.org/cforum/fosi/marriage/ssuap/a0032550.cfm.

45. "Remarriage As God's Gift," *CT*, September 3, 1982, p. 106. Larry Richards, *Remarriage: A Healing Gift from God* (Word, 1981).

46. Les Parrott and Leslie Parrott, *Saving Your Second Marriage Before It Starts: Nine Questions to Ask Before (and After) You Remarry* (Grand Rapids, Mich.: Zondervan, 2001), pp. 17–18.

47. *Annual of the Southern Baptist Convention, 1971* (Nashville: Executive Committee, Southern Baptist Convention, 1971), p. 72. Randall Balmer, *Thy Kingdom Come: How the Religious Right Distorts the Faith and Threatens America: An Evangelical's Lament* (New York: Basic Books, 2006), pp. 10–34. Balmer recalls attending a 1990 conference sponsored by the Ethics and Public Policy Center, and attended by many of the Religious Right's architects. At that conference, attendees casually noted that the Religious Right's origins as an organized political movement lay not in abortion, but in outrage about the federal government's effort, in the mid-1970s, to force Bob Jones University to integrate. Ed Dobson, a one-time colleague of Falwell, who was in attendance at the 1990 meeting, summed up the point: "The Religious New Right did not start because of a concern about abortion.... I sat in the non-smoke-filled back room with the Moral Majority, and I frankly do not remember abortion ever being mentioned as a reason why we ought to do something." Abortion emerged as a key issue later, when during a conference call to discuss the Religious Right's ongoing political strategy, Religious Right leaders were fishing around to determine what issues might successfully galvanize a political moment. Someone on the conference call threw out: "How about abortion?"

48. Grace Elizabeth Hale, "New Right Rebels in a New Left Style: Anti-Abortion Activists, Direct Action, and the Problem of Life," delivered at the American Studies Association conference, Washington, D.C., November 2005. Copy in author's possession.

FOR FURTHER READING

Anderson, Martin. *Revolution.* San Diego: Harcourt, Brace Jovanovich, 1988.

Berkowitz, Edward. *Something Happened: A Political and Cultural Overview of the Seventies.* New York: Columbia University Press, 2006.

Bloom, Allan. *The Closing of the American Mind: How Higher Education Has Failed Democracy and Impoverished the Souls of Today's Students.* New York: Simon & Schuster, 1987.

Blumenthal, Sidney. *Pledging Allegiance: The Last Campaign of the Cold War.* New York: HarperCollins, 1990.

Blumenthal, Sidney. *The Rise of the Counter Establishment: From Conservative Ideology to Political Power.* New York: Times Books, 1986.

Brownlee, W. Elliot, and Hugh Davis Graham, eds. *The Reagan Presidency: Pragmatic Conservatism and Its Legacies.* Lawrence: University Press of Kansas, 2003.

Bruck, Connie. *Predator's Ball: The Junk-Bond Raiders and the Man Who Staked Them.* New York: Simon & Schuster, 1988.

Cannato, Vincent J. *The Ungovernable City: John Lindsay and His Struggle to Save New York.* New York: Basic Books, 2001.

Cannon, Lou. *President Reagan: The Role of a Lifetime.* New York: Simon & Schuster, 1991.

Crespino, Joseph. *In Search of Another Country: Mississippi and the Conservative Counterrevolution.* Princeton: Princeton University Press, 2007.

Critchlow, Donald T. *The Conservative Ascendancy: How the GOP Right Made Political History.* Cambridge, MA: Harvard University Press, 2007.

Critchlow, Donald T. *Phyllis Schlafly and Grassroots Conservatism: A Woman's Crusade.* Princeton: Princeton University Press, 2005.

Dallek, Matthew. *The Right Moment: Ronald Reagan's First Victory and the Decisive Turning Point in American Politics*. New York: Free Press, 2000.

Diggins, John Patrick. *Ronald Reagan: Fate, Freedom, and the Making of History*. New York: W.W. Norton, 2007.

Draper, Theodore. *A Very Thin Line: The Iran-Contra Affairs*. New York: Hill and Wang, 1991.

Edsall, Thomas Byrne, and Mary D. Edsall. *Chain Reaction: The Impact of Race, Rights, and Taxes on American Politics*. New York: W.W. Norton, 1991.

Ehrenreich, Barbara. *The Worst Years of Our Lives: Irreverent Notes from a Decade of Greed*. New York: Pantheon, 1990.

Ehrman, John. *The Eighties: America in the Age of Reagan*. New Haven: Yale University Press, 2005.

Evans, Sara. *Tidal Wave: How Women Changed America at Century's End*. New York: Free Press, 2003.

Faludi, Susan. *Backlash: The Undeclared War Against American Women*. New York: Crown, 1991.

Fischer, Beth A. *The Reagan Reversal: Foreign Policy and the End of the Cold War*. Columbia: University of Missouri Press, 1997.

Fitzgerald, Frances. *Way Out There in the Blue: Reagan, Star Wars, and the End of the Cold War*. New York: Simon & Schuster, 2000.

Friedman, Benjamin. *Day of Reckoning: The Consequences of American Economic Policy under Reagan and After*. New York: Random House, 1988.

Germond, Jack, and Jules Witcover. *Whose Broad Stripes and Bright Stars?: The Trivial Pursuit of the Presidency, 1988*. New York: Warner Books, 1989.

Gilder, George F. *Wealth and Poverty*. New York: Basic Books, 1981.

Hayward, Steven F. *The Age of Reagan: The Fall of the Old Liberal Order, 1964–1980*. Roseville, CA: Prima Publishing, 2001.

Hunter, James Davison. *Culture Wars: The Struggle to Define America*. New York: Basic Books, 1991.

Jenkins, Philip. *Decade of Nightmares: The End of the Sixties and the Making of Eighties America*. New York: Oxford University Press, 2006.

Johnson, Haynes. *Sleepwalking Through History: America in the Reagan Years*. New York: Norton, 1991.

Kimball, Roger. *Tenured Radicals: How Politics Has Corrupted Our Higher Education*. New York: Harper & Row, 1990.

Lettow, Paul. *Ronald Reagan and His Quest to Abolish Nuclear Weapons*. New York: Random House, 2005.

Levine, Lawrence W. *The Opening of the American Mind*. Boston: Beacon Press, 1996.

Lewis, Michael. *Liar's Poker: Rising Through the Wreckage on Wall Street*. New York: W.W. Norton, 1989.

Matlock, Jack F. *Reagan and Gorbachev: How the Cold War Ended*. New York: Random House, 2004.

McInerney, Jay. *Bright Lights, Big City*. New York: Vintage Books, 1984.

Meese, Edwin. *With Reagan: The Inside Story*. Washington: Regnery Gateway, 1992.

Mills, Nicolaus, ed. *Culture in an Age of Money: The Legacy of the 1980s in America*. Chicago: I.R. Dee, 1990.

Morris, Edmund. *Dutch: Memoir of Ronald Reagan*. New York: Random House, 1999.

Murray, Charles A. *Losing Ground: American Social Policy, 1950–1980*. New York: Basic Books, 1984.

Niskanen, William T. *Reaganomics: An Insider's Account of the Policies and the People*. New York: Oxford University Press, 1988.

Noonan, Peggy. *What I Saw at the Revolution: A Political Life in the Reagan Era*. New York: Random House, 1990.

Phillips, Kevin P. *The Politics of Rich and Poor: Wealth and the American Electorate in the Reagan Aftermath*. New York: Random House, 1990.

Phillips-Fein, Kim. *Invisible Hands: The Making of the Conservative Movement from the New Deal to Reagan*. New York: W.W. Norton, 2009.

Reagan, Ronald. *An American Life: The Autobiography*. New York: Simon & Schuster, 1990.

Regan, Donald T. *For the Record: From Wall Street to Washington*. San Diego: Harcourt, Brace Jovanovich, 1988.

Rothenberg, Randall. *The Neoliberals: Creation of the New American Politics*. New York: Simon & Schuster, 1984.

Schaller, Michael. *Right Turn: American Life in the Reagan-Bush Era, 1880–1992*. New York: Oxford University Press, 2007.

Schlesinger, Arthur M., Jr. *The Disuniting of America: Reflections on a Multicultural Society*. New York: W.W. Norton, 1992.

Schneider, Gregory. *The Conservative Century: From Reaction to Revolution*. Lanham, MD: Rowman & Littlefield Publishers, Inc., 2008.

Schulman, Bruce. *The Seventies: The Great Shift in American Culture, Society, and Politics*. New York: Free Press, 2001.

Schulman, Bruce, and Julian E. Zelizer, eds. *Rightward Bound: Making America Conservative in the 1970s*. Cambridge, MA: Harvard University Press, 2008.

Schweizer, Peter. *Reagan's War: The Epic Story of His Forty-Year Struggle and Final Triumph over Communism*. New York: Doubleday, 2002.

Shilts, Randy. *And the Band Played On: Politics, People and the AIDS Epidemic*. New York: St. Martin's Press, 1987.

Shirley, Craig. *Reagan's Revolution: The Untold Story of the Campaign That Started It All*. Nashville, TN: Nelson Current, 2005.

Shultz, George P. *Turmoil and Triumph: My Seven Years as Secretary of State*. New York: Scribner's, 1993.

Skinner, Kiron K., Annelise Anderson, and Martin Anderson, eds. *Reagan in His Own Hand: The Writings of Ronald Reagan That Reveal His Revolutionary Vision for America*. New York: Free Press, 2001.

Speakes, Larry. *Speaking Out: The Reagan Presidency from Inside the White House.* New York: Scribner, 1988.

Stockman, David A. *The Triumph of Politics: How the Reagan Revolution Failed.* New York: Harper & Row, 1986.

Takaki, Ronald. *A Different Mirror: A History of Multicultural America.* Boston: Little, Brown, and Company, 1993.

Troy, Gil. *Morning in America: How Ronald Reagan Invented the 1980's.* Princeton: Princeton University Press, 2005.

Trump, Donald, with Tony Schwartz. *Trump: The Art of the Deal.* New York: Random House, 1987.

Tygiel, Jules. *Ronald Reagan and the Triumph of American Conservatism.* New York: Longman, 2004.

Wanniski, Jude. *The Way the World Works.* New York: Simon & Schuster, 1979.

Weinberger, Caspar W. *Fighting for Peace: Seven Critical Years in the Pentagon.* New York: Warner Books, 1990.

Wilentz, Sean. *The Age of Reagan: A History, 1974–2008.* New York: HarperCollins, 2008.

Wills, Garry. *Reagan's America: Innocents at Home.* Garden City, NY: Doubleday, 1987.

Wilson, William Julius. *The Truly Disadvantaged: The Inner City, the Underclass, and Public Policy.* Chicago: University of Chicago Press, 1987.

Wolfe, Tom. *Bonfire of the Vanities.* New York: Farrar Straus Giroux, 1987.

INDEX

globalization:
 Clinton views on, 66
 neoliberal views on, 55–57,
  59
 in New York City, 74, 80,
  81, 82
 Reagan support for, 4
Goetz, Bernard, 78
Goldwater, Barry, 37, 40
"Good Times" (Chic), 153
Gorbachev, Mikhail:
 at Berlin Wall, 2, 29
 and collapse of Soviet
  Union, 140, 149
 rise to power, 63, 147
 See also Soviet Union
Gore, Al, 64, 67, 162, 163
Gore, Tipper, 162–63
government spending. See
 federal spending
Graham, Billy, 183–84
Gramm-Latta bill, 18
Gramm-Rudman-Hollings
 Budget Act, 34, 63
Great Depression, 128
Great Society social programs,
 3, 10, 24, 52, 55
Greenberg, David, 5
Greenberg, Steve, 7
Greenwich Village, 73, 77
Grenada, 24
Griffin, Susan, 94
Griffith-Joyner, Florence, 90
Griffith, Michael, 79
Gruen, Victor, 173
grunge rock music, 164, 165
Guerrilla Girls, 93
Gulf War, 33, 65, 67, 90
Guns and Roses, 164

Hagin, Kenneth, 191–92
Haircut 100, 158
Hale, Grace, 194
Hargrove, Erwin C., 64
Harris, Barbara C., 90
Harrison, Mike, 154
Hart, Gary, 55, 57–58
Hartsfield, William B., 43
Harvard Business Review, 87
Hawkins, Yusef, 79
Hayek, Friedrich von, 128, 130
Head Start, 17, 64
A Healing Gift from God
 (Richards), 193
health care:
 and Bill Clinton, 66
 and Great Society social
  programs, 3
 liberals views on, 53, 62
"Heard It Through the
 Grapevine" (Troutman),
 155
heavy metal music, 164
Heller, Walter, 129
Helms, Jesse, 189
Heyman, Ira Michael, 99
Hezbollah, 2, 149

Higham, John, 104
Hinckley, John, 11
hip-hop music, 164
Hispanics, 78, 129
Holland, F. Ross, 75
Hollinger, David, 105
Hollywood:
 evoked in Reagan speeches,
  167, 168
 and MTV, 160
 Reagan as actor in, 12, 29
homeowners' associations, 171
homeschooling bill in Oregon,
 189
Hoover, Herbert, 52
Howard Beach, 78, 80
How God Taught Me About
 Prosperity (Hagin), 191–92
Human Lague, 156
Humphrey, Hubert, 55
Hunt, Mary, 91
Hurricane Katrina, 136

immigrants:
 differing religions in, 182
 library use by, 170
 in New York City, 76
individualism:
 in 1980s, 8
 and liberalism, 51
industry:
 neoliberal views on, 55–57
 New York City
  manufacturing, 71, 74, 80
 northeastern
  deindustrialization, 71, 74,
  129, 135
inflation:
 during Reagan
  administration, 32, 54,
  127, 132, 133–34
 and economic theory,
  129–30, 132
 prior to Reagan
  administration, 23, 127,
  129–30, 141
 See also Reaganomics
intellectual affirmative action,
 99–100, 115
interest rates:
 during Reagan presidency,
  32, 134
 prior to Reagan presidency, 23
 See also Reaganomics
Internal Revenue Service (IRS),
 46
Interscope Records, 164
Iran-Contra affair, 7, 35, 63, 149
Iranian hostage crisis, 2, 15, 24,
 53, 54, 141, 153
Iraq. See Gulf War
IRS (Internal Revenue Service),
 46
Israel, 184
Israeli-Lebanon War of 1982,
 149
Israels, Valli, 111

Jackson, Janet, 159
Jackson, Jesse, 58, 60, 64, 66
Jackson, Michael:
 fundraising video for Africa,
  161
 moonwalk, 1
 release of "Thriller" album,
  158–59
 as unifier of pop audiences,
  7, 156, 159
James, Rick, 155
Japan, 56, 129
Jepsen, Roger, 17–18
Jesus, 194
Joel, Billy, 161
John Paul II, Pope, 2
Johnson, Lyndon:
 economy under, 20, 129
 Great Society social
  programs, 3, 10, 24, 52, 55
 and Soviet Union
  containment, 141
 and Vietnam War, 31
Jones, Bob, 183, 184
Journey, 155
Joyner, Florence Griffith, 90
Joyner-Kersee, Jackie, 90

Kamarck, Elaine, 65
Kamen, Paula, 85, 93, 95
Kemp, Jack, 131, 132–33, 135
Kemp-Roth tax cuts, 20
Kennedy, David, 39
Kennedy, John F.:
 assassination of, 19, 31
 on Atlanta, 43
 economic issues, 20, 24, 129
 foreign policy, 141
 impact on presidential
  office, 14
 rookie mistakes, 15
Kerry, John F., 67
Keynesian economics, 23, 55,
 61–62, 66, 128–30
Keynes, John Maynard, 128
Khomeini, Ruhollah, 15
King, Martin Luther, Jr., 43, 194
King, Rodney, 101
King, Ynestra, 94
Kinsley, Michael, 55
Kirk, Paul, 60
Klinghoffer, Leon, 2
Knack, The, 153
Koch, Ed, 5, 72–74, 79, 80
Koehler, John, 145
Kondrashey, Sergei, 146
Koop, C. Everett, 189
Kramer, Larry, 77
Kuttner, Robert, 64
Kuwait, 33

labor, neoliberal views on,
 55–56, 57
labor unions:
 air traffic controllers' strike,
  20, 125–26